W9-CSH-625

DISCARDED

DICTIONARY OF ARTS AND CRAFTS

MIDCENTURY
REFERENCE LIBRARY

DAGOBERT D. RUNES, Ph.D., General Editor

AVAILABLE

Beethoven Encyclopedia
Dictionary of American Grammar
and Usage
Dictionary of American Maxims
Dictionary of American Proverbs
Dictionary of Ancient History
Dictionary of Arts and Crafts
Dictionary of the Arts
Dictionary of Civics and Government
Dictionary of European History
Dictionary of Etiquette
Dictionary of Foreign Words
and Phrases
Dictionary of Early English
Dictionary of Last Words
Dictionary of Latin Literature
Dictionary of Linguistics
Dictionary of Mysticism
Dictionary of Mythology
Dictionary of Pastoral Psychology
Dictionary of Philosophy
Dictionary of Psychoanalysis
Dictionary of Science and Technology

Dictionary of Sociology
Dictionary of Word Origins
Dictionary of World Literature
Encyclopedia of Aberrations
Encyclopedia of the Arts
Encyclopedia of Atomic Energy
Encyclopedia of Criminology
Encyclopedia of Literature
Encyclopedia of Psychology
Encyclopedia of Religion
Encyclopedia of Substitutes and
Synthetics
Encyclopedia of Vocational Guidance
Illustrated Technical Dictionary
Labor Dictionary
Liberal Arts Dictionary
Military and Naval Dictionary
New Dictionary of American History
New Dictionary of Psychology
Protestant Dictionary
Slavonic Encyclopedia
Theatre Dictionary
Tobacco Dictionary

FORTHCOMING

Buddhist Dictionary
Dictionary of American Folklore
Dictionary of the American Indian
Dictionary of the American Language
Dictionary of American Literature
Dictionary of American Men and Places
Dictionary of American Names
Dictionary of American Superstitions
Dictionary of American Synonyms
Dictionary of Anthropology
Dictionary of Astronomy
Dictionary of Dietetics
Dictionary of Discoveries and Inventions
Dictionary of Earth Sciences
Dictionary of Explorations
Dictionary of French Literature
Dictionary of Geography

Dictionary of German Literature
Dictionary of Hebrew Literature
Dictionary of Law
Dictionary of Magic
Dictionary of Mechanics
Dictionary of New Words
Dictionary of Poetics
Dictionary of the Renaissance
Dictionary of Russian Literature
Dictionary of Science
Dictionary of Social Science
Dictionary of Spanish Literature
Encyclopedia of Morals
Personnel Dictionary
Teachers' Dictionary
Writers' Dictionary

PHILOSOPHICAL LIBRARY, INC.
Publishers

15 E. 40th Street   New York 16, N. Y.

Dictionary of Arts and Crafts

By JOHN L. STOUTENBURGH, Jr.

Department of Public Instruction

American Museum of Natural History

College of the Sequoias
Library

PHILOSOPHICAL LIBRARY

New York

Copyright, 1956, by
PHILOSOPHICAL LIBRARY, INC.
15 East 40th Street, New York, N. Y.

R
c. 1
745.03
S 889

Printed in the United States of America

Introduction

The *Dictionary of Arts and Crafts* has been written to fill a need in the arts and crafts field.

A dictionary of arts and crafts should become a tool for the craftsman. It may not look like the tool you are accustomed to but, instead, consider it as a "mental tool."

You may have many interests and may even teach a craft class or have a group of people who look to you for ideas in the field; it is these people that I have kept in mind while collecting material and information for this dictionary.

I speak from experience . . . I, too, have been in the position of saying to myself "What can I possibly do next week?"

This dictionary can't be construed as being the very last word . . . the last word will never be written. The dictionary tries to clarify terms which are used by others rather freely and are taken for granted.

As an example of a rather simple craft let us take block printing. You may know that to cut a block print, the design and especially the lettering should be in reverse so that it will print correctly. Much of your class time is spent explaining how to cut the block and how to ink it and in suggesting ideas for designs, you may in a casual way mention that the design should be reversed . . . but the results you have taken for granted. Members of the group will have letters that are printed backwards and be amazed at what they have done; after all it looked all right when they cut it!

It is not the aim of the *Dictionary of Arts and Crafts* to replace all other craft books, it should become a part of your craft library and act as a key to open new fields of interests to you that you may not have thought of.

There are, however, many ideas and techniques that are explained. Some of the techniques are now obsolete and even some of the materials which are described are no longer in use.

Why then should obsolete and archaic terms and techniques be included, especially when the most recent methods have been described, and are oftentimes far superior?

That question seems to me to be the meat of the fields of arts and crafts. After all, isn't a craft something that is done by hand or made with hand tools and done in the old and original method.

For example, if you are a fine painter, your work deserves the best. Of course, you can buy tubes of paint and create a masterpiece, but think of the satisfaction of creating a painting which is painted with paint pigments that you have created yourself or made in the same way and of the same type of materials as one of the old masters . . . doesn't that add to the spiritual feeling, that strange feeling that one has when in some ancient edifice.

I have not given opinions of crafts and techniques. It is not the aim of this dictionary to pass judgment on any of the arts and crafts. I have tried to present terms which would be useful to the artist and craftsman in many fields. In many cases you will find that some "new" idea or technique has been done centuries before, maybe under a different name.

There will be omissions and you may feel an inner satisfaction in knowing a word or technique that has not been included in this dictionary. It is you who will write the future specific works on arts and crafts.

Because of the people who work in the field and use terms that are familiar to them but not to their neighbors . . . the *"Dictionary of Arts and Crafts"* was created.

For the help that I received from the many people who are happily engaged in arts and crafts I owe a great debt of gratitude. . . . For all those little things which are gained only through experience and actual work in the field of arts and crafts I can only say that they must be experienced to be enjoyed and understood and eventually become the anecdotes which make arts and crafts interesting and rewarding.

I have tried to weave a rug of words to cover the field of

arts and crafts and to tie together all the woof and warp threads into one book. A book which should whet the appetite of the newcomer and the oldtimer alike in the broad and interesting field of arts and crafts.

DICTIONARY OF ARTS AND CRAFTS

A

aaklae: This term applies to a type of fabric made in Europe, made of wool. It was a type of tapestry.

abalone: This shell is found on the west coast of the United States and is used to make small carvings and several types of inlay work.

abalyn: This is a synthetic type of resin (q.v.).

abbatre: A term used in crafts dealing with cloth or fabrics. This is a type of design that appears to be incised (q.v.).

abbozzo: A term used by artists (q.v.). This is a beginning or thumbnail sketch or model or plan for painting or sculpture (q.v.).

aberration: A term used in photography. This is a defect in a lens in a camera. This distortion makes it impossible for a perfect picture to be taken.

abigarrado: In the making of jewelry this term refers to any gem stone that is variegated in its color.

abrasions: When used in connection with photography, abrasions are caused by scratches on the surface of the photographic paper.

abrasive: This term when applied to metal crafts, as well as many other crafts, means a material or substance used to grind or wear down a surface, such as emery or sandpaper, pumice, jeweler's rouge.

absorption: This term is used in the printing crafts, referring to the fact that some types of paper absorb ink faster than others, some stay wet.

abstraction: A term used in the arts. This is a design that is more or less geometric in shape or form. Usually supposed to be pleasing to the eye and provide a mental image, rather than a design or actual copy from nature.

abstractionism: A term used in the arts. Used when describing the method of painting or sculpturing (q.v.) known as abstraction (q.v.).

abutilon: This is a bell shaped flower used in the corsage

1

crafts. The flower will last about three days when prepared correctly.

acacia: A type of bloom used in the corsage crafts. The flowers are yellow and formed in sprays. When correctly prepared, they last about ten days.

academy blue: A mixture of color, made of viridian (q.v.) and ultra-marine.

academy board: This is a type of heavy cardboard that has been coated with a pigment, also known as canvas board. Used by artists in place of regular canvas. Paintings that are intended to last for a great length of time are not usually done on academy board.

academy figure: A term used in the arts. An academy figure is a human figure that is painted smaller than half life size and is painted with a background that enhances the figure.

acaroid: A type of resin; see xanthorrhea.

acca: A type of ancient fabric made possibly in Syria. This fabric was made of silk and gold.

accelerator: A term used in photography. This is a chemical used in the developing process of photography, to hurry the process of development.

accessories: A term used in the arts, meaning objects or figures that have been painted into the background to accent the main theme or figure. Accessories are also used in museum work. When used in this field, they are meant to apply to the objects such as plants, rocks and figures that are placed in an exhibit, especially habitat groups (q.v.) and also in dioramas (q.v.).

accroides gum: This is a resin (q.v.). Also known as acaroid (q.v.).

acerra: This is a type of Oriental container made from metal or from ceramics (q.v.). Used as a container for the burning of incense.

acetate: A salt of acetic acid. Used in various plastics.

acetate film: This is a type of film used in photography, known as safety film because it is a slow burning substance.

achroite: This is a variety of tourmaline (q.v.), a rather colorless variety. This gem stone is no longer in common use.

achromatic: A term used in the arts, denoting the lack of color or a series of greys. There are from six to seven hundred shades of grey.

achromatic lens: This is a type of lens that has been adjusted so that the visual focus coincides with the chemical focus of the picture.

acid: A chemical substance. Many kinds. Used for glass etching, metal engraving.

acid bath: A term used in the crafts of etching (q.v.).

acid blast: In the etching crafts (q.v.), several techniques are used. The acid used in the biting (q.v.) is forced against the plate (q.v.) by a spray.

acid dye: When materials are dyed, various types of dye can be used. Dyes made with an acid dye usually last longer.

acorn doll: The acorn doll is assembled much the same way as the spool doll (q.v.). An acorn is selected for the head, and various sized acorns for the body and the arms and legs of the doll. A nail or large needle is used to string the pieces together. Many other dolls can be made from peanuts, beans, seeds of various kinds and nuts, such as chestnuts, walnuts, etc.

acorn knop: A term used in the metal crafts, especially in the making of pewter (q.v.). The decoration of the knop (q.v.) is made in the shape of an acorn.

Acrawax: A trade name for a wax. Sometimes used in shellac.

acridine: A coal tar product, used in the making of synthetic dyes.

acrolith: A term used by sculptors (q.v.). An acrolith is a figure made of two or more kinds of materials. Such a figure can be made of wood, stone or metal or a combination.

acropodium: This is the raised base that a figure carved by a sculptor (q.v.) is placed on. The acropodium is sometimes carved as a part of the figure itself.

acrotomous: A term used in the jewelry and gem cutting crafts. This is the internal structure of a gem. The internal cleavage should run in the same direction as the table (q.v.) of an acrotomous gem.

acrylic resin: Used in the various crafts, the acrylic resins are used as a film for the coating of surfaces. Also used as a molding compound. This is a thermo-plastic (q.v.). See lucite.

actinic: A term used in photography referring to the light that affects the emulsion (q.v.).

actinometer: An instrument used for measuring the lasting power of certain pigments. Also used to measure the heating power of such objects as the sun's rays.

action: A term used in the arts. Action refers to a painting that has the feeling of motion, running figures or bright flashy colors, etc.

activator: A term used in photography. The activator is a chemical process or ingredient used in the development of a picture. This hurries the process.

adamantine: This is a term used in the gem crafts and refers to the luster (q.v.) of a gem stone.

add: A term used in the printing crafts. Used to describe additional copy that is sent to a printer who already has set the copy in type. This makes changes which sometimes necessitate changes in the complete page.

additive mixing: A term used in photography. Several colors are projected on a screen, thus mixing the light and color for special effects.

addorsed: A term used in heraldry (q.v.). Used to describe the figures on a coat of arms (q.v.) which are turned away from each other.

adjustable ruler: Used in many arts and crafts, the adjustable ruler is made of metal and can be bent. Used for special design work.

adobe: Used in the building crafts. Adobe bricks are made from sun-dried mud with straw mixed in. Made in hot dry areas. The houses are cooler inside because of the thick walls made of this brick.

adoptive: A term used in heraldry (q.v.). Adoptive is used to describe a coat of arms, or bearing (q.q.v.), that is given to a person and not received through the right of descent.

Adrianople red: A rather bright intense red made from the madder plant, also known as Turkey red (q.v.).

adulterant: An adulterant is a term used in the arts. When a foreign substance is added to such materials as paint pigments it becomes an adulterant because it tends to weaken or replace a higher quality substance.

advance sheets: These are stitched or stapled sheets of a publication that are put together for review or other special purpose. This is not a finished job on a publication.

advancing color: A term used in painting, denoting certain warm colors (q.v.), which appear to be closer at hand in a painting.

aegicranes: This is a sculpture (q.v.) term. Refers to the carved heads of goats and rams that were done in ancient Greece.

aerial perspective: A term used in the painting crafts. Aerial perspective is the effect of distance on objects as seen by the eye. The more distant the object, the less detail can be seen and the color tends to be greyish blue to shades of violet or purple.

aerocamera: A type of camera that is made especially for photography from an airplane. These cameras can take large areas of ground at a time and the finished prints can be pieced together to form a large map of an area.

aerugo: This is an artificial bluish-green used as a paint pigment. Also known as verdigris (q.v.).

aery: A term used in the painting crafts, denoting the ethereal quality of the work.

affix: A term used in several crafts to denote small objects that are affixed on the outside of the object, such as flowers or other decorations that are placed on the outside of a ceramic (q.v.) piece.

affronté: A term used in heraldry. This describes the two animals on a coat of arms (q.v.) when they are shown facing each other.

African walnut: A term used in the carving and woodworking crafts. This is a fine textured wood with a grain that interlocks. This hardwood is used for panels, furniture and carving small objects.

aftaba: Used in the metalcrafts. This is a type of pitcher with a long spout used in and around central Asia.

agacella: A term used in heraldry (q.v.). This is an escutcheon (q.v.) that has a representation of a tiger or antelope with hoofs and horns.

agano yaki: A type of ceramic (q.v.) made in the province of Yuzen in Japan.

agaric: A type of black dye made from a fungus that grows in dung. The color is secured by mixing this with iron salts.

agate: The agate is a type of quartz used in the jewelry crafts. This mineral has bands or clouds of various colors.

agate ware: This is a type of ceramic finish. It resembles the gem stone agate (q.v.).

age cracks: These are seen in paintings and in ceramics. Through long periods of time, paint sometimes breaks or cracks. This is caused by parts of a painting drying faster than others. This is also seen on ceramics (q.v.), especially in Oriental ceramics. This effect can be produced by varnishing a painted surface before the paint is dry. This is sometimes done to "age" an object or painting.

aging: A term used in the ceramics crafts, a process of colloidal degeneration.

A-ha: This kachina (q.v.) is found in use on the Second Mesa of the Hopi Indian of the United States. The figure has a green head with eyes of purple and black. Two pieces of colored yarn are fastened across the forehead. The neck is covered with a fox skin. The figure is dressed in the skin of a wildcat. The shoes are red. This kachina is used in the Bean Dance.

Ahöla: This is a type of kachina (q.v.) used in special ceremonies and represents the Germ God known as Alosoka. This type of kachina is supposed to control the growth of all things.

Aholi: This is a type of kachina (q.v.) used in the Hopi Bean Dance. The Aholi is the companion to the Eototo (q.v.).

aiguisce: A term used in heraldry (q.v.). This is a cross on an escutcheon (q.v.) that has pointed or sharp ends which are wider than a forty-five degree angle.

Aiken's metal: A term used in the metalcrafts. This is a type of metal similar to pewter (q.v.) but without bismuth.

ailettes: A term used in heraldry (q.v.). It denotes the small metal shields that were made for use by a knight. They were used in combat, now as a symbol in the form of epaulets.

air bells: A term used in several crafts. In photography, they refer to the small bubbles that appear on the film during the development process. Air bells are found in the making of glass and are sometimes rather difficult to remove.

air brick: This is a type of perforated brick used to provide ventilation in walls.

air drain: A term used in casting (q.v.). When a mold (q.v.)

is made, it is necessary to provide an air drain. If the drain is not provided, it is impossible to pour a compound into a mold and have it completely free from air bubbles.

air dried paper: This is a type of paper used in the arts. The paper is dried rapidly with superheated air.

air shrinkage: A term used in the ceramics crafts. Air shrinkage is caused by the drying out of a ceramic (q.v.). This takes place in a kiln (q.v.).

air space lenses: A term used in photography. These are lenses that are separated by air spaces.

airbrush: This is a tool of the artist and craftsman. It is used to spray fixative (q.v.), paints and varnishes, etc. The airbrush usually works by compressed air, consists of a container to hold the material that will be sprayed out, a small nozzle and a tank of air. The airbrush is usually smaller than the larger gun type that is used to spray walls and other large surfaces.

ala de mosca: A term used in the sculpture arts and crafts (q.v.). This is a fine type of granite, found mainly in Peru.

alabastron: An early small Greek perfume jar or vase. This vase has a small neck and a round bottom so that it had to be supported to keep it upright.

Alaska cypress: A type of softwood used in fine carving.

alberia: A term used in heraldry (q.v.). This term denotes any shield or escutcheon (q.v.) that is plain, without any decoration.

alcohol: This is a distillate of vegetable material. Made mainly of wood for use in the various arts and crafts, as a cleaning agent, a thinner, used in fixatives (q.v.).

alcora: A type of 18th century ceramics (q.v.), a type of Spanish porcelain (q.v.). Floral designs of purple, orange, green and blue are characteristic.

alder: The inner bark of this tree is used to make a red or yellow dye. The inner bark was mixed wth bloodroot (q.v.), wild plum (q.v.) and red—osier dogwood (q.v.). This type of dye was used by the Ojibwa Indians of the Great Lakes region of Canada and the United States. The wood is used for carving, and also for the making of plywood. The wood is rather straight grained and smooth textured.

aldis lens: Used in the photography crafts. A type of lens used in hand cameras.

alembic: A type of glass container common in the art studios of the 15th century. An alembic is used in the distillation of turpentine. The alembic was used by Leonardo da Vinci.

Alencon lace: A type of lace made in the needle-point (q.v.) method. This type of lace was first made in Alencon, France, and is a fine quality of lace.

Alexandria blue: Made of the silicates of copper and lime, this is the famous blue paint pigment used by the ancient Egyptians.

Alexandrite: A type of stone used in the jewelry and gem cutting crafts. This is the most costly of the semi-precious stones. When this stone is cut in a cabochon (q.v.), it shows a dull green in the daylight; under artificial light, the color changes to a red. This is a rather rare stone and is mainly found in India.

alexjejevite: A type of resin found in the Kaluga province of Russia. Used by artists in the making of films for the surface of paintings.

algarovilla: A plant used in the nineteenth century in Spain. Used in the tanning process of leather and also in the making of a rather good grade of ink.

algin: A material that is extracted from sea kelp, gelatin-like in texture. Chemically it is sodium alginate.

algraphy: A photographic term also known as alumino-graphy (q.v.).

alhambra: A type of weaving, resembling the hand woven bed covers that were popular in the 18th century.

alizarin blue: A color used in printing inks. This color does not fade very readily but when exposed to bright light for any length of time, it will turn dark, almost black.

alizarin crimson: This color is made from coal tar (anthracene), a permanent organic pigment. This pigment has a bluish tinge, is rather slow drying and after time and exposure to light, the color darkens.

alkali blue: This is an organic color pigment used in the manufacture of inks used in printing.

alkana: This is a type of dye used in ancient Turkey and Persia. It was made from the ground leaves of the plant

Lausania inermis. In the early days, this dye was used to color horse tails.

alkanet: A strong red dye that is obtained from the roots of the plant Anchusa tinctoria. This dye is used to stain marble and also fabrics.

alkanna: A reddish purple dye made from the plants of an herb, Boraginaceae. Also made from the common red cabbage in Russia.

alkyd resin: This is a type of resin (q.v.). Added to various types of varnish and enamel paints, this is a fast dryer.

alla prima: A painting process. Consists of applying a rather heavy layer of one pigment, rather than several layers.

allerion: A term used in heraldry (q.v.). This is a design that was worn by those who were beaten or disarmed. The design consists of an eagle without beak or feet and the outspread wings have the tips turned down.

alligator glaze: A term used in the ceramics crafts (q.v.). This is a finish that is found on the surface of objects that have been fired in such a way that the surface looks cracked, also known as crackle glaze (q.v.).

allingite: This is a type of fossil resin (q.v.) found mainly in Switzerland, used sometimes in place of amber.

allocamelus: A design used in heraldry (q.v.). The design is made up of the distinctive parts of the camel and the ass, forming a legendary animal.

allochromatic: A term used in the jewelry and gem crafts. Used when referring to a gem that would have no color if it is chemically pure, but because of some element that is in the stone, it has various colors. Stones of this type are known as allochromatic gem stones; quartz and corundum are a few examples.

alloy: In the metal crafts, this refers to the combining of two or more metals. See binary alloy, ternary alloy, quaternary alloy.

allumee: A term used in heraldry (q.v.). This describes any animal in a design that has a red or sparkling eye.

almagra: This is a red variety of ochre (q.v.). Used as a paint pigment and as an ingredient of rouge (q.v.) used in the jewelry and gem crafts.

almandite: Used as a gem stone in the jewelry and gem

crafts; similar to the garnet. A red stone with a crystalline structure, classified as a spinel. An allochromatic (q.v.) gem stone.

almond stone: A term used in the jewelry and gem crafts. Used to describe the gem stone almandite (q.v.).

almond wood: A reddish, fine textured wood used for fine carving. A hardwood, Prunus amygdalus.

aloes wood: This type of wood is also known as paradise wood (q.v.). Used for inlay work, rather difficult to work with. Smooth grain and a smooth texture. The wood splits rather easily.

alpaca: This is an animal found in the high Andes mountains of Bolivia. This animal has long silky hair, known as wool, which is used in weaving. Mixed with other fibers such as cotton.

alquifou: A term used in the ceramics crafts (q.v.). This is a mineral with a lead base, used to make a green glaze. Also known as potter's ore (q.v.).

alsbachite: A type of granite used by sculptors (q.v.). Has large mica crystals and a type of rose garnet.

alto—relievo: A term used in the sculpture (q.v.) techniques. This is a rather high relief. See relief.

altogether: A term used in the arts. This term is used to describe a model used by an artist (q.v.) or sculptor. Posing in the "altogether," means to pose completely nude.

aludel: A term used in the metal crafts and in the ceramics crafts (q.q.v.). This is a type of container or vessel, pear shaped and open at each end.

alumina: A glazing agent (q.v.). Used in ceramics (q.v.) and in the arts. This is an aluminum oxide.

alumina hydrate: This is an artificial light powder, used in printing inks. It is used in tube paints to give them a brushing consistency; it is high in oil absorption.

aluminography: A process used in the printing crafts. Aluminum plates are used in the process of offset (q.v.) printing.

aluminum bronze: This is an alloy (q.v.), a mixture of copper and aluminum. A pale gold in color, this alloy is used in making jewelry and other small metal objects.

aluminum leaf: Used in the bookbinding crafts. Used in place of silver on tooled leather (q.v.).

aluminum powder: Aluminum in powdered form, used in paint pigments and also the making of aluminum paints.

alumocalcite: A term used in the jewelry and gem crafts. This is a variety of opal (q.v.). This stone contains lime and alumina; however, these are impurities and are not desired.

Alvar: A trade name for a synthetic resin (q.v.). Used in the manufacture of phonograph records, varnishes, lacquers and enamels.

ama gatsu: A paper doll made in Japan for purification purposes. These dolls were given to new mothers who rubbed the paper doll on a newborn infant and then returned the doll to the Shinto priest. He then purified the doll and this in turn purified the child.

amalgam gilding: This is a process of gilding metal with a gold amalgam. The surface is coated with amalgam and then through the application of heat, the mercury is driven off, leaving the gold surface.

amaranth: A hardwood with a purple color, from the Guianas.

amassette: Made from animal horn, this is a tool of the ancient artist. In mixing paint pigment, it is used to pile the pigment before it is ground and mixed for use.

amatito: A hematite (q.v.). A fine red pigment is prepared from this mineral that is used mainly in the painting of frescoes (q.v.).

amber: This is a type of fossil resin (q.v.) or mineral. Amber is found mainly along the shores of the Baltic Sea, and very little is found elsewhere in the world. This fossil resin is the hardest natural resin and makes the finest types of varnish. It can be dissolved in linseed oil (q.v.).

ambergris: A waxy secretion that is expelled by certain sick whales. Ambergris can be found on the beach; it has a rather strong odor and is a dark brown color. Used in the manufacture of perfumes, it is very valuable.

amberlite: This is a resin-like material used in the making of a glue that is employed in the making of plywood (q.v.).

ambrite: This is a yellow-grey fossil resin, somewhat like kauri gum (q.v.), found mainly in New Zealand. Used in the jewelry and gem crafts.

America russia: A term used in the bookbinding crafts. This is a type of leather that is made to imitate the leather variety known as Russia leather (q.v.).

American whitewood: A type of wood used in the woodcrafts, with a rather straight grain and smooth texture, from the botanical family of Tilia glabra.

amorphous: When this term is applied to minerals, it means without shape or crystal structure, such as whiting (q.v.).

amphora: This is a type of Greek vase, made of ceramic (q.v.). This vase has a long thin neck. The jar has two handles. The jar was used in ancient Greece to hold oil, grain and wine.

ampulla: A term used in the metal crafts. This is a small religious container made of pewter (q.v.).

amure: This is a weaving term, indicating a type of textile with a twill (q.v.) background. The designs or patterns are made on a Jacquard loom (q.v.).

amyl acetate: Also known as banana oil (q.v.) because of its odor. Used as a solvent for synthetic resins.

amyl formate: A liquid used in many arts and crafts, as in the manufacture of surface films for paintings, and as a paint solvent.

an: Used in the oriental crafts of metal workers. This is a small ornate box used to hold small objects, such as jewelry.

anadem: Used in the corsage and flower crafts. This is a type of wreath or garland that is worn on the head. Usually given in ancient Greece and Rome for special events and winners of games.

anaglypta: A term used in the sculpture crafts (q.v.). This is a type of carving or chiseling done in low relief (q.v.).

anaglyptograph: This is a device or process for producing a drawing or etching (q.v.) on a flat surface. When done with this method, the design has the appearance of having been done in relief (q.v.). The process is known as anaglyptography.

analogous colors: A term used in the arts and the crafts. Analogous colors are colors that resemble each other so much that they can sometimes be mistaken for each other, such as the blues, greens and blue greens, etc.

anamorphosis: A term used in the arts for a technique of drawing or painting. The design is done in such a way that when it is viewed directly it doesn't appear to be anything. But if the design is held at eye-level or other prescribed angle, a picture or design will be clearly seen. Used for hidden messages. Such a drawing could be made of a sailing ship with its many lines; when the drawing is held in a certain way, the lines appear to meet and form words, etc.

anarak: A coat made of oiled skins of animals. Worn by the Eskimo, this coat has a hood and is worn in bad weather and in the kayak (q.v.).

anasazi: A term used to describe the ancient Indian people of the Southwestern United States. A Navajo word meaning the "ancient ones," it refers to the basket makers of about 2000 years ago.

anastigmatic lens: A lens used especially in photography. This lens produces a clear image from edge to edge, and is not distorted around the edges and only clear in the center.

anatastic printing: This type of printing is done from a raised surface. A print is treated with a weak acid and then pressed against a zinc plate (q.v.); this is then etched with acid and printed in much the same way as a lithograph (q.v.).

ancestor images: The spirits of ancestors were sometimes considered by many tribes to be in certain dolls or fetishes (q.v.). Medicine men made many strange shapes with stone and sand and also sticks in which the spirit of the deceased was supposed to reside. Ancestor images and fetishes (q.v.) were carefully guarded by the tribe and children were not permitted to touch these figures or dolls.

anchored cross: A term used in heraldry (q.v.). This is a type of cross that has its ends in the shape of an anchor; this is placed on the bearing (q.v.) of the escutcheon (q.v.).

ancient: A term used in heraldry (q.v.). This is a small flag that is carried at funerals; the pole has a pointed end, and is a sign of public mourning.

andaman marblewood: A fine textured hardwood with fine grey and black bands running through it, used in carving. Sometimes this wood is confused with zebra wood (q.v.).

andiroba: A type of wood used in the wood crafts for veneer and for small carved pieces. Also known as crabwood (q.v.).

angel hair: This is very fine spun glass, used on Christmas trees and for other decoration effects. Sometimes made into a fabric.

angle of view: A term used in photography. This is used to describe the angle from the lens to the film in a camera.

angle worm lines: A term used in Oriental painting. This is a style of painting used especially when painting fabrics. A vertical brush stroke is used, painting from the outside edges to the center.

angora: A rabbit raised for its soft, silky fur. Mainly raised for its fur in France, now raised in America also in large numbers. The fur is white and silky and rather long. Can be spun into yarn and used for special pieces of clothing such as mittens, sweaters, scarfs, etc.

Angstrom unit: A term used in photography. This is a device for the measurement of light waves, which is one ten-millionth of a millimeter. Light rays are from 4,000 to 7,000 Angstrom units in length.

angular field: A term used in photography. This is the angle that is drawn between the opposite ends of the area of sharp focus of a lens and the lens.

Angwushahai-i: A type of Hopi kachina (q.v.). Sometimes seen wearing a white wedding dress. This figure has a green head with crow wings on it.

Angwusnasomtaqa: This is a type of kachina (q. v.). This kachina is also known as the Crow Mother and is used in the Bean Dance. This little figure is sometimes seen carrying a tray of corn on the Second Mesa and is also seen with a yucca whip. The doll itself is green, with a woman's dress and green shoes. The head has a pair of wings and a muff of fox skin.

aniline: This is an oily substance with no color found in coal tar. Used to make aniline dyes (q.v.).

aniline dyes: Used to dye inks, paints, plastics. Originally made from indigo. Now a coal tar product.

aniline color: Aniline colors are made from coal tar derivatives. These colors have been used extensively from the late 18th century. This color is used in some house paints and as a rule the color is not lasting. The aniline colors usually outlast the vegetable colors, however. See aniline dyes.

aniline violet: This is the first organic dye to be manufactured synthetically. The color is a reddish-purple or violet.

animal black: This is a pigment made from the distillation process of degreased animal bones, used by artists (q.v.) in painting and drawing.

animated cartoon: A term used in the arts and also in the crafts for the method. A series of pictures is drawn, each successive picture slightly different from the other. When these pictures are shown or projected in a rapid manner, they appear as one, with motion. This is a rather tedious job when done by hand.

animated dolls: See pantins.

anime: A term used in heraldry (q.v.). This describes any animal that is depicted with fire coming from its mouth.

animé: Also known as copal gum (q.v.). This is a pale brown resin (q.v.). Used in the making of varnish.

annealing: A term used in several crafts. In the crafts of glass making, annealing is done in a leer (q.v.). Here the glass is fused or melted into a single piece. When used in the ceramics (q.v.) crafts, it fuses and hardens the material. When used in the metal crafts, it is used to make metals easier to work with; they are heated and then cooled. This process is repeated several times until the metal is the consistency needed. This process is done by the natives of Africa, who work their own iron for spear, arrow and knife blades.

annodated: A term used in heraldry (q.v.). Used to describe any object on an escutcheon (q.v.) that is turned or twisted in such a manner as to resemble an S.

annual ring: A term used in the crafts of woodworking and related subjects. Annual rings are the result of the growth of a tree, especially in the temperate zones. Each year a tree grows, it leaves a ring or growth ring; these can be counted very accurately and thus the age of a tree that has been cut can be determined.

annulet: This is a ring used on an escutcheon (q.v.). A symbol of nobility used in heraldry (q.v.).

anode: The positive electrode in an electrolytic cell. When electro-plating, it is necessary to have a plate of the type metal that is to be plated on an object. The electric current passes through the plate and removes minute particles which move to the object to be plated.

anomaloscope: A device used in the accurate measurement of color vision.

anserated cross: This is a term used in heraldry. An anserated cross is a representation of a cross that has its upper part made or shaped like the head of an eagle, lion, etc.

anthracene: From coal tar, this is a yellowish crystal, used in the manufacture of a type of aniline dyes (q.v.).

anthrax: A term used in the jewelry and gem crafts. It is a gem stone also known as the carbuncle, (q.v.) a red stone.

antic work: An art term, used to describe any figures, animal or vegetable, that are rather fanciful in design, such as a griffin would be.

anti-halation: A term used in photography, to describe film that has a special backing that is black; this is done to prevent a halo or a circle of bright light on the film, from reflection.

antimacassar: A type of fabric that is made to cover the arms and backs of chairs and couches. The pieces of cloth are placed in such a manner as to protect the fabric of the furniture from hands and hair. The name is derived from a type of hair dressing that was once very popular which was made from macassar oil.

antimony: This is a white lustrous metal, sometimes used in medicine. It is also an alloy used in pewter. See Britannia Metal.

antimony orange: This is a bright, rather permanent color, patented in 1847. A color that is not used as much now as in the past. Antimony orange (Antimony trisulphide) blackens when mixed with lead base paints because of the sulphur in the pigment.

antimony pigments: A type of paint pigment made from lead antimoniate. Used in ancient Egypt and Assyria.

antique: A term used in the printing arts and crafts. This is a style of type wherein the face of the type is of equal thickness.

antique finish: A term used in the printing and paper crafts. An antique finish on a paper is a rather rough surface. Refers to the time paper was made by hand. Now this finish is done by machine.

antique glass: This term is used to describe glass that was made in the early days and used in windows, etc. This glass has ripples and bubbles and after long periods of time, has color through it slightly when viewed at an angle.

antique glaze: This is a type of glaze (q.v.). It is applied to ceramics and then fired; it gives the appearance of age because of the deep color and crackle surface (q.v.).

antique tooling: This is done in the bookbinding crafts; the tools are used to emboss (q.v.) the book cover. No ink or color is used, giving the effect of age.

Antwerp blue: A light variety of Prussian blue (q.v.) about 75% Prussian blue mixed with other pigments such as alumina hydrate. When doing oil painting, this color is not permanent. This is the first synthetic blue made on a large scale.

Antwerp lace: This is a type of lace made in the bobbin method (q.v.) and resembles lace made in the needle-point method (q.v.).

Antwerp red: This pigment is a rather light red color, used in oil painting.

aperture: Used in the various crafts, especially in photography. This is the opening in the camera that lets the light and the image pass through the lens of the camera.

aphrizite: This is a black variety of tourmaline (q.v.) used in the gem crafts.

aplanatic: This is a lens or mirror used in photography that is curved in such a manner as to direct the rays of light in one direction.

apostle spoons: Rather rare spoons made of pewter (q.v.). The knops (q.v.) were made to represent the figures of the apostles.

apple: A type of wood, Pyrus malus, used in the wood crafts. This wood has an irregular grain and a rather smooth texture.

apple green: A color, supposed to represent the color of a green apple, also applied to certain types of Chinese porcelains (q.v.).

applied art: A term with many angles and the ideas of many people. Generally applied art is that art which is applied or added to the work of others, or the extra ornamentation. This covers many fields of arts and crafts.

applied decoration: A term used to describe any added work that is applied to an object already made. Such as a chair which is already made and has an added design cut out or glued on its surface.

applied design: Another term which is not always understood or used correctly. This is the modeling or painting of an object already made. The design or embellishment is added to the finished product and is then called applied decoration (q.v.).

applique: This is a type of sewing craft. Applique is used on many types of cloth. The design is made up of various pieces of cloth of different colors. These pieces are laid on the base cloth and are sewn in place. Sometimes several layers of cloth are used. Each color is cut so that it exposes the layer directly beneath it and so the final cloth is rather thick or thin, depending on the number of colors used. This type of sewing is done by certain American Indian tribes of the United States.

appointé: A term used in heraldry (q.v.). This term is used to describe two objects on an escutcheon (q.v.) which have their extremities touching.

apulian ware: A type of ceramic (q.v.) of ancient Greece. A rather egg shaped mouth on the vase was shaped into the neck.

aqua fortis: Also known as nitric acid (q.v.). Used in many arts and crafts, such as etching (q.v.).

aqua regia: This is a mixture used to test and to dissolve gold. It is made of nitric acid and hydrochloric acid.

aquamarine: A gem stone used in the gem crafts. It has a light blue green color.

aquatint: This is an intaglio process (q.v.). Aquatint is a process of etching (q.v.) whereby the plate (q.v.) is coated with a resinous material in the form of a powder. This prevents the acid from eating or biting in a solid etched line. The process is repeated over and over. The result is a plate with tones on it that resemble a wash drawing, thus the name aqua-tint.

aquatint pen process: The making of an aquatint (q.v.) so that it looks as if it has been done with a pen or brush.

aquatone: A printing process, using thin plates of aluminum and a plastic coating; also known as Lichtdruck and photo-gelatine (q.q.v.).

Arabic gum: See gum Arabic. Used in inks and adhesives and in many other crafts.

archetto: A term used in the craft of ceramics (q.v.). This is a device used for the smoothing of the clay in the process of molding (q.v.).

argent: A term used in heraldry. This is the silver color that is used to show metals such as spears, swords, etc.

Argentina: A type of ceramics (q.v.). The surface is coated with unglazed porcelain (q.v.).

Argentine glass: This is a type of glass that has incrustations of dry porcelain; the glass is transparent.

argile: A type of French clay, used in ceramics (q.v.).

argilla: A type of decomposed granite rock. Used in the making of porcelains (q.v.). This is also a paint ingredient, used in the printing crafts and used as a wash on clay walls in the Far East. Known also by the name of kaolin (q.v.).

argyle: This is a knitted design, usually in a diamond shape. Three colors are usually used. Argyle designs are seen mainly on men's socks.

arm palette: A type of palette (q.v.) with an added cut out area that allows the palette to rest on the arm as well as the thumb. See palette.

armature: An armature is used in the Japanese craft of kanshitsu. It is also used in sculpturing (q.v.). This is a frame or shape made from wire mesh, pipe or heavy wire. It is used as a skeleton to hold clay or plaster. For small models, pipe cleaners can be used.

Armenian bole: A pigment, made of red earth, sometimes known as Venetian red (q.v.). It may also be used as clay.

armorial bearings: This is a term used in heraldry. Used to define the bearings (q.v.) or design of the owner.

armure: A term used in the textile crafts. This is any raised or pebbled pattern or design on a material.

arnaudon's green: This is a color used in painting, chromium oxide green.

Arochem resin: A trade name for a type of resin (q.v.). Used in paints and varnishes.

Arras: A type of French tapestry, used for the coverings of walls. Named from the city in France where it was made.

arriswise: A term used in heraldry. This is a cube-like design that is placed on the escutcheon (q.v.) in such a manner that it faces front showing the top and two sides; used to depict altars.

art of light: A term used where light is used as the medium of expression, also known as lumia (q.v.).

artifact: A term used to describe any tool or object that is constructed by man for his use, such as an arrowpoint, etc.

artificial soft porcelain: A type of porcelain (q.v.). This porcelain is covered with a lead glaze (q.v.) and resembles glass.

artisan: This is a person who has industrial skill, a person who follows a set standard or a way of doing something. He knows a certain trade, such as a carpenter who is able to build a set of stairs.

artist: An artist is a person who creates. He uses his imagination and his eyes, to paint, sketch or model an actual view or what he feels the scene may look like in his mind. This differs from an artisan (q.v.).

arts and crafts: The term arts and crafts is used rather loosely by many people. This Dictionary of Arts and Crafts is aimed at the how of a craft and not the interpretation or the art aspect, where we try to find the meaning behind a craft. For example, American Indian bead work; the art part of this craft comes in when we try to find the meaning in the designs and colors. The craft part of the bead work comes in when we try to do the bead work in the Indian method. Arts and crafts lumped together applies also to an article that is handmade and where ingenuity and skill come into the picture. See crafts.

asbestine: This is an inert pigment, a type of talc (hydrated magnesium silicate). Asbestine is used to prevent liquid paints from becoming hard and caked. It has the ability to remain in suspension.

asbestos: A mineral with silky-like hairs in it. A fireproof material, woven into many types of cloth. Used to cover heating pipes and boilers. Also used in the making of models—see maché. Can be ground or made into sheets.

asbestos cement: A mixture of cement and shredded asbestos (q.v.). Mixed with water and made into a paste.

ash ultramarine: A paint pigment made from the residue of lapis lazuli (q.v.), sodium aluminium silicate, and some sulphur. Used as a neutral tint for sky effects.

ashberry metal: This is a type of pewter (q.v.) which contains about 25% antimony. This makes a very hard pewter, used for kitchen articles.

aspect: A term used in heraldry (q.v.). Aspect is a term used to describe the position of a bird or animal on an escutcheon (q.v.). Full aspect is facing front.

asphalt: A dark bituminous mixture, found in nature and also made synthetically.

asphaltum: A dark brown mixture of asphalt and oil or turpentine. At one time asphaltum was used as a glazing color. In the antique crafts, this substance is used to age a painting, as it gives a surface that is wrinkled and cracked.

asteriated sapphire: Because of the crystalline structure of this sapphire (q.v.) the rays of reflected light appear to form a star; also known as a star sapphire. Used in the jewelry and gem crafts.

astigmatism: This is a term used in photography. Denotes a lens in a camera that does not produce a clear picture or image from the edge to the center but is rather distorted. See anastigmatic.

astrakhan: This is a grade of karakul lamb (q.v.), not the best grade of karakul lamb skin. The term is also used to describe imitations of the real karakul.

atelier: A term used to describe the workshop or studio of an artist.

atmospheric: A term used in the arts, especially in paintings showing large areas of space, such as sky and seas.

aubusson: A type of weaving done on rugs. All of the design lines are parallel to the warp threads (q.v.). The rug has to be sewn together by hand.

augmentation: A term used in heraldry. This describes a grant from a ruler to a person for an additional charge (q.v.) on his coat of arms (q.v.).

aureolin: This is a bright yellow, made of cobalt-potassium nitrite. This pigment is used in tempera, oil and water colors. It was first compounded by N. W. Fisher of Breslau, Germany, in 1830 and first used as a paint pigment in 1852.

auriphrygia: This is a type of embroidery (q.v.), done in gold and found mainly on the lower parts of robes worn by ecclesiasticals. This type of embroidery goes back to the 12th century.

aurora yellow: Cadmium yellow, a type of paint pigment.

Australian walnut: This dark brown hardwood has a straight grain with an even texture. From the tree Endiandra palmerstoni. Used in the wood crafts.

author's alterations: A term used in the book crafts. This term is used when referring to the changes made by an author after a book has been set in type. These changes are made in composition and text.

author's portrait: A practice no longer common. The portrait of the author of the book was printed facing the title page of the book.

autochrome: This is the first screen plate that was made and used successfully in color work. Introduced in Lyons, France, in 1907.

autodidact: A term used to describe an artist who is self taught and took no lessons.

automatic film transport: A term used to describe the method by which film is advanced or moved in a camera, from one exposure to another.

auxiliary lens: A term used in photography. This is a lens that is added to a camera, to enlarge or reduce an image.

aventurine: A type of glass, sometimes used in the jewelry and gem crafts. This glass has a coat of glaze which is brown; when reflected light passes through it, the glass appears to be filled with gold spangles. This glass is made with copper and the addition of peroxide of iron.

avodire: This is light African hardwood. It is used by the Africans to do fine carving.

awata yaki: This is a rather good grade of pottery made in the city of Kyoto, Japan.

awl: A tool used in many crafts. A sharp pointed tool. Similar to a common ice pick.

ax cuts: A painting technique done in China. The brush is passed over the surface in such a manner that it leaves a sharp ax-like angle. Also known as hogback (q.v.).

ax stone: A variety of jade (q.v.) used in carving small objects.

Axminster: This is a type of rug, invented in 1876, named after the city in England where it was first made. The term is now used to apply to any heavy pile (q.v.) rugs. They are now made by machine; the loops are done faster by machine than by the old hand methods.

Aya: This is a type of Hopi kachina (q.v.). This is a type of kachina that belongs to the Wawarus (q.v.). Usually painted white or red, but may be painted other colors. This figure carries a yucca whip.

ayous: This wood is similar to Avodire (q.v.) but a great deal softer. It has a definite striped grain.

ayr stone: A stone used for the polishing of metals and also marble pieces. Used in the metal and sculpturing crafts.

azalea: The blooms from this plant may be used in the corsage (q.v.) crafts. Pick only the flowers or buds as needed, place the stem of the flower in a shallow dish in which there is a solution of peppermint oil, about ½ teaspoon. The blooms should last about three to four days.

azodiphenyl: A coal tar product of a deep blue. Used in the dyeing of fabrics. Also known as coupier blue (q.v.).

azure: A fine blue pigment, this is a form of glass colored with oxide of cobalt and then ground to a powder. Used in the coloring of porcelain. Known also as smalt (q.v.).

azure stone: This stone is also known in the jewelry and gem crafts as lapis lazuli (q.v.).

azurite: A rather rare pigment of a deep blue. This has now been replaced by cobalt and cerulean blue (q.v.). Azurite is a basic copper carbonate, does not work well with oils. A better pigment to use with water colors.

B

babel quartz: A type of crystal used in the making of glass.

babul gum: Used as a substitute for gum arabic (q.v.). A white powder used also in the making of inks.

bachelor: A term used in heraldry (q.v.). This is an order of knighthood conferred in England.

bachiru: A technique of the ivory carver. The surface of the ivory is tinted one color and then the design is cut in, thus exposing another surface and another color. This type of carving is done in Japan.

back: This term, when used in the bookbinding crafts, refers to the back part of a book. This part covers the headband (q.v.).

back focus: A term used in photography. This is the distance from the rear of the lens to the film. Used when distant objects are photographed.

back painting: A process of the arts, especially of mezzotint (q.v.). This consists of affixing a print to a glass surface in such a way that it appears to have been painted on glass.

backing: A term used in the bookbinding crafts. This is the hammering or pounding process by which the back (q.v.) of the book is grooved so that the cover may be finished.

backing paper: A term used in photography. A photograph is mounted or backed with a heavy paper or cloth to make it more durable.

backing up: This is a printing term. Backing up is the printing of a paper on the reverse side or opposite the side that has already been printed on.

Bagdad cloth: A silk cloth that has gold threads woven through it. Used for special occasions.

Bakelite: A trade name for a plastic material used in many arts and crafts. Available in many forms.

baking: A process of many arts and crafts. Consists of heating until the object fuses or forms together. See firing (q.v.).

balance: When used in photography, balance refers to the symmetry in a picture. The objects are shown so that they complement each other.

balaustre: This orange-colored wood comes from South America.

balbriggan: In the textile crafts, this term is used for a fabric made of cotton. Now also applied to certain unbleached cloth.

balearic boxwood: Known also as boxwood (q.v.). This is a fine type of wood used for carving and in the making of woodcuts (q.v.).

ball and wedge: A term used in the metal crafts. Used especially in the crafts involving the use of pewter. This is a type of knop (q.v.).

ball clay: A rather plastic clay. Also known as fat clay (q.v.).

ball knopped: This is a small ball on the tip of a spoon. Especially used on objects made of pewter (q.v.). See knop.

ball mill: This is a device used in the ceramics crafts (q.v.). The ball mill is made with a porcelain (q.v.) lining. It has small hard pebbles inside. Used to grind clay finely.

ball peen hammer: A type of hammer used in metal crafts. One side of the hammer has the conventional head and the other side has a peen or round head. Used to pound metal surfaces to give a pebblelike surface.

ballista: A military weapon. Used in heraldry (q.v.), and is shown as two upright posts with a bar across, loaded on one end.

balloon: This is a device of the cartoonist. It is made in the shape of a balloon over the head of the individual in the cartoon, with a line extended to the person's mouth.

balsa: This rather soft wood comes from South America. It is the lightest of all woods, straight grained and with a coarse texture. This light creamy colored wood is used in many ways, as in making models, either in thin strips or carved from the block.

balsa wood dolls: Dolls can be carved from the soft South American wood known as balsa wood (q.v.). Dolls can be carved to resemble the Hopi Indian Kachina doll (q.v.).

bamboo: A plant that is actually a grass. Used in many crafts, for the making of furniture, fish poles and containers.

banana oil: So called because of its odor. This is the sweet oil of amyl acetate (q.v.). Used in resins, varnish and other films.

bandana: Usually red and white, a large cloth used for the neck or head or just used as a handkerchief. Originated in India.

bander: A brush used in ceramics (q.v.). Used to apply a stripe on a ceramic piece.

banderole: A term used in heraldry (q.v.). This is a small flag that is flown near the tip of a lance.

banding wheel: A device used in ceramics and sculpturing (q.q.v.). A wheel with concentric circles on its surface, used to make a perfect circle. This differs from a gentleman (q.v.).

bands: A term used in bookbinding. These are the cords upon which the pages of a book are stitched, thus collecting the signatures (q.v.).

banko yaki: A type of kitchen ware made of clay in the Ise province of Japan.

barb: A term used in the metal and jewelry crafts. This is any rough edge that is produced on the surface of any object, such as in etching or engraving (q.q.v.).

barberry: The root of this plant is used in the finishing of Morocco leather (q.v.). The root produces a rich yellow dye.

barbotine: A term used in the ceramics crafts (q.v.). This is a thin clay surface or paste that is applied in low relief (q.v.) on the surface.

baren: A device used in block printing. Consists of a block made of a variety of materials. The object is to make a tool that can be pressed or rubbed on the paper which is placed on an inked block print (q.v.). Thus through correct and even pressure, a print can be made.

barium yellow: A light greenish-yellow pigment. Does not mix with water. This sulphur-colored pigment has been used since the early nineteenth century. Barium yellow is a permanent pigment.

barmá: A tool of the ivory carver. This is a type drill used to make very deep cuts in the ivory. The point is usually shaped with a V.

barometer: A simple barometer can be made with blue litmus paper (q.v.). A design can be made and as part of the design, be sure to include a piece of blue litmus paper. When it is damp the paper turns a pink color.

barré: A term used in heraldry (q.v.). This term is used to describe an escutcheon or shield (q.q.v.) that has bars or lines across its surface.

baryta: A term no longer used, it is a form of barium. This pigment is used as an adulterant in cheap paints. Used in the early eighteenth century.

baryta water: Used in fresco painting (q.v.). A lime and water wash used on a wall before a fresco is painted.

basalt ware: Also known as black ware (q.v.), this is a type of stone ware, usually black in color. Made famous by Josiah Wedgwood.

base: A term used in the lapidary and jewelry crafts. The base is the lower half of a gem stone which has been cut. This is the part that is below the girdle (q.v.). It is also known as the pavilion (q.v.). Used in photography. This is the glass plate or the film upon which the emulsion (q.v.) is applied.

basketmaker: The Indians of the American Southwest who preceded the Pueblo civilizations.

base metal: This term refers to the metals which will mix or combine with the gas, oxygen.

bas-relief: A term used in sculpture (q.v.). Bas-relief is a term that denotes a low relief or carving. See relief.

basswood: This Canadian and American wood is very soft and can be easily carved. The grain of basswood is even and straight.

bastard file: One of many files used in the crafts. This file has a very rough surface.

bastard teak: From the tree Butea frondosa. A yellow dye is made from the flowers of this tree. Used in the dyeing of fabrics.

bastard title: Also known as the fly title (q.v.). This is the page in the front of the book containing only the title and no other printed matter.

bat: A term used in ceramics (q.v.). This is a gelatine-like substance which is applied to porcelain (q.v.) or pottery. This is applied over the glaze and then the design is incised or cut on this surface and then fired (q.v.).

batch: A term used in glass-making. This is the final mixture of materials used in making glass; next the glass is fused with heat.

bated: This term when used in the leather crafts is a method of removing the lime and the flesh. A solution is used containing enzymes which act on the flesh. This method makes the hide have a tough grain and a fine grade of leather.

batey: This is a fine type of embroidery (q.v.). Gold and silver threads are used.

bath: This term, when used in the etching (q.v.) crafts, refers to the mixture used to etch (q.v.) a plate (q.v.). See: nitric acid; perchloride of iron.

batik: A technique of dyeing fabrics. The design is made on the cloth, the parts that are to be dyed are left and the rest is painted with wax. The cloth is dipped in dye. It is then boiled to remove the wax, or a hot iron is pressed over it and several layers of paper are placed under it to absorb the wax. Batik is known mainly in connection with the products made in the Malay area.

bats: A term used to describe the ledges or shelves in a kiln (q.v.). Usually made of iron.

batting block: A term used in the ceramics crafts (q.v.). This is a flat block or table top, usually made of plaster (q.v.). Used to beat or wedge clay (q.v.). It then goes to the gentleman (q.v.).

battleship linoleum: Used in the block printing crafts (q.v.). This material is the best suited of the linoleums. This linoleum (q.v.) is uniform in color and texture and thick enough to cut. The color of the linoleum is usually gray or brown. It can be had in any size, usually no wider than six feet. Blocks (q.v.) suitable for cutting can be purchased ready made, glued on wood; sometimes the surface has been coated white so that the design (q.v.) can be seen more readily.

bay laurel: A wood with a fine texture and a straight grain. Used in carving and inlay work. Known also by the name of laurel (q.v.).

bayberry: A low bush which has grey berries. These berries contain much wax. The bayberries are boiled in water, the wax floats to the surface where it can be skimmed off and used for the making of bayberry candles.

bead crafts: Many types of beads can be used and the list is

long of ideas and use of beads. The American Indians are well
known for their bead work, especially the Indians of the western part of the United States. Beads were used to trade with
the Indians, they in turn made lasting designs on buckskin
(q.v.). The Indian used human hair and horsehair for threads.
A beaded belt is rather simple to make. Make a simple loom
(q.v.) or buy a ready-made loom. String the amount of threads
or cords that you will need to make the belt wide enough. Plan
a design first on graph paper (q.v.). Next use a needle and
thread the beads in and out and weave them in place.

beaker: A term used in metal crafts, especially pewter (q.v.).
A vessel with the sides ascending out from the base.

beam splitter: A term used in photography. This is a device
used on a camera which is doing three-color work. This sepa-
rates the colors and causes three identical images to appear.

bean bag: A craft game can be made by sewing two squares
of cloth together about four inches square. Leave one end open
and fill the pocket with beans or small stones. Sew this together and you have what is known as a bean bag. This is
tossed at a target that has several holes large enough to receive the bags. Those that are thrown into the holes are the
ones that score.

bean oil: A pale yellow oil used in many arts and crafts. See
soya bean oil.

bearings: A term used in heraldry. The bearings were placed
on the escutcheon (q.v.). They were a design that belonged to
its owner, also known as a charge (q.v.).

beater: A term used in weaving (q.v.). A device used to beat
the weft threads (q.v.) as they are passed through the warp
threads (q.v.). This is done to make the cloth tight and even.

beer: Beer is used with epsom salts to make a coating on
glass which resembles a frosted window. Use a can of beer and
a half can of epsom salts. This can be painted directly on glass.
Warm water will remove it.

beeswax: A wax secured from melted honeycombs. It is
usually found in two grades, the yellowish and the white
bleached wax; the latter is used in the making of artificial
flowers and plants or where the white color is important. Beeswax has a melting point of 63 to 66° C.

Beetle resin: A trade name for a urea-formaldehyde resin. Used in certain textile and paint products.

beige: A light tan. This term is used to describe a fabric that is in its undyed form or natural.

bekko ware: A type of ceramics (q.v.). The pattern somewhat resembles the tortoise shell. This type of ceramic is made in Japan.

bell metal: This is an alloy (q.v.). Used in the bell-making crafts. The metal is made from tin and copper, used mainly for the making of bells.

Belleek china: A type of American ceramics (q.v.). Named for the well-known Belleek Porcelain Works in Ireland.

bellows camera: A type of camera that can be folded when not in use.

Ben Day: This is an art process, named for its inventor. The process involves sheets or screens of various patterns and designs. These sheets can be used separately or in combination with each other; they adhere to the surface that they are applied to. For example, we have a cube, drawn in pen and ink. To bring out the cube, we might want to shade it on one side; rather than make a wash over it, or inking in one side, and its shadow, we would use Ben Day. The sheet is applied over the cube and the parts we want shaded, we would leave covered, the rest can be cut away. Ben Day is used mainly for illustrations that are to be used for reproduction and provides the small dots which would be impossible to draw.

Benare work: A type of engraved (q.v.), ornamental work done on metal. Done mainly in the Benares area of India.

bendigo pottery: A type of ceramics (q.v.), made in Australia. Rather coarse body with the designs done in relief (q.v.).

Bengal: A type of cotton cloth, woven with a striped design.

bengaline: A type of corded cloth, similar to pique (q.v.). Usually made of silk and cotton or silk and wool.

benitoite: Used in the jewelry and gem crafts. A mineral, blue in color, barium-titanium silicate. Comes mainly from the California area.

benteak: This is a type of wood used for carving. This type of wood is also known as nana (q.v.). The grain of this wood is rather straight with a coarse texture. The color is a reddish brown.

bentonite: Used in the ceramics crafts (q.v.). This is a clay-like mineral that comes in various colors. Swells greatly when wet. Also known as colloidal clay and wilkinite (q.q.v.).

benzene: A product of the distillation of petroleum. Highly inflammable, this colorless liquid is used as a solvent and as an ingredient in paint and varnish removers.

benzoin: A gum resin from Sumatra and Siam. Used in varnishes and various lacquers.

benzol: Derived from coal tar. A solvent for resins and rubber products, such as rubber cement. Sometimes known as benzene.

beque: A term used in heraldry (q.v.). This term is used to describe any bird that is depicted on a shield or escutcheon (q.q.v.). The bill of the bird should have a beak of a color that is different from the rest of the bird.

Berlin blue: The first blue pigment that was made synthetically. Made in Germany in the eighteenth century. Known better by the name of Prussian blue (q.v.).

Berlin iron: Used in the metal crafts and in the jewelry crafts. This is a soft type of iron that contains phosphorus. Used in the making of small castings.

beveling: When working with leather, the edge of the object being made is usually beveled. Beveling is done with a beveling tool (q.v.). This tool cuts along the outer edge of the leather and thus makes a smooth somewhat rounded edge.

beveling tool: A tool used in the craft of leather working. This tool is like a small gouge with a sharp V shape point. It is used to cut along the edge of leather; this helps to prevent the leather from curling. The cut should be made evenly and with one long continuous strip.

bezant: This is a gold medallion, used in heraldry (q.v.). It is placed on the shield or escutcheon (q.q.v.).

bezel: When making jewelry, the bezel is the metal ring that holds the stone.

biacca: A paint pigment, also known as white lead (q.v.).

bianco sangiovanni: A pigment used in the craft of fresco painting, made of calcium hydroxide and calcium carbonate. The color is white.

bias cutting: Cutting in a diagonal direction. In the craft of lampshade making, this is important. Material used on a lampshade should always be cut on the bias or angle. This is to make the material stretch evenly on the frame.

bilge hoop: A type of iron hoop used in the making of barrels. See hoops.

bimbelotier: This term is used to describe a person who makes toys and who works only in metals.

binary alloy: A term used in the metal crafts. This is used to denote a mixture of two metals or elements. See alloy.

binding: As used in the craft of lampshade making, this is a material or tape used as a foundation on the frame of the shade. It provides a means of fastening the shade with threads or other means that will not hold on the metal frame.

binding wire: This soft wire has many uses, such as in metal crafts and in model crafts. It can be used to bind or hold something in place until it has been soldered. Another use is to stretch it and use it in the making of artificial plants and flowers.

birka: A tool of the ivory carver; this tool has a square or triangular point, made of metal.

biscuit: A term used in ceramics (q.v.). This is a term used to describe a piece that has been fired (q.v.) without glaze and is considered to be finished in this state. See bisque.

biscuit kiln: A kiln (q.v.) used in the firing of biscuit or bisque (q.q.v.).

bismuth: In the metal crafts, bismuth is used as an alloy to harden metals, especially pewter (q.v.). It also lowers the melting point of the metal it is used with.

bismuth white: Used early in the nineteenth century; not as poisonous as zinc white. This pigment darkens when it comes in contact with other paints and pigments that contain sulphur.

bisque: A term used in ceramics (q.v.). The term bisque is used to describe ceramics that have been fired in a kiln (q.v.) and are then decorated with a glaze (q.v.) and again fired. See biscuit.

bistre: This pigment is made from the ashes of charred beech wood. Only used with water colors, this pigment fades rather fast; it was in use from about the middle of the eighteenth century.

bite: A term used in the etching (q.v.) crafts. This term is used to describe what the various acids do to a plate (q.v.). It bites or eats its way into the metal surface that is exposed to action of the acids.

bitstone: Fine grains of quartz that are placed in a kiln (q.v.). This bitstone is placed on the smooth sagger (q.v.). Used to help keep the pieces from sliding or moving in the kiln.

bitten pattern: A bitten pattern is a pattern that was used by the Ojibwa Indians of the Great Lakes region of Canada and the United States. This was a design that was bitten with the eye teeth. These marks were bitten into thin sheets of birch bark. The pattern was used later on by the Indians for bead work designs, quill work, etc. Similar work is done by sign painters with a metal wheel known as a pounce wheel (q.v.).

bizet: A term used in the jewelry and gem crafts. This is the part of the brilliant (q.v.) between the girdle and the table (q.q.v.). The bizet has 32 facets.

black horn: Jewelry is made from black horns. Some of this jewelry is inlaid with pearl and ivory.

black lead: A paint pigment, also known as graphite (q.v.).

black oxide of cobalt: A type of pigment, used in ceramic crafts (q.v.). When applied as a glaze it changes to a dark blue when the ceramic is fired (q.v.).

black oxide of iron: A type of permanent pigment. A pigment that has been developed in the twentieth century.

black oxide of manganese: This is a dark brown pigment, used as a drier in varnish and paints.

black ware: A type of stone ware made famous by Josiah Wedgwood, also known as basalt ware (q.v.).

blackpot: A rather coarse type of English ceramic (q.v.) which is unglazed.

blazonry: This is a term used in heraldry (q.v.). This is a representation of a coat of arms (q.v.) that is shown in full color.

bleed: A printing term. To bleed an illustration on a page, the illustration is printed right to the edge of the page. When the page is trimmed, there is no margin left and the illustration is said to bleed or run off the page.

bleeding: A term used in the arts. Bleeding, a term used to describe what happens when one color "bleeds" through another color. For example, a surface is painted with red; next the red surface is painted with white. The red will bleed through and cause the white to have streaks or patches of red or pink.

blending: A term used in weaving and other cloth crafts. The blending is usually done at the time the thread or yarn is made. Wool and cotton fibers are twisted together, or camel's hair and wool, etc.

blind tooled: A term used in the bookbinding crafts. This consists of uncolored tooled leather; no gold or other color is used to enhance the design that is tooled (q.v.) on the leather.

block books: An early method of printing books. Each page of type had to be cut from wood and then printed as a block print (q.v.). The type (q.v.) was carved and could not be removed and used over to make up other words.

block printing: See linoleum printing.

blocks: See linoleum printing.

blood albumin: Used in textile painting, this is a natural dye made from the serum obtained from ox blood.

blood root: This plant was used by the Ojibwa Indians of the Great Lakes region of Canada and the United States. These Indians used this dye to color porcupine quills (q.v.). The color was red. When the fresh roots were used, the dye was yellow. The dye was also used to color wooden objects.

bloom: A term used in the arts and crafts. Bloom is the haze that sometimes appears on the surface of a painting or other surface. Seen on shellacked surfaces. This is caused by moisture in the air or on the surface that has been coated.

blow over: A term used in the making of glass objects. The blow over is the excess glass that extends over the mold; this is later broken away.

blow-up: A term used in photography and engraving crafts. The blow-up is an enlargement of a picture or other illustration.

blown oil: Linseed oil (q.v.), thickened by mixing it with oxygen which is blown or forced through it.

blueprints: Regular blueprint paper can be used to make many simple designs with many objects, such as leaves, wire, etc. Make a frame from a small piece of glass, sand the edge or cover edge with tape so that it will be easier to handle. Next cut a stiff piece of cardboard the same size as the glass. This should be fastened at one end so that it will be hinged to the glass. To print a leaf, for example, lay the leaf on the glass. Next lay a sheet of blueprint paper on the leaf, being sure that the paper is placed with the coated side down. Next use several clothes pins to clamp the paper to the glass. Next turn over the glass and open the cardboard flap. This will expose the blueprint paper to the sunlight. Leave this exposed several minutes. When the paper turns blue, remove it and wash the surface of the paper with clear water. When the coating has been thoroughly washed away, dry the blueprint paper with a blotter or between several sheets of newspaper.

blunger: A device used in the ceramics crafts (q.v.). This device is used to wedge clay (q.v.). The device consists of a tank or container with mechanical arms that revolve.

blurb: In the book crafts, a blurb is a term coined by Gelett Burgess, and is used on the jacket of a book and carries advertising, such as statements from interested parties about the worth of the book.

boarding: When used in the leather crafts, boarding means a process of folding the tanned leather over itself and rolling it back and forth with a board. This process brings out the fine grain of the leather.

bobbin method: A method of making lace (q.v.). Also known as the pillow method (q.v.).

bocasine: A type of fabric used in the bookbinding crafts. This fabric is similar to buckram (q.v.).

bodkin: A tool used in leather work. It is used to enlarge the hole and to apply a snap fastener or eyelet in the leather.

body stain: This term is used in the ceramics crafts. This applies to the color pigment that is added to the moist clay while mixing. This differs from glaze (q.v.), which is applied to the outside of a ceramic piece.

Bohemian glass: A type of very hard glass, made with a base of lime rather than lead, used in the making of mirrors and chemical apparatus.

Bohemian ruby: A term used in the jewelry and gem crafts. This name is used by jewelers when they cut rose quartz (q.v.) and use it as a gem stone. See Bohemian topaz.

Bohemian topaz: Used in the jewelry and gem crafts. This is yellow quartz when it is cut as a gem. See Bohemian ruby.

bole: This is a pigment which is used as a size or ground (q.q.v.) (a base) when applying gold leaf (q.v.). See gold size.

bolt: A term used in the bookbinding crafts. This is the fold on the outer edge of folded paper in a book; this is cut away and thus the pages can be opened in sequence.

bone black: A pigment made of charred bone, used since early Roman times.

bone brown: This pigment is made from bone which has been burned and ground; it also contains particles that are not yet completely decomposed. As a primitive pigment this can be used. The color, however, is not permanent.

bone flesher: A bone flesher is made by the American Indian. It is made from the tibia or shin bone of a deer or other large animal. The edge of this bone is cut on a slant. See flesher.

book pallet: A tool used in the bookbinding crafts. Used for the tooling of book covers and also to spread gold leaf (q.v.).

book press: A device that is used in the bookbinding crafts. This is a press that is used to hold a book tightly so that the cover can be applied and shaped.

bookbinder: A person who designs and produces the covers for books. Covers may be made of any number of materials, wood, paper, cloth. A bookbinder assembles books and binds them together.

bookplates: This is a plate or label that contains the name of the owner of a book. The bookplate is usually pasted on one of the front pages. See ex libris.

borax slate: When soldering, a good flux can be made of borax and water. This is rubbed on a slate surface.

border: This term is used in many crafts. In the making of rugs, this is the outer edge which surrounds the center or the field of the rug. When used in the printing crafts, borders are characters of type of various kinds used around illustrations and along the edges of the pages, etc.

bort: An impure diamond, used mainly in cutting and abrasive tools in the jewelry and gem cutting crafts.

botany: Used in fabrics, this term is used to define a fine type of wool from Botany Bay in Australia. Also applied to any fabric made of a fine grade of wool.

botch: A term used in the jewelry crafts to describe a worthless opal (q.v.).

bottle cap mat: To make a mat to use outside a door, bottle caps can be used. Nail rows of bottle caps, crinkled edge up, on a board until the complete surface is covered. Hose with water to clean the mat.

bottony: A term used in heraldry (q.v.). This term is used when applied to a shield or escutcheon (q.q.v.) upon which a cross is shown. This cross has its points terminating in small crosslets.

boucharde: A term used by a sculptor (q.v.). This is a tool which is used to apply a finish to sculptured pieces. It is a hammer that has a head that is rough and is formed in grooves or ridges.

bouquet: A bouquet is a group or large floral arrangement. A bouquet should be carried and not worn on the shoulder like a corsage (q.v.). A bouquet is given at the end of a show, graduation or to a bride.

bourges: Sheets of acetate paper used by artists, coated with tones of greys or colors. Placed over photos, enables artist to bring out certain objects in a photograph. Printed in color shades and used to make color layouts which can be used by the engraver.

bow-pen: A pen or pencil, similar to a compass, with one end a sharp point. Used for special drawing problems.

box animals: Animals can be made from all sorts of boxes. See paper box animals.

boxwood: Two varieties of boxwood are used; the Turkish wood is to be desired first, next the West Indian variety. The wood is hard, fine, close grained and very hard to work. Boxwood is used to make fine wood cut engraving (q.v.). It has a pale cream color and grows very slowly.

braid: Mostly made from cotton, these are straight lengths that are manufactured in various colors and used on lampshades. They are used to cover seams. Other examples of braids are: gimp (q.v.) made of silk with fancy edges; Vandyke braid, a braid that has a zig-zag shape or made in curves; Russia braid, another type made of silk; silk cord, heavier than the Russia braid, and used to decorate edges.

braided papyrus: Braided papyrus was found in tombs of the ancient Egyptians. The papyrus was braided and made into a crude form of doll, this was covered with hand woven linen. These papyrus (q.v.) dolls were buried with children.

braided rug: This is a rug, usually made from scrap rags which are braided together into a long cord. This cord is then coiled and sewn together to form an oval rug, or one of whatever shape is desired. Also known as a rag rug.

Braille: This is a type of printing in relief (q.v.). This is printing that is done without ink. The raised symbols are "read" by the blind. The fingers are run lightly over the surface and the various dots form words that the blind can read.

brait: In the jewelry and gem crafts, this is an unpolished and uncut diamond.

brass: As used in the metal crafts, brass is an alloy of copper. Brass is made of 65 per cent copper and 35 per cent zinc.

brass type: Used in the book crafts. Brass type is used to apply gold leaf (q.v.) to the surface of a book cover.

brayer: This is a tool used in the printing and intaglio (q.v.) crafts for spreading ink. A brayer consists of a roller with a handle. Of course this is rather more involved on a large printing press, but the same results are desired; the picking up of ink and applying it in a thin smooth film on a plate (q.v.) or block (q.v.).

brazier: A device used to hold hot coals, used in the metalcrafts, especially by those working with brass.

Brazil Wood: This is a type of wood from Brazil. When prepared, Brazil wood yields a red dye, not quite as strong as aniline colors (q.v.).

Brazilian emerald: Used in the lapidary arts and crafts. This name is used by jewelers for the green variety of tourmaline (q.v.).

bread crafts: Various types of stale bread can be used to make interesting flowers and shapes. These may be cut, dyed and then soaked in shellac or other material. Ornamental pins can be made from bread. The field for this craft is rather broad as far as designs go.

breathing tube: This is a device used in gilding (q.v.), especially with gold leaf (q.v.). The breathing tube is used to apply the needed moisture to the bole (q.v.). There is enough moisture in the breath to make the bole sufficiently adhesive.

brick kiln: This is a type of kiln (q.v.). This kiln is shaped like an igloo. Used for the baking of bricks used in building.

brilliant: This is a term used in the lapidary and gem crafts. This is a type of cut that is made on a gem stone. There should be fifty-eight facets (q.v.) on the gem, thirty-three cuts on the crown (q.v.) and twenty-five on the base (q.v.).

bring up: A term used in the printing crafts. This term is used to describe what is done to type that is not registering correctly. Thin pieces of paper are placed under the type to bring it up.

Bristol board: This is a fine variety of drawing board, which usually has a rather smooth finish. First made in Bristol, England. This drawing board can be used on either side. Used for printing, airbrush, line drawings, etc.

Britannia Metal: This is a metal, a fine type of pewter, containing 92 per cent tin, 6 per cent antimony (q.v.) and 2 per cent copper. Britannia Metal is a trade name.

broadloom: This term is used in the weaving crafts, especially in the weaving of rugs. A broadloom carpet is woven at least 54 inches wide.

broadside: A printing term, used to describe a large unfolded sheet, printed on one side only.

brocade: Brocade is a term that is generally applied to a cloth of heavy silk. The surface of this silk is covered with a design, usually of gold or silver thread. This gives the design a rather raised look.

broken pick: This is a term used in weaving. A broken pick causes a streak across the cloth, caused by a missing pick (q.v.).

bromide paper: A slow silver bromide emulsion paper (q.v.). This paper is used for the making of enlargements.

bronze: Bronze is an alloy of copper, with tin and some other types of metals in very small amounts.

bronzed glass: This is a deep green glass that has been exposed to acid vapors, which makes it rather iridescent.

brown spots: A term used in photography. This is a defect in the developer, caused by oxidization or impurities in the water that the negative was washed in.

brunissoir: This is a type of burnisher (q.v.) that is used on pewter (q.v.).

brush: A tool of the arts and crafts. Fine brushes are made from the tail hairs of Asiatic mink, known as kolinsky, found mainly in northern Russia; the hairs are a reddish yellow. Other fine brushes are known as camel hair, this is actually the hair of the squirrel found mainly in Siberia and Russia. The rather coarse brushes are made from pig bristle. Chinese brushes are made from goat and wolf hair.

brush washer: This is a device used to hold brushes while they are immersed in a cleaning solution. This device consists of a spring which is stretched so the handles of the brushes are held firmly in place by the coils of the spring.

bubinga: A type of African Rosewood (q.v.). This wood is hard with an even texture. The color is red.

buckram: A material used in the making of lampshades, used by itself or in conjunction with other materials. Made of cotton or linen.

buckskin: A soft leather whose use by the American Indian is well known. The Indian had many methods of preparing various skins. One method was to skin the animal and scrape as much as possible with sharp knives made of flint. The hide was then soaked in a solution of water and lye; the lye was secured from wood ashes from their fires. This method removed the hair and flesh that remained. The hide was then smoked for several days and then worked until it was soft and pliable. The Eskimo women softened the leather by chewing. Most of the leather work was done by women in the far north.

bud: A type of knop (q.v.) used in the metal crafts, especially the making of pewter (q.v.).

buff leather: Probably made from the skin of the buffalo, hence the name of buff leather. Also made from oxen skins. This is a rather flexible, natural colored leather. Used for the making of bags and belts. Used in the Middle Ages for the making of light armour.

buff stick: A device used in the gem crafts. The buff stick is a small stick covered with leather or velvet and charged with emery, used for the polishing of gem stones.

buff ware: A type of ceramics (q.v.). Made mainly of clay with the addition of other materials to give it strength. This type of ware is never decorated.

buffing: This is a mechanical method of raising a soft fuzzy surface on leather; this type of leather is known as suede (q.v.).

bullion: This is a term in the glass-making crafts. The bullion is a spot or bull's eye (q.v.) in the center of a glass pane. This is known as crown glass (q.v.).

bullion bar: This is a bar or rod used in the glass-making crafts. This is used to hold a tube or other shape that is being worked into some special shape.

bull's eye: A term in glass-making crafts also known as bullion (q.v.).

bullsticker: This is a tool used in the craft of wood-engraving. The blade is made of hard steel. Round on one side and curved to a sharp edge on the other side, the shape is somewhat like a tear drop.

bung: A term used in ceramics (q.v.); this is a tier of saggers (q.v.) which is loaded with ceramic pieces.

bur oak: The inner bark of this tree was used by the Ojibwa Indians of the Greak Lakes region of the United States and Canada. The bark was mixed with hazel burs (q.v.) and the bark of the butternut tree. Sometimes earth was also mixed with these barks. The resulting dye was black. This dye was used to color porcupine quills (q.v.).

burin: A type of graver (q.v.). Used in the craft of wood-engraving. Also used in metal engraving, such as drypoint (q.v.).

burlap: A type of cloth made from jute (q.v.). A rather rough type of cloth used in many crafts, such as bookbinding, rug making, weaving, etc.

burls: A burl is a growth that is found on the trunks of trees. These may be cut off and hollowed out. When cut thin, they make a simple drinking cup. These burl drinking cups were made in early colonial America, and also by the American Indians.

burning: This term is used in ceramics (q.v.). The term is used in connection with the firing process; burning usually takes place with the temperature from 1700 to 2100 degrees Fahrenheit.

burnish: To burnish metal is to give it a high polish by various methods, either by hand or mechanical means.

burnisher: A tool used in the etching crafts (q.v.). A rounded tool used for removing shading and scratches.

burnt ochre: This pigment is ochre (q.v.) that has been baked until it has a brick red color; this pigment is quite permanent.

burnt sienna: This pigment is made by baking sienna (q.v.). This is a very permanent pigment with a reddish-brown color. It can be used in all painting techniques.

burr: A term used in engraving (q.v.); this is the rough edge that is left by the graver (q.v.).

butternut: A carving wood from America. Somewhat resembling walnut, it has a yellow grey color.

butternut dye: The root of this tree was used with the bark of the hazel tree (q.v.) to dye rushes used in basket work. When just the inner bark of the tree was used, the resulting dye was brown. This dye was made by the Ojibwa Indians of the Great Lakes region of Canada and the United States.

button-hole stitch: Also known as the layover or Cordova stitch (q.v.) when used in the leather crafts. This is a knotted stitch, usually found on the cut edges of leather. To measure how much lacing is needed, multiply the amount of edge to be stitched by six, this will give you ample lacing. The button-hole stitch is also used in embroidery.

C

cable release: A term used in photography. This is a device used on a camera to actuate the shutter on a camera. Because the cable absorbs some of the slight movement of the operator, this results in a steady picture.

cable stitch: A type of raised stitch; this stitch resembles twisted rope on the surface of the finished cloth.

cabochon: Cabochon is a term used in the cutting and polishing of gem stones. A cabochon when cut and polished has a rounded surface with no facets (q.v.).

cabosh: A term used in heraldry. This is any charge (q.v.) that shows the head of a beast. This is placed on an escutcheon (q.v.).

cadmium: This is a pigment, a metal related to zinc. It is a permanent type of pigment and is used to make yellows, reds, and oranges and other bright colors. Cadmium is a pigment that is now found in many commercial paints.

caduceus: A term used in heraldry to signify two serpents entwined around a staff. Shown on shields and escutcheons (q.q.v.).

caledonian brown: A pigment made of earth. Not very permanent and a little-used pigment today.

calfskin: This is a type of leather that is obtained from the hide of a calf. Used in bookbinding (q.v.) and other crafts that use leather.

calico: Named after a trading city in India. This is a plain type of woven cotton cloth. Can be printed in colors or in a single color.

calligraphy: This is more of an art than a craft. Calligraphy is fine printing or writing which is done by hand. This is practiced mostly in the orient. It is done with special inks, brushes and papers such as jade tablet paper (q.v.).

callitype: This is a printing term, used to describe a plate (q.v.) made from a page that has been typewritten.

calvary cross: A term used in heraldry. This is a cross that is placed on a shield or escutcheon (q.q.v.). The cross is mounted at the head of three steps. These three steps represent faith, hope and charity.

cambric: A fine cloth. Made originally of linen only, now made of cotton. Named for the French town where it was first made, Cambrai.

came: A joint in a stained glass window (q.v.). This is a grooved metal strip, used generally for all leaded windows.

camellia: The blooms of this plant are used in the craft of corsage (q.v.) making. When the plant has been picked, soak the stems in a solution of two quarts of water to which a ¼ teaspoon of boric acid has been added. The blooms should last about four days.

cameo: A term used in the jewelry crafts. A cameo is a carved surface applied to a surface of another color. Used for small ornamental jewelry. Cameos are sometimes carved from certain tropical conches; the top layer is cut away thus exposing a lower layer of another color.

cameo printing: A term used in the printing crafts. This is used when printing is done from a raised surface.

cameo ware: A type of ceramics (q.v.). This is a two-color ceramic with the designs or figures in relief (q.v.).

camphor wood: This type of wood comes from the island of Formosa.

candelilla wax: This wax is next in hardness to carnauba wax (q.v.). This wax is obtained from a weed that grows in Mexico and Texas. Its melting point is 67 to 71° C.

candid photography: This is the taking of pictures quickly and usually without the knowledge of the person or persons who are being photographed. Small cameras are used for this type of photography.

candlenut oil: See lumbang oil.

candlestick: Made in many shapes and sizes. Usually considered to be rather long and narrower on the top end.

cane: There are over 300 species of plants that may be called cane; it is a type of grass. Cane used for weaving and basketry purposes is a long climbing vine-like plant over 100 feet in length. It is found in jungle and swampy areas of India, Java, Sarawak, Malay and Africa. This is a very difficult plant to harvest as the flagella or tentacles of the plant are armed with very sharp spines. Most of the cane is found in the wild state. Stalks are cut into lengths of about twenty feet, then graded and soaked in a silicate solution. This brings out the glossy surface texture. Cane comes in a number of widths, the small size known as carriage superfine, fine fine, fine, medium, common, narrow binder, wide binder. There are many types and shapes of cane, known by the names of Sarawak (q.v.), Palembang (q.v.), Malacca (q.v.).

cantharid luster: A term used in ceramics. This term defines any glaze (q.v.) that has the greenish-blue iridescence of the Spanish fly.

canton crepe: A type of rather heavy cloth made from silk and rayon.

canvas: This term is applied to many fabrics and does not mean any specific cloth. It is usually a coarse material used for sails, tents, oil paintings and awnings. In the painting crafts, linen cloth is the best type, this comes in various grades with the warp and woof being equal in strength in both directions. To prepare a canvas for use as an oil painting, it is necessary to properly size (q.v.) the canvas. White lead (q.v.) in oil or white lead and zinc (q.v.) in proportions of from 40% to 60% of either make an excellent size. This mixture may be thinned with turpentine. Oil paint should never come in contact with the canvas as it will cause the canvas to rot. Before size is applied, the canvas should be stretched on a frame and wet with water until it is tight; after it becomes dry, then apply the size.

canvas board: A term used in the arts. See academy board.

canvas pliers: A tool of the artist (q.v.). Used for pulling a canvas (q.v.) tightly on a frame, prior to using the canvas for a painting.

canvas sketching pin: A device of the artist (q.v.). A double pointed pin, made in such a way that it will separate wet paintings or other drawings which are not yet dry.

cape diamond: Used in the jewelry and gem crafts. This is a yellowish diamond.

cape ivory: A soft variety of ivory. Used for carving. This ivory takes a high polish.

cape ruby: Used in the gem crafts. This is a ruby red garnet found in the diamond mines of South Africa.

capes: See feather capes, made by the ancient Inca Indians.

cappagh brown: A type of pigment made from Irish earth, this pigment is a permanent type.

caput mortuum: This is a type of pigment, made from a blue-red oxide of iron. The term is an ancient one and is in very little use today.

caracoly: This is an alloy (q.v.). Made from copper, gold and silver, first used by the people of the Caribbean area.

carat: In the measuring of gem stone size or weight the term carat is used. One carat equals ⅕ of a gram. The diamond is measured in points, thus a diamond that has ½ carat has 50 points. Karat (q.v.) is a unit of measure used with gold.

carat goods: A trade term used in the gem and jewelry crafts. This term is used to describe parcels of diamonds that are about the average weight of one carat (q.v.) each.

carbon black: This pigment is made as a result of burning natural gas. This is a very permanent pigment; it drys slowly and does not mix well with other colors as it has a tendency to separate. This black is better than lampblack and ivory black.

carbon paper: This is a type paper used for the making of exact copies, especially typewritten sheets. A sheet of carbon paper is placed over a sheet of paper with its coated side down, next a sheet of paper is placed over this. The top sheet will receive the ink from the typewriter, the exact impression will be made on the bottom sheet of paper. Carbon papers are made in several ways. One method is to coat a paper on one side with a thin coating of wax and lampblack or carbon.

carbon steel: This is a type of alloy steel that is used to make various tools. It is a metal that has been hardened by tempering and annealing (q.v.).

carbuncle: A red stone found mainly in the West Indies. Used in the gem-crafts. A red stone, also known as an anthrax (q.v.).

cardiglio marble: A type of marble used by sculptors (q.v.). Found mainly on the island of Corsica. This is a rather cloudy grey marble.

carding: A process of brushing such fibers as wool so that they become soft and rather straight. This is done with a carding comb. The soft resulting roll is used to spin into cords or threads.

caricature: This is a type of drawing done by an artist (q.v.). The artist takes certain outstanding points or features and overemphasizes them to a grotesque point. However a caricature should be done in such a way that the person or object can be recognized because of the parts that are selected, and fit only that person or object. Often seen in cartoons (q.v.).

carmine: This color is made from the cochineal, an insect from South America. Used in paints and as a dye.

carnauba wax: This is a very hard wax, obtained from the leaves of a palm found growing in Brazil. Its melting point is 83 to 86° C.

carpet: Used in the weaving crafts. This is a rather heavy covering for a floor. A carpet today is considered to reach from wall to wall and is usually fastened to the floor. See rug.

carthame: An orange dye made from the dried petals of the Carthamus tinctorius. This same plant is used to produce a siccative (q.v.) known as safflower oil (q.v.). Besides the use of this plant in the arts, it is also used in the making of cosmetics.

cartography: This is the art of making maps—drawing, collecting and preparing the finished map.

cartoon: A term used in the arts. This is an exact drawing, done for a mural (q.v.) or for other decorations. Done first so that an idea can be seen as it would appear in the finished job. A cartoon is also a drawing or reproduction done for a newspaper or magazine, sometimes done in caricature (q.v.). Cartoons usually tell a story or a joke and are generally supposed to be funny.

cartouche: When this term is used in heraldry, it refers to the Italian escutcheons (q.v.) in particular. In Italy, the shield or escutcheon (q.q.v.) is usually egg shaped or equally curved on both ends.

carving: This term is used in many arts and crafts. Carving is done on many materials, wood, stone, ivory. Carving may be done on a small scale with a small knife and this we know as whittling (q.v.). Woodcarving we mean to be on a larger and more elaborate scale, using more tools, chisels, etc.

case: A term used in the bookbinding crafts. The case is the cover of a book considered apart from the book itself.

case work: A term in the bookbinding crafts. This is the technique or process of fastening a book in its cover or case (q.v.). It can be sewn or stitched.

cased glass: A type of flashed glass (q.v.). Cased glass is made of two layers of glass, either glass may be clear or one may be colored, used for special effects and for stained glass (q.v.) windows.

casein: This is a product of skim milk that has been allowed to become sour, it is then separated from the water. There are three general commercial grades of casein, self-soured, acid and rennet casein. Casein is sold as a yellowish powder and is used as a form of glue. To mix casein, do so in any container that is not metal, mix with water and let stand for two or three hours, add clear ammonia, drop by drop, and at the same time stir until it is well mixed. Mix only enough for use as the material does not keep for any great length of time.

cashmere: A fine and rather rare hair from the undercoat of cashmere goats found in Asia, mainly in the Himalayas.

casing: A term used in glass making. This term is used when two layers of glass are fused together; one glass is invariably colored. See cased glass.

casing in: This is a term used in the bookbinding crafts. This is the process of applying the cover to a book. When a leather cover is put on a book, the casing in is done while the leather is soft and pliable, such as it would be when it is coated with glue or paste.

cassel yellow: A paint pigment made from lead oxide and chloride. Known also as patent yellow.

Cassius purple: A paint pigment, discovered by a German chemist, Andreas Cassius. Used in the making of ruby glass (q.v.). Made from chloride of gold and tin.

casting: A term used in many crafts, especially in ceramics and metalcrafts. This is a shape that is the result of pouring some compound into a mold (q.v.). The result will be a duplicate of the object from which the original mold was made.

casting clay: A fine type of clay used in the making of cast ceramics (q.v.).

casting plaster: A fine white plaster, used in the making of molds (q.v.) and for the making of castings (q.v.).

casting slip: A slip used in ceramics (q.q.v.). Used in the casting of molds (q.v.); this is a fine screened clay, rather liquid, which is poured in and out of the mold.

castor oil: This oil is obtained from the seeds of the plant known as Ricinus communis; this plant, grown in tropical countries, is well known and is grown by many people as background planting in yards and estates. The castor oil is used as a medicine and mixes completely with alcohol, turpentine and all other vegetable oils. Castor oil is used in plastics and cellulose lacquers.

Castung: A trade name for a processed oil made from oil obtained from the castor oil plant. Used in the making of inks, plastics and films for paintings and sculptured (q.v.) pieces.

cat gold: A variety of mica with a rather gold color.

catgut: Never made from cats, this material is made from the intestines of sheep and goats, sometimes from those of the horse. Name probably derived from the small violin or fiddle known as a kit fiddle. The intestines are dried and twisted.

cathedral glass: A type of glass with a rippled or patterned glass. The surface texture is applied at the time the glass is made. See stained glass.

catlinite: A red clay found in parts of Minnesota. Used by the American Indians for the making of pipes, and known as pipestone.

cat's eye: Used in the jewelry and gem crafts. This is a variety of chrysoberyl (q.v.). Sometimes the door of certain tropical snails is called cat's eye and used for the making of rings, etc.

cattail: The heads of the cattail will last indefinitely if they are painted with clear shellac or clear nail polish. To freshen the cattail, soak the stems in water in which a small amount of vinegar has been added.

cattail mats: The Ojibwa Indians of the Great Lakes area of Canada and the United States used the cattail to make simple shelters. The cattails were cut and sewn together with the fiber from the basswood. These leaves were overlapped so that they would shed rain. They were made into wigwams (q.v.).

cave pearl: A substance found in the deposits of caves, having the composition of a true pearl (q.v.) but an irregular shape.

cedarite: A fossil resin, used as a substitute for amber (q.v.), found mainly in the Saskatchewan river deposits of Canada.

celadon: The porcelain made in China is named celadon porcelain, because of its color. This is a pigment made from a green earth, celadonite, which is an iron silicate.

cellophane: A cellulose material. Made in thin sheets, used in many crafts and in the arts for covering various objects. Cellophane comes clear and in many colors and thicknesses. It can be mixed with fibers.

cellophane jewelry: Simple necklaces can be made from cellophane. Roll the cellophane into tubes, roll or wrap it around a pencil or other small round object. Cement the edges with Duco cement (q.v.) or Scotch tape (q.v.). When the tubes are tight, remove the pencil and you will now have a cellophane tube. Cut this tube into short lengths and string them with a contrasting color yarn or string.

Cellosolve: A trade name for a solvent, made from ethylene glycol mono-ethyl ether. Used in many crafts such as leather, textiles, printing and in the painting crafts.

celluloid etching: A very satisfactory etching (q.v.) can be made on a plate (q.v.) made of celluloid. A rather thick piece of celluloid should be used. A drawing or photograph can be placed under the sheet and then the surface of the celluloid can be scratched with some sharp tool. The plate can be printed the same as any other of the etching plates. The ink should be wiped off after the plate has been used as it is almost impossible to remove hard dried ink. The plate can be cleaned with a cleaner that will dissolve the ink, such as benzine.

cellulose: Found in the cell walls of plants. This substance is used in many arts and crafts. Used in the making of paper, weaving fibers, paints, etc.

celure: A term used by sculptors (q.v.). This is any decoration that is done in relief (q.v.) on the walls or ceiling of a room.

cement: There are many kinds; it is mainly the result of burned and ground lime. Also means a glue or adhesive.

ceramic case: A mold made from a solid block of plaster, used in the making of the model or working mold.

ceramics: This term is used generally when clay is used and fired (q.v.). This is a general term. Used since ancient times, the ceramics craft has been practiced in all parts of the world. The clay is fired (q.v.) in a kiln (q.v.), no matter how crude, and even sometimes just sun baked until it is hard. A ceramic does not have to be useful, it can be ornamental, such as a small decorative figure.

ceramist: A person who is devoted to the arts and crafts of ceramics. The maker, designer, collector or researcher in the field of ceramics (q.v.).

ceresin: This is a type of wax, white or with a yellow tinge. Sometimes this wax is used as a substitute for beeswax (q.v.). The various grades of this wax melt from 61 to 80° C.

cerography: This is a painting technique done by the ancient Romans. The paint pigments were mixed with hot beeswax and then applied to the painting surface. Wax tablets were also made in this method.

cerulean blue: A pigment made of cobalt and tin oxide. A rather bright blue and is a permanent pigment for all types of art. First used around 1805.

ceruse: This is another name for white lead. However, it is no longer in common use.

Ceylon ivory: A white to pink ivory, used for fine carving; does not crack easily when carved.

chalchuite: A blue-green turquoise (q.v.), used in the gem crafts. Found in Mexico and New Mexico.

chalk: A calcium carbonate; when it is pure and white it is known as precipitated chalk. Most pastels are made from chalk. It has the same chemical makeup as limestone, marble and whiting (q.v.).

chalking: A term used in the arts, this is the action of certain paint pigments which dry out and become chalky and rub off.

chamois: This is a very old method of leather preparation. The leather is washed many times and then with the application of oil, it is pounded and re-washed and more oil applied and then the process is repeated. The result is a fine soft leather. Chamois feels and looks like "buckskin" (q.v.). This type of leather is used to wash and polish automobiles and other surfaces; it absorbs water and does not leave any lint on the surface. The dirt may be washed out of it as you would wash a cloth. Chamois is also a name given to the pigment ochre (q.v.). The term is now obsolete for this use.

College of the Sequoias Library

chamois skin doll: Chamois (q.v.) has been used since the early American Indian days. To make a chamois doll: Start with a ball of cotton or a ball of cloth, wrap this with the chamois and tie tightly, this will form the head of the doll; proceed to stuff more of the doll and you will now have the chest and waist. Next cut pieces of the chamois and roll them to make small tubes, either solid or with a stuffing of cotton or cloth, these will form the arms and legs. Next sew these to the body of the doll. Clothes can be made of chamois and put on the doll; this will make him look as if he is an early settler, in buckskin (q.v.) clothes. Eyes, nose and mouth can be made from thread or sew some bright beads on the chamois.

champain: A term used in heraldry. This is a mark placed on the shield or escutcheon (q.q.v.). This is a sign of dishonor, such as the killing of an enemy who has surrendered, drunkenness, rape, etc.

channel black: A natural black pigment collected from burned gas, used in the making of inks, paints, crayons, black leathers. Also used as a separator in molds used in casting (q.q.v.).

chaplet: A term used in heraldry, denoting the garland or wreath of leaves found on a coat of arms (q.v.). A chaplet shows that its owner has had outstanding military prowess.

char: A black pigment made from animal bones.

charcoal: Usually made from willow wood. The wood is charred and used to make sketches and rough in paintings.

charcoal drawing: A type of drawing, in black or shades thereof. Done with sticks of charcoal (q.v.). Usually done on charcoal paper (q.v.).

charcoal paper: A white, rather soft paper with a rough surface, used by the artist (q.v.) for the making of drawings, especially with charcoal and pastels (q.v.). Also used for watercolors. This paper has a high rag content.

charge: A term used in heraldry. A charge is a design that covers part or all of an escutcheon (q.v.). The proper charge (q.v.) and the common charge (q.v.) are the two main classifications.

chased metal: This is metal that has a design on its surface. This design is made with a graver (q.v.). It is either raised or indented, depending on the size, type and purpose that the metal is to be used for. Early armor was chased with designs. This type of technique sometimes included the addition of color which was applied by a technique known as inlaying (q.v.).

chasing: This term is used in the metal crafts. The surface of the metal is pounded with a hammer or with a punch to give a rough surface, pebble-like, such as would be done on a metal tray or dish.

châssis: A frame used by artists (q.v.) for the stretching of canvas (q.v.) used in painting.

chatón: This is a rather coarse diamond, used in the gem crafts.

chatoyant: A term used in the jewelry and gem crafts. Used to describe a gem stone that has a luster that changes as in the cat's eye (q.v.).

Chaveyo: This is a type of kachina (q.v.) made by the Hopi Indians of the United States. The head of this kachina is painted black; it has a mark on its forehead that represents the footprint of a bird. He has half moons on his cheeks. In his hand he carries a knife. This kachina appears in the spring and comes when Hopi Indian children are bad.

checker board: A term used in weaving. This is a style of weaving in equal squares of high and low relief (q.v.).

cheese box drum: A simple drum can be made for children out of a discarded cheese box. Of course there are various sizes when it comes to cheese boxes, so I would suggest a box to go with the size of the child. A large cheese box can be covered with rawhide (q.v.) or you can do a cheap, quick job with tough brown wrapping paper. This paper can be oiled or painted with wax. A design can be painted or drawn on the surface if you desire. You can stretch the paper over the surface and then Scotch tape (q.v.) it or use masking tape (q.v.) around the edge. Drumsticks (q.v.) can be made.

chelsea filter: A device used in the detection of fake emeralds (q.v.). This device consists of a dichromatic color filter that transmits only two wave-length colors or deep red and yellow-green.

chemical porcelain: This is a type of porcelain (q.v.) of high quality, used in chemical laboratories, as it resists chemicals and extreme heat changes.

chemigraphy: Used in the etching and engraving crafts (q.v.). This is mechanical engraving using chemicals.

chemitype: A technique of map making. The etched lines are coated with wax and then filled with metal. The zinc plate is then eaten away with acid. This leaves the lines in relief (q.v.).

chenille: A fabric made of cotton or other fibers, recognized because of the tufts of ridges that run through it. Usually seen in the form of mats, bed spreads, etc.

chevron: A term used in heraldry. This is one of the nine ordinaries (q.v.). The chevron is shown one fifth the size of the shield or escutcheon (q.q.v.).

chi: A term applied to ceramics made in the Orient which applies to any ceramic (q.v.) that has been painted with lacquer (q.v.).

chiffon: A light weight, soft finished fabric, such as light weight hose, gauze, etc.

chih: This is a type of Chinese paper. Generally made from bamboo, rice, mulberry, or straw. The color is white.

Chilkat: A mainland tribe of Canadian Indians who weave blankets from the hair of mountain goats and the fibers of the cedar.

china: A broad term which embraces all varieties of dinnerware. Originally meant only ceramic pieces (q.v.) from China that were vitrified (q.v.).

china clay: This is used with other pigments in the craft of pottery making. It tends to give other pigments a muddy appearance.

china marking pencil: A china marking pencil is used to write on china and glass ware. It is sometimes used in the lithograph crafts (q.v.). See lithograph pencil.

chinchilla: A small animal found in the high South American mountains. This small rodent is difficult to raise and so the value of its fur is very high. Used for the making of coats, gloves, etc.

chine: The top edge of the barrel stave (q.v.), grooved to receive the top of the barrel. This is done by a cooper (q.v.).

chine silk: A cloth with colored warp threads (q.v.). Used for many purposes, it can be printed, dyed, etc.

Chinese bean oil: A pale yellow oil, used in the arts and crafts. See bean oil.

Chinese ink: Also known as India ink (q.v.).

Chinese insect wax: This wax is used as a substitute for beeswax (q.v.). Made in much the same way as shellac (q.v.). The wax itself is rather hard and has a melting point of 79 to 83° C. This wax comes from Japan and China.

Chinese pencil: A tool of the engraver and the etcher, a brush with strong sharp bristles. Used for stirring the acid used in etching. This has replaced the use of a feather.

Chinese white: A fine white paint pigment, made from zinc oxide. Used mainly in the making of inks.

Chinese wood oil: A drying oil used in the arts. See tung oil.

Chinese yellow: A fine yellow pigment, see king's yellow.

chinkinbori: A term used in the arts. Refers to anything done by the Japanese lacquer process with the use of shallow engravings which have been traced with gold.

chinoiserie: An art term, used to refer to anything originated or created that is peculiar to the Chinese.

chint: This is a Hindu word for chintz (q.v.).

chintz: This is a type of fabric. There are many variations and patterns. Generally, chintz has an all over pattern, and is sometimes glazed. The name was originally a Hindu word known as chint. Commercial use changed the name to chintz. This is a cotton fabric.

chip: Used in the jewelry and gem crafts. A chip is a small gem stone that is usually placed in a setting around a better cut stone. This term is especially applied for use when referring to the diamond.

chip carving: This is a type of relief (q.v.) carving done mainly in wood. A sharp tool is used to chisel or chip out a design. The design is made up of many small cuts, usually triangular in shape. Sometimes, enamel or other material is inlaid (q.v.).

chiriji: A Japanese technique of painting. Gold dust is sprinkled on a wet surface of lacquer, usually black.

chisel: A tool used in woodworking crafts. Also used in the cutting of a block print. A chisel has a sharp flat point, the cut that is made is flat and even such as this / or this =.

chisel draft: A term used in sculpturing. This is a cut

guide line done on stone. This serves as a guide for further cutting.

chitte: A variety of chintz (q.v.).

chloromelanite: Used in the gem crafts, this is a black variety of jade (q.v.), sometimes a dark green.

chokeberry: The inner bark from this plant was used by the Ojibwa Indians of the Great Lakes region of Canada and the United States. A dye was made from this bark, the resulting color being red.

chrome colors: These are synthetically prepared paint pigments. Chrome yellow is the best known. These are crystalline pigments and not too permanent.

chrome green: This pigment is a mixture of Prussian blue (q.v.) and chrome yellow. This is not a permanent pigment.

chrome tanning: Chemicals which are the chrome salts used in the process of tanning give rise to the term, chrome tanning.

chrome yellow: See chrome colors.

chrysoberyl: Known in the gem crafts also as cat's eye (q.v.) and chrysolite. This is a mineral with an aluminum base.

chrysocolla: A green pigment made from a mineral, copper silicate. Used in early times as a paint pigment. It was replaced with Egyptian Green (q.v.).

chu sha: A red or vermilion paint pigment used in China. A mineral pigment made from cinnabar (q.v.).

chuban: This is a type of wood cut done in Japan. This wood cut is somewhat larger than a koban (q.v.).

chulga: A plant used in the tanning of leather, used by the Arabs.

churi: A tool of the ivory carver. Somewhat shaped like a saw, the tool has teeth on one side and a smooth sharp edge on the other. Used for the cutting up of ivory before it is to be carved.

cinnabar: A red pigment with an orange tinge. Found in use in early Assyria and ancient Greece. This pigment is now no longer in use and is considered obsolete.

circular kiln: This is a type of kiln (q.v.). Used much as the tunnel kiln (q.v.). The kiln is arranged in such a way that pieces can be moved in and out of the kiln without waiting for it to cool completely.

circular knit: This type of knitting is done by a machine with a set number of needles which are arranged in a circle. As the machine knits, the material comes out from the bottom in a long tube.

cire perdue: A technique of casting (q.v.), known also as the "lost wax method." An object is modeled in wax, this is then coated with plaster or other material. Hot or molten metal is then poured in and the melted wax is forced out. The metal hardens and replaces the wax. The outer mold is broken away leaving an exact impression of the original.

ciseleur: A term used in the metal crafts. This is one who does chasing (q.v.) of the metal, especially in bronze.

ciselure: This is the art or the process of chasing (q.v.) on metals.

cistern: A term used by those in the glass-making crafts. This is a device into which the glass is ladled prior to pouring in the making of plate glass (q.v.).

citron yellow: This term is usually applied to any light yellow. This pigment has a zinc base.

clamp wheel: A term used in the crafts of ceramics and sculpturing. This is a small banding wheel (q.v.) that can be clamped to a table.

clamping press: In the bookbinding crafts a clamping press is used to hold the pages tightly in place.

clarendon: A term used in printing, this is a style of type. A rather thick style of type.

claw: This is a setting used in the gem crafts. This is a device that looks like a claw or hooks which are bent in such a way as to hold a gem tightly in place on a ring or bracelet.

clay: A material used in the arts and crafts, especially in the ceramics and sculpturing crafts (q.q.v.). Clay is a natural material from the earth. Made mainly of hydrated silicates of aluminum, although there are many other types of materials called clays. Clay can be sun dried or fired (q.v.). When this is done the clay dehydrates and it becomes hard.

clay crock: A large container made of clay. Used by sculptors and ceramists for the keeping of clay in a moist form for later use. Usually holds about fifteen pounds of wet clay.

clear melting: A term used in the making of blown glass. Clear melting is a term used to define the process of keeping the glass in a molten state long enough for the impurities to settle. Somewhat like the method of cold stoking (q.v.).

Clinchfield: A trade name for an extender for paints and varnishes. A variety of China clay (q.v.), a form of aluminum silicate.

clock: A type of embroidery (q.v.), used to conceal the sewn seams around the ankle of a sock.

cloff: A term in the metal crafts, especially in the working of pewter (q.v.). These are small pieces of pewter that are left over from the making of an object. These scraps are later used for applique (q.v.).

cloutage: A term used in leather crafts. It means the use of fancy nails to decorate leather work. These nails are of two types; one that is shaped as a common nail and is used to decorate trunks, boxes, etc. The other type nail is split, with a shape much like a rivet; this is used on belts, bags and other objects that are soft and cannot be nailed.

coal tar: A thick substance which results from the distillation of coal. There are thousands of products made from coal tar products. Dyes are one of the products.

coat of arms: The origin of this term goes back to the 12th century. A coat of arms was a design that was placed on the front of a suit of armor. It was a "coat over arms," and changed to coat of arms.

coated paper: This is a special type of paper. Coated paper is used for engravings (q.v.). The surface of the paper is coated under pressure with a film of clay. See enamel paper.

cob dolls: Simple dolls can be made from corn cobs. Dry the cob and remove the corn. The cob may be cut in various shapes and dressed with the husks of the corn or with cloth.

cobalt: This term applies to many types of paint pigments made from a base of the ore, cobalt. Cobalt blue, etc.

cobalt blue: Made of cobalt oxide and aluminum oxide with phosphoric acid. A variety of ultramarine blue is used as an imitation of cobalt blue in cheaper paints. Cobalt blue is a permanent type of pigment.

cobalt green: Made of a mixture of zinc oxide and cobalt zincate. This is a bright green pigment tinged with blue.

cobalt violet: A permanent pigment made from cobalt phosphate, it is also made from cobalt arsenite. Its use started in the early nineteenth century. Most of the cobalt violet pigments are made with the cobalt arsenite; they should be used with care because they are poisonous. Cobalt violet is a pigment that has been in use since about 1860.

cochineal: A dye similar to kermes (q.v.). This is a pigment made from an insect that is found in Mexico on the cactus plant. The body of the insect is used to make a red dye.

cocobolo: A tough hard wood with a red color from Panama and Nicaragua. This wood is used to make the handles of knives.

coelanaglyphic: A term used in sculpturing, refers to hollow relief (q.v.).

coiffure doll: In 1763, dolls were made by the French hairdressers. These dolls showed the latest styles of hairdressing. They were sent all over Europe and were used by the hairdresser to make the latest styles. The hair styles of these coiffure dolls were registered to insure that they be done correctly.

coil method: A term used in ceramics (q.v.). This method is used to make objects of clay. The moist clay is made into a long thin roll, about the thickness of a pencil. This long strip is placed on a clay base and coiled in a circle on top of itself until the desired shape is made. This is then smoothed. The coils can usually be seen on the inside of bowls and other objects made with this method.

coin silver: Silver coins are 90 per cent silver and 10 per cent copper. Coin silver has a melting point of 1615 F. When testing coin silver, nitric acid is used; the resulting color will be black.

cold forest: A term used in Chinese painting to denote trees that are painted without their leaves.

cold stoking: A term used in glass making. This is done by lowering the temperature of the oven or furnace until the glass is of the consistency of glass that can be blown. A process also known as clear melting (q.v.).

colloidal clay: Used to increase the plasticity of clays used in the ceramics crafts (q.v.). Known also as bentonite and wilkinite (q.v.).

collage: The cutting of pictures and placing them together to form a new picture known then as a montage (q.v.).

collate: A term used in the bookbinding and the printing and allied crafts. This means to assemble a book or pamphlet or sheets in the correct order for final binding, stapling, etc.

collet: A term used in the craft of glass making. This is the part that sticks to the pontil (q.v.) used for the removal of the glass object from the pot.

collotype: A printing technique, known as photo gelatine or aquatone (q.q.v.).

colophon: A printing and book art term. This is the last page of the book, used for production facts such as typography, typeface, number of copies, etc.

color: This is the general effect of the difference in the various hues on the eye. Colors are made from various pigments (q.v.) and dyes.

color aquatint: Used in the art of aquatint (q.v.). This is the use of a color plate for each color used in the aquatint.

color mill: A device used by the artists (q.v.). This device was used to mix pigment, oils and thinners into paint that can be used by the artist.

color value: This is the amount of light and dark in a color. The more light, the higher the value.

commercial art: This is the type art done for commercial purposes. Such art as: advertising layout, package designs, illustrations of all sorts for use in posters, etc.

common board: This is a sawmill designation and is applied to rough cut (q.v.) wood. A board is one inch thick and from four to eighteen inches wide.

common charge: A common charge is a type of charge (q.v.) used in heraldry (q.v.). This is a design or representation on an escutcheon (q.v.) that is not the original design but one that has been added, such as the figures of persons or animals.

Community Putz: A community project in Pennsylvania, done around the Christmas holidays. Sometimes called a putz (q.v.).

composing rule: A tool of the printer. Used when making up lines of type. This rule has a small projection on the end which is held against the type until it has been justified. See **justification.**

compound fabric. A fabric that has more than one warp. Used in the weaving crafts (q.v.).

concave: A concave lens is a lens that curves inward. This lens is thicker around the edge and tapers toward the center where it becomes considerably thinner. See convex.

concave relief. See hollow relief.

conch shell: This is a gastropod, used in the crafts. The shell is cut or carved to make fine cameos (q.v.). Used also for making trumpets or horns.

conchoidal: A term used in the jewelry and gem crafts. This term is used to describe a stone that has a concave or convex fracture. Useful when a cabochon is cut (q.v.).

condensing: A term used in the printing crafts. This is the use of very narrow letters. Done so that more type can be got into an allotted space.

condensing lens: A device used in photography. Used to more evenly distribute the amount of light that projects through the lens.

cone: A term used in the craft of ceramic making (q.v.). A cone is a stack that comes out of a kiln (q.v.). Cones are also test pieces of clay. They are used to test the heat of a kiln, known also as pyrometric cones (q.v.).

confetti ribbon: The common confetti ribbon can be used to make mats and coasters for glasses. Glue several rolls together to form the mats.

configurated glass: A type of glass with a pattern, usually not a transparent glass. The surface pattern is applied at the time the glass is made.

confluent colors: A term used in the arts. These are colors that blend with each other in such a way that no definite dividing line between the colors can be seen.

contact print: A term used in photography. A contact print is a print made exactly the same size as the negative. Done by placing the negative directly on the print paper.

continuous filament: A type of fiber or filament used in the weaving crafts. This is a synthetic fiber, made in one long thread and is not made up of many small fibers.

continuous kiln: See circular kiln and tunnel kiln.

contoura: This is a device used for small copying work. Such as the copying of the pages of a book.

converging lens: A lens used in photography. This lens is thicker in the center; this differs from the convex lens (q.v.).

convertible lens: These are lenses used in photography. They can be used together or as separate lenses.

convex: A convex lens is a lens that curves out from the center. This type of lens is thick in the center and tapers out at the edge. This differs from a concave (q.v.) lens.

cool colors: A term used in the printing and painting crafts. These are the colors and shades of blues, violets and shades of greens. These contrast with the warm colors (q.v.).

cooper: A highly skilled craftsman. These are the people who make barrels.

cooper's adze: A tool of the cooper (q.v.). This is shaped somewhat like an ax with the blade set at right angle to the handle. It was used to shave the edge of the wood in the making of barrel staves.

copal gum: This is a hard resin-like substance. Secured from living trees. Used in the making of varnish. Can be mixed with linseed oil (q.v.) and turpentine to make a varnish.

copal varnish: This is an oil resin varnish. It is made by combining resin, linseed oil and lead or manganese for a drier. These are cooked at high temperatures. Copal varnish has a tendency to darken and crack with age, especially when combined with other paints or varnishes.

coping: A term used by the sculptor (q.v.). Coping is done on marble slabs. This is the trimming and smoothing that is done on marble base boards, etc.

copper: A metal used in many crafts; used in sheets it can be hammered into shapes or designs. Used for etching (q.v.). Copper salts used in paint pigments.

copper etching: This is done in the etching crafts (q.v.). The plate of copper is covered with a wax layer or varnish. The design is then scratched through this thin layer. Next acid is applied to the surface which bites (q.v.) into the lines and thus etches the plate. Printing is then done from the plate; first remove the coating from the plate.

copper screen: Plain copper screen, the type used to screen windows and doors, can be used to make smart craft objects. The screen can be cut to fit in a picture frame and form a background for a shadow box (q.v.) or some cut out picture.

The screen can be used in the same way as a copper plate that is to be hammered and thus have a different design that is in relief (q.v.).

Coptic bone doll: There were many strange dolls from upper Egypt. The Coptic bone dolls were carved from bone and had flat tops on their heads. The arms were made so that they would move. The eyes of these dolls were grooved and painted black. Nose and mouth were made rather small. Real human hair was used on these dolls, earrings and necklaces for the dolls were made of bronze.

copy: A term used in printing, especially in newspaper and book publishing. Copy is the written or typed matter that is given to a printer to be set in type or to be reproduced in any other manner.

Cordova: A type leather named after the city of Cordova in Spain. Cordovan leather is usually made of horsehide. This type of leather was known as early as 1400.

cordwainer: A word of French derivation. It designated a section of the city where the leather workers had their shops. See Cordova.

core yarn: This is a type of yarn which has a covering of another type twisted around it, thus concealing the inner core.

cork chickens: To make a cork chicken, take a cork. Use a stiff wire or a pipe cleaner (q.v.) and make legs and feet for the chicken, force these wires into the cork. Use a small cork for a head and wire or duco (q.v.) the cork in place. Cover this form with feathers, use care so that the feathers will overlap and look natural. The feathers may be dyed as you desire (see feather dye).

cork dolls: Simple dolls can be made from old or new bottle corks. Use a large cork for the head and other smaller corks can be strung together to make arms and legs. An icepick can be used to make a hole through the cork; instead of string or thread, a rubber band can be used and this will make a doll that can be bent and will snap back in shape.

corn cob dart: A simple dart can be made from a nail, corn cob and three feathers. Cut the head off of the nail and force the nail into the narrow end of the cob. Glue should be applied in the hole, or some plastic wood (q.v.). Glue the feather in a triangular form on the fat end of the cob. You will now have a fine dart. File the point so that it will stick. Use care when throwing these darts as they are very dangerous.

corn husk dolls: The hair of the corn husk doll is made from dried corn silk, the hat made from dried blossoms, the body of the doll is made from a dry corn cob, the costume and the hat are made from the husks of the corn. Some dolls are made completely from the corn husk. The husk is wet first and then it can be worked and bent without breaking. Make a small ball of husk and wrap it with husk, this will form the head. The body of the doll can be made from strips of the husk, these are folded in half and bent to form a slight X; this is tied in the center to form the body and the waist of the doll. This may be left as is and you will have a girl doll; split the husk in the center and bind the bottoms and you will have a boy doll.

Cornish stone: Also known as kaolin (q.v.).

corners: A term used in the bookbinding crafts. Used to cover the corners of books, especially half and three-quarter bindings.

corrigenda: A term used in the book crafts. These are mistakes or errors that have been discovered after the book has been printed and can no longer be changed. These are added on a sheet in the book known as an insert or errata (q.q.v.).

corsage: The making of a corsage is known all over the world. Some are very simple, others are very ornate and very difficult to make. A corsage may be made from fresh flowers, dried or waxed, or of many other materials. Generally, a corsage is made for a special occasion, such as a marriage, birthday. They are sometimes placed on the top of a gift box. There are many ways to make a corsage, because there are many, many types of blooms to use. Each flower requires its own method of fastening. Some flowers have very weak stems, or none at all, others have tough stems and can be used as is. The corsage should be designed to fit the occasion, the colors should harmonize. The tools needed to make a corsage are rather simple: Scissors, pliers, pruning shears, needle and thread, a punch such as ice pick, green covered wire and a tape that will stretch, scotch tape and other variously colored ribbons, cords and strings. When making the corsage, keep in mind how the flowers grow naturally and then form and fasten them in a natural way, blooms up and the stems down. See: Wiring, taping, dyeing flowers, corsage forms, size.

corundum: Corundum stones are various types of powders and dusts from various stones; these are made into wheels, and sandpapers, which are used for polishing and smoothing rough surfaces.

cosmetic bismuth: This is a white powder used in the making of white paint pigments. Known also as pearl white (q.v.). Used in the making of artificial pearls.

costume jewelry: A term used to describe jewelry that is made with metals other than gold, silver, etc. Also the non-use of valuable gem stones, using synthetic gems instead. Most of the metals are plated.

cotton: The fibers from this plant are used in many ways. Cotton has been cultivated as early as 3000 B.C. Its use was developed by the Moors in Spain around 912 A.D. Was also in use in pre-Inca times in Peru around 200 B.C. Called by the Greeks the "wool of the bushes."

count: A weaving term, this is the number of warp and filling threads (q.q.v.) to the square inch.

counter etch: To prepare a zinc used for etching (q.v.), it must be counter etched. This is done by placing the plate in a solution of acid and powdered alum. About five tablespoonfuls, a teaspoon of nitric acid and the rest water, make about a quart of solution. Pour the solution into a flat glass container. Let the plate soak about two minutes. Use care when removing the plate from the solution, wash the plate clean under running water. Lay the plate on a flat surface and fan dry. The plate now has a very sensitive surface that is ready for drawing, which is done with a lithograph pencil (q.v.).

countersink: Countersink is a term used in many crafts where parts are fitted together with bolts, rivets, nails or screws. To make a smooth surface on an object, it is necessary to gouge or bevel the surface so that the head of the fastener will be flush with the surface. Nails are driven into wood with a countersink, a small tool with a blunt point about the size of the nail. Putty is then applied to cover the nail completely.

couped chevron: A term used in heraldry. This is a chevron (q.v.) which does not reach the edge of the escutcheon (q.v.).

coupier blue: A dark blue dye, somewhat like indigo blue. Made from coal tar products. Also known as azodiphenyl (q.v.).

couple-close: This is a small type of chevron used in heraldry (q.q.v.).

courbaril plum: A type of hardwood used in the woodworking crafts, also known as locust (q.v.).

cover case: A term to denote the cover or the front of a book.

crabwood: A slightly reddish wood with a smooth grain, used in carving and furniture, from the family Carapa guianensis.

cracking: In the crafts of painting, some painting cracks and soon has a design that resembles an alligator's skin. There are many reasons for this cracking; some paintings have underpaints that have more oil than the surface paint. Canvas that has been bent and rolled also cracks, extreme temperature changes, especially cold, affect the surfaces of paintings. The use of the wrong pigments and materials such as asphaltum (q.v.), that change with time, may be a cause.

crackle glaze: A term used in ceramics crafts (q.v.), also known as alligator glaze (q.v.). These cracks are sometimes desired to impart a rather interesting design on the surface. No two pieces will fire (q.v.) the same. This crackle treatment is sometimes done to give the ceramic a look of age.

crackled glass: This is a type of surface that is applied to glass during the process of manufacture. The surface is made in such a manner that it looks cracked. This glass is not transparent.

crackled ware: A type of ceramic (q.v.). This is seen in many ceramic pieces from China. Parts of a piece are sometimes fired (q.v.) so that they will be partially crackled.

Cracowes: A shoe of the Middle Ages was made with a long point or toe. These shoes were known as Cracowes.

crafts: The term crafts as used in this dictionary applies to the method of doing or constructing an object or device, usually by hand and with native materials. A craft is sometimes a skill that is handed on from generation to generation, such as the making of glass flowers or the making of iron tools with crude facilities. A craft of the present era does not always take skill and sometimes the use of very simple materials such as a paper cup made into a dish to hold nuts is considered to be a craft. A true craft should involve many techniques and be a worthwhile project, and should result in a lasting object rather than a "busy" project. See arts and crafts.

crawling: A term used in ceramics (q.v.). This is the running or crawling of the glaze (q.v.). This leaves parts of the piece un-glazed.

crayon: A tool of the artist and the craftsman. Usually made of different kinds of waxes, mixed with pigments or dyes. Their first use was in the 16th century.

crayon leaf prints: A simple method and a very effective method of making leaf prints is with crayons. Lay a leaf on a flat surface, make sure the bottom or vein side is facing up. Next lay a paper, tracing paper or regular writing paper on top of the leaf. Select a crayon and color the surface of the paper, rub in several directions so that the complete outline of the leaf will appear. Several colors can be used to give the leaf a fall coloration. Next cut out the leaf and mount in a scrap book. Label the leaf.

crazing: A term used in the arts. Crazing is the cracking of paint or the glaze in ceramics (q.q.v.). Also known as crackle.

creasing: A term of the bookbinder. This is the creasing or bending of the sheets of a book so that they will lie flat.

crepe: A type of cloth with a crinkled surface. Done by mechanical means or with chemicals.

crepe paper: A rather cheap crinkled paper. Used for decorations. Special heavy grades are used in the making of artificial flowers. Colored crepe paper can be soaked in water, this will result in a simple dye of the same color as the paper.

crest: A term used in heraldry (q.v.). This was a mark or seal; this is not a coat-of-arms (q.v.).

cretonne: A rather heavy fabric made of cotton, sometimes has a ribbed weave. Used for drapes. Pattern only on one side due to the thickness of the cloth.

cri: A term used in the metal crafts. This is the sound made when good pewter is bent. Sometimes used as a test by experts when testing pewter (q.v.).

crib: A term used in the doll making crafts. A group of people of the sixteenth and seventeenth century made religious groups of dolls. A different craftsman made each figure, tree and animals, these figures were made of wood and painted. At Christmas time, these cribs were brought out and people made tours of the various cribs to admire them. As time went on, these figures became more realistic and the sisters of the various convents made clothes for the dolls. Real hair and sometimes real jewels were used on the figures. Cribs are now made mostly in one place, Tyrol.

cribble: Used in the intaglio and etching crafts (q.q.v.). These are small dots or holes used for decoration.

crinkled glass: This is a type of blown glass. Also known as kinkled glass (q.v.).

crinoline: A type of rather stiff fabric. Originally made of horsehair, used in such things as hoop skirts.

crocus: A type of iron oxide, used for polishing metals. Also known as rouge.

croisant: A term used in heraldry (q.v.). This is a cross which ends in crescents. Placed on a shield or escutcheon (q.q.v.).

cropping: A term used in several arts and crafts. This is the cutting away or blotting out of parts of a picture or drawing that are not wanted.

cross dyeing: A type of dyeing whereby only certain fibers absorb a dye, such as wool and cotton, one absorbing a dye while the other does not, etc.

cross stitch: An embroidery stitch, the stitch resembles an X.

crosslet: A term used in heraldry (q.v.). This is a cross on a shield or escutcheon (q.q.v.). This cross has its three points ending in smaller crosses.

crown: A term used in heraldry (q.v.). This is a crown worn by a ruler, which usually has four arched bars. Sometimes surmounted by a cross or a globe. In the lapidary crafts, the crown is the upper portion of a gem stone. This is considered the part that is above the girdle (q.v.).

crown glass: This is a type of early window glass. This glass was made with a blowpipe method. See nose hole (q.v.). This is a rather hard glass with a circular flow in it.

crozing: A technique of the cooper (q.v.). Crozing is cutting the groove in the top of a barrel in which the top or bottom lid will fit.

crucible: A container, used in the metal crafts, to hold various molten metals. The crucible is made of fire clay and sometimes of graphite (q.v.).

cryptocrystalline: Used in the jewelry and gem crafts. This is a gem stone that is made up of crystals in a mass; these crystals are on the inside and thus hidden.

crystal: Known also as flint glass (q.v.). This is a fine type of glass.

culet: A term used in the gem crafts. This is the lower part of a gem stone that has a brilliant cut (q.v.).

cupellation: This is the heat process by which gold, silver and other valuable metals are separated from impurities.

cushion stitch: Used in the sewing crafts, this is a stitch used in embroidery (q.v.). This stitch, made of short straight lines, is used to make the backgrounds on material, used in the sewing of decorative scenes.

cut: A term used in the printing crafts. This is any type of relief engraving, usually made of metal. Properly called plates (q.v.).

cutting a block print: A block print (q.v.) is a design (q.v.) cut in reverse, usually on the surface of linoleum (q.v.) or on the surface of Plastigraph (q.v.). To cut a block print requires that the design be rather bold and simple, very few fine lines, such as would be found in an etching (q.v.). Tools used to cut block prints have to be sharp and any surface not wanted must be cut away so that the ink will not adhere to it. The part that is wanted, should be left. Letters must be cut in reverse; to check the letters, use a mirror, if the letters can be read correctly in the mirror they will print correctly: if not, the block must be done over. Mistakes in a block print are hard to correct, if at all. Cutting a Plasti-print (q.v.), a similar process to linoleum block cutting, is a bit easier when it comes to making a correction, because of the nature of the material. New material can be added on the surface to replace a part that has been accidentally cut away. Gouges (q.v.) which are somewhat like chisels and veiners (q.v.) are used, sometimes an old razor blade will be a help. The block should be warm or at room temperature so that it will cut more easily, this will prevent chipping of the surface also.

cutting reed: Round reeds should be cut on a slant. This makes them easier to thread in and out when using them to weave with. Cutting the reed on a slant also makes the object look more professional.

cyclamen: The bloom should be pulled from the bulb, the stem should be soaked and cut under water. The flower is used in the corsage (q.v.) crafts. The blooms should last about four days.

cynotype: A print made, either blue or brown. Made on a sensitized paper. Used for the making of copies of originals. See blueprint.

D

dabber: A dabber is used in the printing or engraving (q.v.) crafts. This is a pad used to apply ink to the surface of an etching (q.v.). Also made in the form of a stiff brush, much in the shape of an old shaving brush, which serves the purpose. Also known as a poona (q.v.).

damar: This is gathered from trees found in Java, Sumatra. The two main varieties of this substance, No. 1 Singapore and Batavia, come in assorted pieces and are a light yellow color. This damar resin makes a fine varnish for paintings. Sometimes spelled dammar.

damascene: A technique of the metal craftsman. This is the inlaying (q.v.) of one metal on top of another, forming a design.

damasked: A term used in heraldry (q.v.). This is a shield or escutcheon (q.q.v.) which is completely covered with squares. Also known as diapered.

damp book: A damp book refers to the paper that is used in the etching (q.v.) crafts. When the plate is ready to be printed, it is necessary to dampen the paper before use. This is done by dipping the paper in clear water and then placing it on blotting paper, a sheet of paper and a sheet of blotting paper. When the amount of paper is reached, a weight should be placed on top of the pile. The paper is now ready to use. See intaglio.

dapping: This method is used in jewelry and metal crafts. Dapping is done with a dapping block (q.v.), when the surface is to be raised, it is turned over and a dapping tool (q.v.) and matching size hole in the dapping block is selected. The object is then pounded until the desired shape is secured.

dapping block: A small block of lead or steel, the surface of which is indented with many hollows, each of a set size. The dapping block is used in the metal and jewelry crafts. See Dapping.

dapping tool: This is a small tool used in the metal and jewelry crafts. It has a ball point, made of steel, and has various sizes which fit into the various indentations on the surface of the dapping block (q.v.). The tool is hit lightly with a small hammer.

darned embroidery: A type of embroidery (q.v.). The open spaces are filled in with other threads, which makes a solid fabric.

daruma: A type of doll made in China and Japan. This doll is made of papier-mâché and is weighted in such a way that when it is knocked over, it will again stand up.

Davey's grey: A paint pigment made from clay or ground slate, used to reduce the tones, used instead of black.

dead clay: Used in the crafts. This is clay that has dried out or has had water in it and is now dry. When hit, this clay sounds with a dull thud.

dead dipping: Used in the metal crafts. This is the dipping of metals into an acid for a set period of time, this removes the finish and dulls the surface.

death mask: A mask, usually made of plaster. Applied to the face of the dead, this cast is used later on to make an exact likeness. See life mask.

decalcomania: This is an art and a process, used in many crafts. Used in the ceramics crafts (q.v.). The design is placed on a dish or bowl and is then fired (q.v.), this causes the color to fuse with the dish or bowl surface and become a part of it, the base of the decalcomania is removed or burned away.

deckle: This is a type of paper with a rather rough edge. Used in printing cards, special announcements and certain books. This edge is seen on handmade paper.

declivant: A term used in heraldry. This is a snake or serpent that is shown on a shield or escutcheon (q.q.v.). The tail of this animal is shown pointing straight down.

decoupage: The use of paper cut-outs to form a new picture. Used for the decoration of table tops, etc. Similar to inlaid (q.v.) work. Sometimes rather abstract forms are made with the addition of string, bits of metal, etc.

dees: These are a type of metal fastener used on bags and other types of leather objects that will have a strap. It is semicircular in shape with one side flat and split so that it may be inserted in the leather.

deep color: A term used in the arts. A deep color does not show the presence of black, such as the dark greens and blues.

deerfoot: A tool used in the leather crafts. The shape of the tool suggests the deer foot, hence the name. This tool is used to get into corners and hard to get at depressions, such as the insides of a pocketbook.

de-hairing: This means just what it says, the removal of hair from the hides of animals. This is done by hand or with the aid of chemicals, such as lime in solution; the hide is placed in large revolving vats. This method loosens the hair. The lime also makes the hide more easily treated with the tanning chemicals. Other chemicals such as arsenic and sodium are also used.

Delft blue: The well-known blue color found in the Low countries of Europe. This pigment is made from the mixing of indigo and ultramarine (q.q.v.). Used in the ceramics and tile crafts.

delphinium: The blue flowers of this plant are used in the craft of corsage (q.v.) making. The individual florets are picked and used. The stem should be soaked in water to which a teaspoonful of alcohol has been added. The blooms should last about two days.

demi-relief: A term used in sculpture. Demi-relief denotes a carving in relief (q.v.) that is half or medium relief.

dendrochronology: This is the science or study of dating ruins, trees and objects that have been made from wood. Dr. A. E. Douglass is credited with the discovery and development of tree ring dating. Each year most trees grow a new ring. The dark ring shows the summer growth and the light ring the spring growth. By counting these rings it is possible to date a tree or an object made from it. The wide rings denote a rainy year and thus faster growth, tight rings tend to show a dry season.

denier: A term used in the sewing and cloth crafts. This is the degree of fineness in cloth such as silk, rayon, nylon.

dental cut: A term used in the jewelry and gem crafts. This is a cut made on a gem stone which leaves two rows of facets (q.v.).

dentelle: A leather crafts and bookbinding term. This is the lacing or tooled border that resembles a row of teeth.

deodar: Also known as Himalayan cedar (Cedrus deodara). A tree found in India, with soft wood used for carving. Rather difficult to glue because of the oil in the wood.

design: This is a sketch or layout for a drawing or illustration, or for the construction of some object. In art, a design is sometimes the interpretation of an artist (q.v.) of some object or scene.

detail: These are the small minute parts of a model, photograph or other object. A term applied to the making of small models and dioramas (q.v.).

device: A term used in heraldry. This is a scene or motto on a coat-of-arms (q.v.).

devil's cloth: A jute fiber, silky and white. Sometimes used as a substitute for silk. From the plant Abroma augusta, found in the Pacific area.

devitrified glass: A type of glass that has been subjected to great heat which renders it hard and opaque. Done to prevent it from forming crystals.

dexter base point: A term used in heraldry. This is the lower corner of the dexter side of a shield or escutcheon (q.q.v.).

dexter chief point: This is the upper right side of the dexter side. A term used in heraldry. This applies to shields and escutcheons (q.q.v.).

dexter side: A term used in heraldry. This is the right side of the shield or escutcheon (q.q.v.). See sinister, dexter chief point, and dexter base point.

dextrin: This is a type of glue or adhesive. Dextrin is derived from starch and mixed with sugar. Used as a sizing for paper. Used in many crafts that call for powdered glue. Mixed with plaster of paris (q.v.), whiting (q.v.) and asbestos shreds or shredded paper to make a pulp used in modeling and in the making of dioramas.

diadem: A term used in heraldry. This is an arch that is shown rising from a crown.

diamond: This is a crystal form of carbon. This is the hardest mineral. Used as a gem stone; imperfect stones are used for cutting and boring tools. Pure diamonds are colorless.

diamond cut glass: This is glass that has been cut on its surface in such a way that its surface is covered with a design, made up of small diamond or pyramid shaped points.

diamond glass: See flitters.

diamond-point knop: Used in the metal crafts. This is a knop (q.v.) with a diamond shape. Used when referring to the metal pewter (q.v.).

diamond type: This is the smallest size type, used in the printing of foot notes, small books, etc.

diapered: A term used in heraldry (q.v.). This is a shield or escutcheon (q.q.v.) that is covered with squares or lozenges (q.v.).

diaphaneity: A term used in the jewelry and gem crafts. This is the amount of light that is transmitted through a gem stone.

diatomaceous earth: This is a type of clay, used as a filler in some types of paint. Under the microscope, diatomaceous earth shows that it is made up of millions of tiny skeletons from ancient times.

diazotized dye: This is used in the crafts involving fabrics. This is a dye that is applied to mixed materials or fibers, such as a cloth made with cotton and wool. The cloth is treated with a nitrous acid to make the dye fast.

dictaphone wax: Old dictaphone records can be melted and the wax used in many crafts.

die: A device, usually made of metal. Used for stamping a design or letter on a softer surface, such as leather.

dimension stuff: This is a term used to designate a type of rough lumber. The wood has been rough cut (q.v.) and is two inches thick and is from four to twelve inches wide.

diorama: A diorama is a small scale, three dimensional exhibit on any subject.

dipping: The process of coating objects with paint or slip (q.v.).

discharge printing: Done on cloth. This is a process of printing on cloth that has been dyed. This is done with chemicals which are later dissolved and thus produce a design or pattern.

disposable palette: A type of palette (q.v.). Made up of many sheets; as the artist finishes a painting, he can tear off a sheet. This does away with cleaning and scraping a palette for future use.

dividers: This is a steel tool used to measure, similar to, and used somewhat as, the regular compass.

dividing brass: Thin sheets of brass, used as separators in making molds. Used by sculptors and other craftsmen.

dobby: A small loom (q.v.). Used to weave small figures.

dodging: A term used in photography. This is a method of holding back light in such a way that a certain part of a photograph will stand out from the rest. This is done with the hand or several types of devices.

doeskin: A cotton cloth that is napped (q.v.). Used as a backing for artificial leather. Term also applied to any wool with a short nap.

dogwood red-osier: A red dye was made from the inner bark of this tree. The Ojibwa Indians of the Great Lakes region of the United States and Canada used this inner bark along with birch, oak and cedar bark (q.v.) ashes to make this dye. The Ojibwa used this dye to color porcupine quills red.

doki: A term used in the ceramics of Japan. This is any type of earthenware that is not glazed (q.q.v.).

doll bean bags: These are simple dolls to make and are fun to use. The materials that you will need are simple, needle and thread and some bright cloth, and beans, dried and hard, any kind will do. Draw a simple outline on the cloth, or trace the outline of a gingerbread man (see edible dolls) on the cloth, cut out two pieces, one for the front and one for the back. Next sew the doll together, leaving a part open so that you can insert the beans. Use a funnel to pour in the beans, this will help keep them going in the right direction and not on the floor. Doll heads may be made firm by pushing some beans into the head and then sewing across the neck, this will keep the beans in the head and keep its shape. A target made with holes larger than the doll can be made and then marked for a score. The bean bag doll can be thrown at the target and those that go through the holes count on the score.

dominant color: The main or key color that stands out from all of the others in a painting or illustration. Used in the arts.

dosa: A size (q.v.). Made of glue and alum, used mainly in Japan.

double brilliant: A type of brilliant cut (q.v.). Consists of two rows of diamond shaped cuts and three rows of triangular facets (q.v.).

double end tool: A tool of the artist and sculptor (q.q.v.). Consists of a wooden handle with a heavy wire shape extending from each end. Used for modeling in clay or other soft substance. These tools have many shapes and sizes, depending on the size and type of work to be done.

double loop stitch: A type of knotted lacing. This is a rather heavy type of stitch or lace. Used in the leather crafts.

doubling: A term used in heraldry. This is a small drape that is seen on a coat-of-arms. Denotes special favor from a ruler.

doublure: A term used in the bookbinding crafts. The doublure is the back cover, next to the end sheet (q.v.).

doups: A weaving term used to describe the loops formed in the upper and lower part of the cord heddle on a primitive loom.

dowels: A dowel is a peg of wood that fits tightly in a hole that has been bored into two pieces of wood. The wood is bored in such a way that the dowel will hold the two pieces together to form a larger board or panel. See painting panel.

down draft kiln: A type of kiln used in the ceramics crafts (q.q.v.). This kiln is arranged so that the heat will come down from the top.

drafting paper: This is a hard surfaced paper, usually sized (q.v.). Used for the making of drawings, usually accurate or mechanical drawings, done in ink.

dragging: A technique of painting. A paint brush heavy with paint is brushed heavily over a painting. This leaves a small amount of color or pigment at the end of the stroke. Used in the dry brush technique (q.v.).

dragon's blood: A red resin which comes from trees in Batavia and also from Singapore. Not a true paint pigment. This resin does not dissolve well in turpentine. Alcohol, mineral spirits and benzol are the best solvents for this resin. Dragon's Blood is used to color varnishes and its ruby red has been known and used since ancient Roman times. Used in the engraving (q.v.) arts & crafts.

drawing: A pictorial representation of an idea or a scene or object. Done with many types of mediums, ink, paint, charcoal, pencil, etc. A drawing is usually done by an artist (q.v.).

drawing metal: This is the process done in the metalcrafts. Metal is extended or stretched as in the making of wire or in the making of artificial plants, the wire is stretched and later glued to form the veins of leaves.

drawing pencils: Special types of pencils are used by the artist and craftsman. The softest is 6B, HB is medium soft, 2H is hard to 9H, the hardest. Used for pencil sketching and drawing in the field of mechanical drawing. A correctly drawn picture should have been drawn with pressure enough to be able to feel with the fingers on the under side of the paper.

drawn clay: Clay that has been heated, dried or fired (q.v.). This causes it to draw or shrink.

drawplate: This is a piece of steel with holes of various sizes. When used in metal crafts it is useful for reducing the size of wires. A wire may be pulled through the drawplate and the edge cuts or scrapes the wire. This tool is also useful in the making of artificial flowers.

drenching: After the flesh has been removed from a hide, it becomes necessary to further clean the hide. This is done by the method of drenching; the hide is placed in a weak acid solution to remove what is left and also the lime. It is then bated (q.v.).

dressed wood: Dressed wood is wood that has come from the lumber mill as rough cut (q.v.) and is run through a machine that removes the saw marks and the fibers. This dressing usually takes off about 1/8 of an inch of the surface. This lumber is marked and designates how it is prepared, such as D1S which means, "dressed on one side," or S1S which means that the piece has been "surfaced on one side," etc. D1E means that the lumber has been "dressed on one edge."

driers: Certain materials are added to paints to make them dry faster, these are called driers. These driers act to force the paint to absorb oxygen more readily. Generally, driers are not good for the paint and shorten its life when used. Their use in paint should be done by experts. Cobalt linoleate and linseed oil is the best type of drier as it does not darken much with age.

driftwood: This is a wood that has been found along the shores of our oceans, also lakes and ponds, but is generally considered to be found in the ocean. Driftwood is usually a grey color and worn smooth as a result of the action of the waves and action of the sand. Driftwood is used as a decoration as it is found. It is used with flowers to form a pleasing design. Sometimes the imagination can be used and with a dab of paint here and there, the wood can be turned into an animal of some sort. Driftwood can be used in the lamp crafts; here it is used as a base for a lamp, bookends, etc.

drop stitch: A fault in a knitted fabric. Sometimes desired, however, for a special effect.

dross: A term used in the metal crafts. This is the sludge or impurities that are found on the surface of molten metals.

drum stick: A simple drum stick can be made from a stick about eight inches long. At one end you can twist cotton or roll a tight ball of rawhide (q.v.). This can be tied. When using rawhide, it is best to use it wet so that it will stretch and when dry, it will become very tight and hard.

dry: A term that denotes a piece of ceramic has been glazed (q.v.) insufficiently.

dry brush painting: This is a technique of painting. Very little paint is used on a brush and the painting is done with a rather dry brush, hence the name. It is used for special effects, such as smoke, clouds, shading, etc.

dry color: Paint pigment that is dry, in a powder or in cake or stick form. Can be mixed with various liquids later on.

dry mounting: This is a technique used in the mounting of photographs. A tissue that is covered with a thin coating of shellac is used. The photograph is pressed on this surface and heat is applied. This cements the print to the mounting board. It is then trimmed and framed or used as it is.

dry writing: A recent printing development using static electricity, also known as Xerography (q.v.).

drying oils: These are oils used in painting crafts. Such oils as linseed (q.v.), and others are used to hurry or delay the drying of various paints.

drypoint: A term used in the intaglio (q.v.) crafts. This craft is done with a tool with a rather sharp but slightly rounded point called an etching needle (q.v.). The design is cut or scratched into the surface of the plate which has been previously prepared for the intaglio crafts.

Duco cement: A trade name for a clear cement. Used in many crafts.

ductile: In the metal crafts, this refers to the metals that can be drawn or stretched.

dugout: A canoe, made from a single hollowed-out log. This can be hollowed by burning or cut out with an ax. Made in many parts of the world.

dummy: Used in several arts and crafts. This is a sample, usually done by hand to give an idea of the finished product. Books are sometimes printed in dummy form and used as a selling medium, etc. This is a plan of the final product.

duplex paper: A type of paper that is finished on opposite sides with different colors. Sometimes meant to be paper with a different type finish on one side, such as a gloss finish on one side and matte finish on the other.

duramen: A term used in the woodcrafts. This is the heartwood of a tree.

dust cover: A cover that is applied over the jacket or book cover that is provided with a book by a publisher.

Dutch file: A term used in the gem crafts. The Dutch file is rather fine and is used in the first rough forming of a gem stone. See needle file.

Dutch metal: Dutch metal is a finish that is applied on book covers. This is not a permanent color. The material is usually imitation gold.

Dutch pink: Made from the plant buckthorn, the berries are used to make a type of yellow pigment. This is not a permanent color, however.

dye: This is a solution that can be fixed or suspended in a medium and used to color an object. Not granular as is pigment (q.v.).

dyeing flowers: Many flowers will respond to dyeing. When making corsages (q.v.) it is sometimes desirable to dye the blooms or to tint them a pastel (q.v.) shade. Flowers such as sweet peas, carnations and daffodils will take liquid dye very readily. Pick the flower and let it start to become limp, then place the stems in the dye solution, the flower will then "drink" the liquid with the dye which will then change the color of the bloom. Some blooms, such as the lilies and the gardenias will take a powdered dye, this may be applied in a rather simple manner: Place the part to be dyed in a paper bag and add the powdered color, hold the bag tightly at its mouth and gently shake. This method will apply an even color to the petals. Tintex (q.v.), a type of liquid dye, can be used. Grass and dry pods may be sprayed with color. The mixture is half alcohol and half shellac with the desired color added. The plant can be dipped in this mixture or it may be sprayed on.

E

eagle feather: American Indians in various parts of the country wore eagle feathers. These feathers had special meanings, affected by where they were worn, how they were marked or clipped. The Ojibwa Indians of the Great Lakes region of Canada and the United States had such feathers. A feather that was tipped with horse hair dyed red was a sign that the wearer had completed some personal bravery. It also signified that the wearer had secured a scalp. A feather that was split denoted a wound. A red spot on the feather showed that the wearer had been wounded by firearms. Turkey feathers were sometimes used if eagle feathers were not available.

eagle wood: Also known as aloes wood (q.v.). Used for inlay work (q.v.).

ear dishes: These are flat metal dishes, shaped somewhat like ears. Made in Europe.

earth colors: These are colors that are usually the various shades of browns and dark greens.

earthenware: Ceramics that are made of clay or other earth matter, that are fired, baked or hardened in the sun are considered to be earthenware. Earthenware objects are usually porous and opaque and have a rather coarse texture. Porcelain (q.v.) is not considered as earthenware.

easel: This is a tool of the artist. The easel is made of a number of materials, sometimes wood, sometimes aluminum. Used to hold a painting or sketch while the artist (q.v.) paints or sketches. The easel is usually three-legged and adjustable for height.

East Indian walnut: This coarse-textured, straight-grained wood comes from India. Used for fine carving. (Albizzia libbek).

ebony: A tropical hard wood. This wood has a straight even grain and texture. The heartwood is black and is used for fine carvings.

eccentric cutter: A tool of the ivory carver. This is a small drill-like tool used to cut small shapes that are difficult to cut with other tools.

échoppe: This is a beveled needle used by early etchers (q.v.).

eclecticism: A term used by artists to describe the technique of borrowing certain parts or styles of another artist, this is then incorporated into one's own painting. But in doing so, the first artist's technique still can be recognized.

ecorché: This is a figure used by a sculptor (q.v.). The figure shows the muscles of the human body.

ecru: A light tan, such as a light eggshell color.

ectype: A term of the visual arts; refers to any copy of the artist's original.

ecuelle: A small rather flat dish, usually made of pewter (q.v.) or other metals. The shape is similar to the porringer (q.v.).

edelzinn: This is a class of rather rare pewter (q.v.), made in the form of large plates; these plates have large cast designs on their surfaces.

edge bolt: Used in the bookbinding crafts. This refers to the folded and un-cut pages in a bound book.

edge creaser: A term used in the leather crafts. This is a tool of the leather craftsman. Used to crease and smooth the edges of a finished leather piece.

edible dolls: See picture bread.

edition: A term used in the book arts. This is the form in which a book is first issued, not the number of copies that are printed.

edition binding: This is a term used in the bookbinding crafts. An edition binding is an edition of a book that is prepared by machine. The whole book is assembled by machine. The book is glued, sewn and stamped with a design.

effare: A term used in heraldry. This is used to describe a lion or other animal that is reared on its hind legs as if in rage or fear.

egg tempera: The use of egg yolk in tempera painting has been long known. The yolk is first separated from the white, great care should be used to remove all traces of the white of the egg. The tempera may then be ground with the yolk to the consistency of tube oil paints. It is now ready for use; water may be added to the mixture and the brush should be dipped in water to keep the paint at a workable stage. Egg tempera paint should not be applied to a surface very thickly. Eggs should be fresh, light or dark yolk makes no difference; the egg tempera can be kept for about three days in a covered jar. It should also be kept moist as it becomes very hard when exposed to the air.

egg white: Egg white may be used in the painting crafts. It may be hardened with formalin; when it is used as a size on picture frames it works well with gold leaf, and also is used on gesso (q.v.) and leather to hold gold leaf.

eggshell: Used in the arts to describe a shade or color, or matte finish (q.v.). Rather light tan in color.

eggshell finish: A printing term. Describes a type of paper used in printing. Rather firm but not smooth finish.

eggshell ornaments: Ornaments can be made for a Christmas tree from eggshells. Punch a hole in each end of an egg and blow the insides out. This will leave you with a hollow and clean egg shell. This can be painted with glue and rolled in glitter (q.v.) or sequins (q.v.) or other material that has a sparkle. Faces can be painted on the eggs also or paper designs can be glued on the surface.

eggshell porcelain: This is a type of porcelain (q.v.). So very thin that light can be seen through it.

E-gorai ware: A type of Korean ceramics (q.v.). The surface under the glaze is painted with designs, usually floral.

Egyptian blue: This is made from copper silicates. Egyptian blue, used in Egypt from about three thousand B.C., is one of the earliest known artificial pigments. This blue is well known because of the porcelain (q.v.) beads found in the Egyptian tombs. This pigment has been changed and improved down through the centuries and is now sold under the names of Italian Blue and Pompeian Blue.

Egyptian brown: This is a type of pigment that is no longer in use. Also known as the pigment mummy (q.v.).

Egyptian jasper: This is a type of jasper, brown in color, found in Egypt. See jasper.

eidograph: This is an instrument of the artist, similar to the pantograph (q.v.).

e-kotoba: A type of painting done on a scroll. Made in Japan, they contain both painting and lettering or text.

electrical porcelain: This type of porcelain (q.v.) is used on electrical insulators. The glaze and the clay are fired (q.v.) only once.

electro: A rather common name for the etched plate (q.v.) used in printing.

electroplate gold: When gold is electroplated it usually deposits a very thin layer of gold on the object. The layer of gold is about 1/1,000,000 of an inch thick. Plated gold does not wear well and cannot be used where the surface will be worn.

electrotype: This is a printing term. Also known as an electro. This process consists of coating a surface, such as lead, with a metal to make it hard and more lasting when used in printing. Electros are also plated with copper. The surface of a lead plate is coated by an electric process. The plate is immersed in a salt solution and electric current is passed through the solution. When this is done, fine particles of the metal are deposited on the surface of the plate. This is done until the plate is coated the desired thickness.

electrum: This is an alloy (q.v.) of gold and silver, used for fine casting.

element: A term used by artists. The element is the base of a paint used for painting.

elemi: This is a type of resin from trees in Luzon, also known as Manila elemi.

elephant ears: A type of sponge used in crafts using molds and casts. This sponge is used to smooth over the marks of the molds.

elfenbeinschwartz: Also known as ivory black (q.v.), this is a paint pigment made from the charred or burned chips of ivory.

e-maki: A type of Japanese scroll; this scroll didn't always contain text.

emblazon: A term used in heraldry (q.v.). See blazonry.

emblem book: This is a volume of woodcuts (q.v.). They should have captions under them or should tell a story.

embossed: An embossed design is a design that is raised from the surface slightly, more of an impression.

embossed printing: This is a type of printing done without ink. Done as for the blind, in braille, the letters or symbols are raised or embossed.

embossing: In the craft of leather working, embossing is a method of raising the design on the leather above the rest of the surface. This design is kept in place in many instances by backing the design with plaster of paris (q.v.), sawdust or other filler.

embossing wheel: This is a type of tool used in leather crafts, as well as other crafts. It consists of a handle with a wheel at one end, such as a cog wheel; it has sharp teeth, which when rolled over the surface of the leather, leave a track on the surface. The embossing wheel comes in a great variety of designs and shapes. When using the embossing wheel, it is best to dampen the leather first so that the design will "take."

embroidery: Embroidery is done with a small needle. The work is done on a woven cloth. The threads are raised on the surface due to the type of stitch. Embroidery is done with silk, gold and cotton threads.

embrued: A term used in heraldry (q.v.). This shows the figure on an escutcheon (q.v.), the figure has a bloody mouth or a bloody weapon, the result of action with an enemy.

embryo shell: A type of thumb knop (q.v.). This was made usually from pewter and represented a cockle shell or scallop without the ridges.

embuia: This is a type of hardwood used in the woodworking crafts.

emerald: A precious stone used in the jewelry and gem crafts. Green in color and sometimes rather transparent. Found in North Carolina, Siberia and in Colombia in South America.

emerald green: This brilliant color pigment, a bright bluish green, is very permanent. Made from copper aceto-arsenite, this pigment is very poisonous. It was discovered in Sweden in the late seventeen hundreds. It is also known as Paris green.

emery: This is used as a polishing agent for stones, tools and other implements. Made in various sizes, emery is finely ground corundum stone (q.v.).

empaistic: This term is used to describe any surface that is inlaid (q.v.). This is used for any surface such as wood, leather, etc.

empaled: A term used in heraldry. This is a shield or escutcheon (q.q.v.) that is divided in the center. Used by two families that can bear arms. The man on the right or the dexter side (q.v.) and the wife on the left or sinister side (q.v.).

emulsion: A term used in painting. This applies when several types of liquids are suspended together. Such a mixture is egg, oil and watery albumen together in a mixture known as egg tempera (q.v.). In photography the term emulsion is used. This is a layer of chemicals that are sensitive to light on the surface of a paper. They consist of one or more types of silver halides that have been treated with gelatine (q.v.).

enamel: This is a type of paint or varnish that dries to a hard shiny finish and also is known for its quick drying ability.

enamel: A material that is fused to the surface of the object to be enameled. The surface is covered with an opaque glass and heat is applied until the glass melts and fuses with the surface that it is laid on. Enamel paint differs in that it is not necessary to bake it to the surface although a mild heat helps it to become hard, as on automobiles. Enamel is applied to many surfaces, especially those that are used in and around water.

enamel glass: A type of glass that has had enamel applied to its surface while it was being made.

enamel glass painting: The glass surface is first painted with enamel and then fired in a kiln or muffle (q.q.v.).

enamel kiln: This is a type of kiln (q.v.). Used to bake enamel on a surface. This type of kiln does not have the high temperatures of a ceramics kiln (q.v.).

enamel paper: This is a special type of paper, also known as a coated paper (q.v.). The surface of this paper has been coated with a fine clay which is pressed into the paper under pressure rollers.

encaustic painting: This is a painting technique. It involves the use of heat to apply the medium. Beeswax (q.v.) is mixed with various pigments and then applied to the surface. This type of painting is also known as cerography (q.v.).

encaustic tile: This is a type of tile that is made of one type of clay and backed with another kind.

end sheet: A bookbinding term. This is the last sheet in a book next to the doublure (q.v.).

endpapers: Also known as end sheets, these are the first and last sheets of the signature (q.v.). These are sometimes decorated by hand in special editions (q.v.).

English hawker doll: This was a type of doll made of wood. At the end of the eighteenth century, these dolls were also known as pedlar dolls (q.v.).

English red: This is a well-known red paint pigment. This is a red iron oxide. Also known as Venetian red (q.v.).

English white: See whiting.

Engobe: A technique of the ceramic (q.v.) arts. The object is coated with a slip known as engobe. This slip is used to conceal the surface of the object. Interesting results can be obtained by cutting away a design through the outer slip (q.v.).

engraved: This is a process of incising lines on a plate. See intaglio (q.v.).

engraver's metal: This is an alloy (q.v.). Used in color printing. The plate is made from tin, antimony and lead.

engrossing ink: This is a type of waterproof ink, jet black. Similar to India ink (q.v.). This ink is used for lettering on documents such as diplomas, etc.

enhanced: This is the raising of an ordinary (q.v.) from its proper place on a shield or escutcheon (q.q.v.).

enlargement: A term used in photography; when a negative (q.v.) is projected to a larger scale and the image is made larger, the resulting print made from the negative is known as an enlargement.

eosine: This is an ink, very bright scarlet. Used in the late eighteen hundreds. This red ink tends to fade when exposed to sunlight.

Eototo: A type of kachina (q.v.). Used in the Hopi Bean Dance, this kachina is the chief of all of the kachinas.

epidendrum: The spray-like blooms of this plant may be used in the corsage (q.v.) crafts. Used with other flowers, these blooms make a striking corsage. The blooms will last about ten days.

epigraphy: The study of the art of carving on stone or hard metals. Epigraphy is the study of the texts or symbols that have been cut on some hard surface.

epsom salts: Used with beer (q.v.) to make frosted windows.

er ch'ing: A blue paint pigment used in China. Made from the mineral azurite (q.v.). Used in Chinese painting mainly for the backgrounds, such as hills and mountains.

erifon: An inorganic substance made from titanium and antimony salts. Erifon is used to fireproof materials such as cotton and rayon. First developed in nineteen forty-nine.

erinoid: Also known as lactoid (q.v.), this plastic substance is made from casein (q.v.). It is used for the making of small objects such as buttons and other small articles.

errata: A term used in the bookbinding crafts. This is a list of the errors that have been found in a book which can no longer be changed. This list is printed on a sheet of paper and pasted in the front of the book, known as an insert (q.v.).

escutcheon: A term used in heraldry. This term applies to the design of the shield which makes up the background.

esnafs: This is a term that is used to denote a guild of craftsmen of the Slovakian countries. To advance in this guild, each member must complete a work of art or masterpiece which must be passed by a board made up of other guild members.

esparto: This is a type of grass found in England. Esparto is used in the manufacture of a rather strong paper.

esquisse: A term used by artists (q.v.). This is a rough layout or sketch also known as a thumbnail sketch.

essonite: Used in the jewelry and gem crafts, essonite is a class of zircon. The stone is a brownish color similar to garnet.

estaimier: This term refers to the person who works with and designs pewter (q.v.). This includes the making of the alloy (q.v.).

estain: A term used in pewter making (q.v.). This is the finest quality of pewter.

ester gums: This is a synthetic resin (q.v.). Used as a substitute for kauri gum (q.v.). Ester gums are used in the making of varnishes (q.v.).

étain aigre: A term used in the pewter (q.v.) crafts. This term denotes a rather poor quality of pewter. This term is also used to describe the alloy (q.v.) used in the pewter.

etched plate: See electrotype, or electro.

etching: This is a type of intaglio (q.v.) craft. The design to be made is done on a plate (q.v.). This is then etched with nitric acid (q.v.) or perchloride of iron (q.v.). The ink is then rubbed over the surface of the plate and then wiped clean.

This leaves the ink only in the cut grooves of the plate. The damp paper is then pressed or rolled tightly on the plate. This forces the paper to absorb the ink. A test for a real etching can be made by the simple method of feeling it lightly. The design will be slightly raised.

etching embroidery: This is a type of decoration that was done on silk. The design was placed on the silk with a water-proof ink such as India ink (q.v.). The design was made to imitate an etching (q.v.).

etching ground: This ground is the surface that is applied to a copper plate or other plate that is used in the etching (q.v.) crafts. There are various commercial grounds on the market that can be used. Beeswax, asphaltum (q.v.), are a few that can be used. The surface of the plate must be covered so that the acid which is used to etch, will not eat away the plate or the parts that are wanted. The ground provides a protective coating.

etching needle: See etching tool.

etching paper: This paper is made with very little size (q.v.) or coating. Etching paper is rather soft.

etching press: This is a roll type press used to make prints or impressions from an etched plate (q.v.).

etching tool: Etching tools vary in size and shape. The points should not be sharp, but rather round so that they will cut easily through the etching ground (q.v.). Tools may be purchased, or they may be made. Old mechanical drawing instruments make fine etching tools. Darning needles can be used. Old phonograph needles can be used and held in a pen holder or mechanical pencil.

Etchuseto yaki: This is a rather low grade of ceramics (q.v.) made in the Etchu province, Japan.

ethanal: A substance used in photography and plastics and several of the arts and crafts. Known as acetaldehyde.

euphoria: A term applied to an artist (q.v.). This is a state of mind, a feeling of jubilation or satisfaction upon having created a work of art.

even folio: This is the left side of a book that is open and faces the reader, also known as the verso (q.v.). See recto, or odd folio.

ewer: A type of wide-mouthed pitcher, sometimes made of

pewter (q.v.), also made of ceramic (q.v.). The spout is rather large.

ex libris: A term used internationally. This is a small plate that is placed at the front of the book, usually pasted in; the name of the owner is included also.

execution: Applied to the arts, this is the act of developing a painting or sculptured piece (q.v.).

exogen: This term is used in wood crafts. This term applies to trees that grow with annual rings, known as growth rings. The study of tree ring growth is known as dendrochronology (q.v.).

exposure: A term used in photography. This is the length of time that light is allowed to fall on the plate or film (q.v.).

exposure latitude: This is the variation in various types of films (q.v.). Some are faster, others slower.

exposure meter: This is a device used in photography. This instrument measures the amount of light that a certain object reflects. This is measured and then scaled to apply to certain films so that the correct amount of light will be admitted through the lens of the camera.

extended cover: A term used in the printing and bookbinding crafts. An extended cover is one that extends or is slightly larger than the inside pages of the book. This differs from a trimmed flush (q.v.).

extender: A term used in the arts. This is a substance that is added to paints to extend or spread a color or pigment. When too much extender is added, the pigment becomes lighter or does not cover as well, it then becomes an adulterant (q.v.).

extra cloth: A term used in the bookbinding crafts. Extra cloth is cloth that is dark or heavy in color, used to conceal the weave or type of cloth used on a cover of a book.

extruded: Extruded, in the metal crafts refers to the metals that have been forced or pushed through a die or small hole or through a drawplate (q.v.).

extrusion process: Also known as the Lee process (q.v.). This is a method of forcing certain metals and alloys (q.v.) through a hole or mold. This is done with cold metals.

eyestone: A term used in the jewelry and gem crafts. An eyestone is a variety of agate (q.v.). This gem stone has spots in it that have a brighter color than the rest of the stone.

ezo: A term used by Japanese artists; the term is used to describe the general painting of portraits.

ezteri: This is a kind of bloodstone or greenish jasper with red veins. Used in the jewelry and gem crafts; found in South America.

F

fabric: A term used to describe all material that has been made or woven together or felted as rabbit hair in the making of felt.

Fabrikoid: This is an imitation leather. It is a waterproof fabric with a cloth base. Fabrikoid is a trade name.

face: The right side of a cloth or fabric as opposed to the under side.

facets: When cutting and polishing gem stones, the facets are the minute surfaces that are cut and polished; there are set standards for the number of facets that are cut on the various stones. See cabochon.

faenza: A fine white enamel used in the ceramics crafts (q.q.v.).

faience: A term generally applied to any glazed earthenware (q.q.v.). Also applied to a porcelain that is applied to the outside of buildings.

faille: A type of ribbed, soft cloth, made of silk, rayon or cotton. Ribs are quite wide and flat.

false amethyst: The name given to the purple or violet fluorite. Used in the gem crafts.

false biting: A term used in etching (q.v.). This is a bite (q.v.) done by mistake, through carelessness or a defective ground (q.v.).

fan brush: A type of brush shaped like a fan with soft animal bristles. Used for the painting of grasses, hair, etc.

fan painting: The art of painting on fans has been an Oriental practice for many years. Watercolors are usually used, scenes, animals and flowers are depicted.

fast color: This term is applied to any color that will not fade or wash out. A fabric that is dyed with a fast dye or color will not run or fade in the bright light, heat or cold.

fat clay: A type of very plastic clay used in the ceramics

fat liquor: This is a mixture of soap, water and various

93

oils, such as neat's-foot oil, cod oil and also egg yolk. This liquor is used to help replace the fats and oils that have been removed from a hide in the tanning process. In large plants, the hide is placed in this mixture and tumbled about in large vats or drums.

feather brush: A feather brush is used in the etching (q.v.) crafts. A long feather from any large bird such as a turkey, chicken, etc. can be used. When the plate (q.v.) is placed in the bath (q.v.), small bubbles form over the etched (q.v.) part. These bubbles should be lightly brushed away so that the acid can bite (q.v.) the plate.

feather capes: The ancient Inca Indians were fine feather craftsmen. To make a feather cape, you must first have a cloth cut to the desired size and shape. The ancient Incas used parrot feathers. No doubt you will have to dye chicken feathers and this can be done simply (see feather dye). Each feather will have to be sewn on the cloth separately and overlapped so that the base of each previous feather will not show.

feather dye: To dye feathers for feather crafts, mix a half gallon of water with a half pound of lime. Stir this well and when it is completely mixed add the feathers that you wish to dye. Let them soak for at least three days. Remove them from this solution after three days and then wash them gently in warm water. Next put the feathers in the color dye you desire, when they have soaked a short time, remove them and spread out to dry, or place in a cloth bag and shake dry.

featherweight paper: A thin, light weight paper used for cheap printing jobs.

feldspar: A mineral used in the making of glazes (q.v.).

felt crafts: Many types of arts and crafts involve the use of felts of various sizes and colors. Felt is made of many kinds of fibers that are pressed together to form a mat or felt. Used on the bottoms of bookends. Used as a story-telling device, using cut-out figures to tell a story. As the story is told the pieces are fitted together and laid on a large felt surface which they adhere to. Small hats and ornaments such as letters are cut from felt and sewed on other fabrics.

Ferrite: This is a trade name for the pigment of yellow iron oxide.

fess: This is an ordinary in heraldry (q.q.v.). This is a band placed horizontally on the shield or escutcheon (q.q.v.).

fess point: A term used in heraldry. The fess point is the direct center of a shield or escutcheon.

fetish doll: This was a type of doll made by the ancients and used by the medicine men of the tribe, among many primitive peoples. A fetish doll was considered to have certain spirits in it and was considered to be very sacred. Fetish dolls were sometimes believed to have the spirit of an ancestor in them and were known as "ancestor images" (q.v.).

fettling knife: A sharp rather flexible knife, used in the ceramics (q.v.) and model crafts. Used to remove the cast marks and for carving the soft clay or other modeling material.

fictile: A material rather plastic in consistency, capable of being molded as clay; able to be molded by hand rather than by mechanical means.

field: A term used in heraldry. This is the surface upon which the charge or bearing (q.q.v.) is placed or blazoned (q.v.).

figurine: A small figure or a group of figures, usually done in clay and fired (q.v.).

filigree: Rather intricate metal craft work, done with small wires, scrolls and twists. Done in silver and gold using thin threads, interwoven and twisted to form designs of flowers, etc. A term used to describe any fine or delicate pattern done in other crafts or in the arts, such as the drawing of the branches of a tree in winter.

fillers: Used in the rug and carpet making crafts. These are extra threads run with the woof and weft cords (q.q.v.). The fillers are used to make the rug or carpet (q.q.v.) fuller in weight and stiffness.

fillet: This term means the part where the two surfaces meet on a curved surface of a pattern. Also a tool of the bookbinder, a device that is pushed or rolled on the surface of a cover of a book and leaves small marks to show where a design is to be placed. Also the ornamental gold line that is sometimes placed on the covers of a book.

filling: Used in the textile crafts. Filling, also known as the woof (q.v.), is the yarn that runs at right angles to the warp (q.v.).

film: A term used in photography. The film is a gelatin coating that is sensitive to light and thus retains an image which is projected on it.

film line cutter: A tool of the craftsman who does silk screen (q.v.). This tool cuts the line and peels the film at the same time. Also known as a line cutter (q.v.).

film speed: This is the degree of sensitivity that certain films are capable of.

filter: This is a type of lens or glass used to filter out certain colors, or used in a projector to project certain colors of light.

fine arts: Meant to include more than the know-how and the techniques of the arts and the crafts. More of the appreciation and expression of the arts, such arts as dancing, drama, painting, sculpture, architecture, literature and music.

fine binding: Usually done by hand, with hand tanned leather, gold stamped leathers, etc.

finger drawing: As done in China. The finger is dipped in the paint and used as one would use a brush to paint with. This differs from finger painting (q.v.).

finger painting: A technique of painting. This differs from finger drawing (q.v.). Finger painting is done on paper that has been dipped in water and laid on a flat surface. Next small gobs of paint pigment are placed on the surface and smeared around to form designs and pictures. Nails, elbows, and fingers are used. No two pictures will be alike.

finishing: A term used in the bookbinding crafts. This process is performed when the book is finished and the cover is ready to receive its design and title.

fiorite: A variety of opal (q.v.). Used in the jewelry and gem crafts.

fir: A type of wood used mainly in making musical instruments. A rather soft straight-grained wood. The wood is rather brittle and care must be used to keep it from splitting.

fire opal: This is a type of opal used in the gem crafts. This opal has rather deep red reflections through it.

fireball: A term used in heraldry (q.v.). Depicted as an oval shape. Used in the early days as a weapon.

firebrick: This is a type of fire resistant brick used in kilns (q.v.) and in many types of stoves and fireplaces and boilers. Firebricks are made of fireclay (q.v.).

fireclay: This is a type of clay that is very resistant to fire. Used to make kilns (q.v.) and firebricks (q.v.).

firing: This is a method used in the ceramics crafts (q.v.). Clay is fired or fused together so that it becomes one. It is glazed (q.v.) with color when it is fired at great temperatures in a kiln (q.v.).

first water: A term used in the gem crafts. This applies to the best quality, such as a fine diamond.

fish glue: Usually sold in a liquid form and can be used as it is without heating. A fine grade of fish glue is known as Isinglass (q.v.).

fish scale crafts: Fish scales make interesting material to work with in the crafts. Fish scales may be purchased from hobby stores, or you may collect your own. Scrape the scales from various size fish, wash the scales in water and then dry them. You may also dye them with various types of dyes. When dry they are ready to be glued into various shapes, such as flowers, etc. They may be used in the making of ear rings, etc.

fishtail: This is a type of setting done in the jewelry crafts. A fishtail setting is one in which the gemstones are set in such a way, that they look continuous with no dividing parts. This setting is sometimes used in a wedding band. The stones are held from the sides and below.

fitchee: A term used in heraldry. This is a type cross on a shield or escutcheon (q.q.v.) which has a sharp point and the cross part ending in bud-like points.

fivecolor ware: A type of Chinese ceramic (q.v.). This type of porcelain (q.v.) is done in violet, red, yellow, green and blue.

fix: In the pastel arts, it is necessary to fix the drawing to prevent the drawing from being rubbed or brushed away. A fixative can be purchased or a good fixative may be made: Soak about ½ oz. of casein in about 5 oz. of water, no less than six hours, next add drop by drop, pure ammonia (not cloudy household ammonia), when this is well mixed, add a half pint of alcohol and enough water to make a solution of about a quart. To spray a picture with fixative, have the picture flat and do not spray too heavily as it will run. Use care so that drops or streamlines (q.v.) won't form on the surface.

fixative: See fix.

fixed: A term of the crafts. Fixed refers mainly to a color that is fast (q.v.) and will not change.

fixing: A term used in photography. This is the treating of a film or plate so that it will cease to be sensitive to light after it has been exposed to light and developed.

flake aluminum: Known also as aluminum powder. This powdered form of aluminum is used in the manufacture of paints and varnishes.

flake white: This is a high quality of white lead (q.v.).

flaking: In the crafts of painting, there are some paints that flake or become brittle and chip off. This is sometimes the result of moisture reaching the paint from the undersurface through the canvas.

flame black: This is a rather low grade of black carbon, made by burning mineral oil and coal tars.

flashed: A term used in the ceramic crafts. A flashed ceramic is one that is discolored on its surface. This discoloration is the result of contact directly with flames.

flashed glass: A type of glass usually found in stained glass (q.v.) windows. This glass is made by coating the surface of one piece of glass with another glass or several coats of glass, also known as cased glass (q.v.). The surface is then etched away and reveals the undercoats of glass.

flax: A soft, silky fiber about three inches long. This fiber comes from the inside of the flax plant. Used in the making of linen.

flatware: A term used in ceramics (q.v.). Flatware is a type of ceramic that is made rather flat, such as saucers, dishes, and other flat types. See hollow ware.

flesh split: Some leathers are too thick to work and have to be split. When the split half is on the inner or flesh side, this is called a flesh split. See "grain split."

fleshing: When fresh skins are used in the leather crafts, it is necessary to remove the flesh and hair. This is done by hand or by mechanical means (fleshing machine, q.v.). The fleshing is done with a two-handled curved knife, the hide is placed over a curved wooden "horse" and is scraped clean. The remaining flesh is removed by drenching (q.v.) or by bating (q.v.).

fleshing machine: A mechanical device for the removal of the flesh side of a hide. Fleshing (q.v.).

fletcher: A craftsman who makes arrows or, as they are also known, stele (q.v.).

fleury: A term in heraldry. This is a design on the shield or escutcheon (q.q.v.). It is a cross with its points ending in a flower or fleur-de-lis.

flint: A quartz or silica used in the making of porcelain (q.v.) or other enamel ware.

flint glass: This is the finest type of glass made. Used for lenses and fine glass ware. This glass scratches easily and is very brittle.

flitters: Flitters are used in the printing crafts. They can be made from a variety of materials, bronze or gold powder or mica. They give the printed material a luster. Used on greeting cards and special announcements.

floral jewelry: Floral jewelry is somewhat like corsage (q.v.) making. Bracelets and necklaces can be made from flower blooms. String the blooms with wire or with a waxed cord or thread. A bow may be added to the floral jewelry to add color.

florentine lace: In the craft of leather working, this is a type of lacing. Florentine lacing is simple; knot types of lacing are not used with Florentine, which is a kidskin.

florentine lake: This, when used in the painting crafts, refers to a red pigment.

flotant: A term used in heraldry. This is a design, such as a flag, which is shown waving in the breeze.

flowerpot: Many flowerpots can be decorated with paint or placed in small woven baskets. A flowerpot is porous and is made of a fired clay.

flowers: Flowers are used in the making of corsages. Some flowers can be dried and used to make shadow pictures.

fluting: Fluting is the grooves or cuts made on the surface of metal.

flux: When the soldering of metals is done, flux is needed so that the two parts will adhere. It prevents the oxidation of the metals at the point of the solder.

fly leaf: This is a blank leaf or page at the beginning or the end of a book. See end paper.

fly title: A term used in the printing crafts. See bastard title.

f-number: A term used in photography. This is the size of the opening on the lens of a camera.

foil: Any thin sheet of malleable material, usually metallic, such as tin foil, gold, silver, lead, etc. Used in many crafts and arts, for book covers, signs, etc.

folio: Used in the bookbinding crafts, this term applies to the number of pages in a book. See odd folio and even folio.

font: A term used by the printer. This is a set of a style of type. When a letter differs from another in style and size, it is said to be from the wrong font.

foot: Used in many crafts, this is the base or the bottom of an object.

fore edge: The fore edge is a bookbinding term and refers to the sheets that are cut in such a manner as to form the pages that will be opened when reading the book.

forget-me-not: The blooms from this plant can be used in the corsage (q.v.) crafts. When the flower is picked, place the stem in boiling water to a depth of about one inch, leave for two minutes. The bloom should last three or four days.

format: This is the size, style and shape of the book. If several books are published as a series and they are alike in size, style and shape they are said to have the same format.

forms: The shape and form of a corsage. The making of a corsage (q.v.) involves several crafts. The arrangement of the blooms in a corsage (q.v.) is important, for style and for the occasion. The form of the corsage is the finished outline of the corsage. There are circles, curved or half moon form, square (q.v.), rectangle (q.v.), Hogarth (q.v.), and other variations of these forms.

Formvar: A trade name for a synthetic resin used in the making of various types of films. Used as a layer in safety glass. Used in the making of varnishes and lacquers.

forwarding the book: This bookbinding term is used to cover the process that a book goes through when it is ready to have the cover fastened on.

fourchee: A term used in heraldry. This is a cross that ends in a forklike point on each of its extremities. Placed on the shield or escutcheon (q.q.v.).

foxed: In the paper and bookbinding crafts, this term is used to describe the yellowish spots that are left on paper as a result of water or of dampness.

fracture: A jewelry and gem crafts term. This is the type of break in a mineral or stone, such as the conchoidal (q.v.) as seen in glass. Jade has a splinter-like fracture.

frame: A term used in photography. A frame is a single picture or image. Sound motion pictures are moved at 24 frames a second. Silent pictures pass at 16 frames a second. Present television passes at one frame a second.

franc-quartier: A term used in heraldry. This is one of the ordinaries (q.v.). See quarter.

frankfort black: A black paint pigment made from the yeast in spent wine. The pigment makes a blue black when mixed with a good grade of white pigment.

free form: A term used in the arts and in some crafts. This is a design (q.v.) or shape either drawn or carved, which resembles a thought or idea of the artist, who sees his thought in the finished product. The idea is not always apparent to the observer.

free lance art: A term used to describe work done by an artist for several people on his own. His time is not relegated to one concern.

freestone: Used in sculpturing, this is a stone that does not fracture (q.v.) or split. This results when the stone has no grain. Ideal for a sculptor who cuts in many directions in his work.

french chalk: This has various uses in many crafts, also known as talc (q.v.). It is used as a separator in molds, in cosmetics and as a dryer for the surface of Plastigraph (q.v.) plates.

french curve: A tool of the artist. This is not a true circle but a finely curved device used to make smooth curved lines, both inside and outside.

french fat oil: This is an ingredient of overglaze (q.v.). Used in the ceramics crafts.

fresco: Fresco painting is a process of painting on a wet or freshly prepared plaster surface. The paint pigments penetrate the surface and as they dry, they become a part of the surface painted. Pigments that are water ground are used, the surface becomes very hard and is a very permanent type of painting, without reflection and a surface that can be washed. The color pigments become cemented to the lime particles of the plaster and thus become a part of each other.

fresco secco: A painting method, especially mural painting (q.v.). The surface is prepared with a mixture of baryta water (q.v.) and glue. This is then painted as a fresco (q.v.). This is similar to a fresco but does not last or have the quality of a true fresco.

fringe: Used in weaving and rug-making. These are the cut ends of the warp threads (q.v.). The result of weaving (q.v.). These threads or cords are knotted to prevent the rug from becoming unraveled.

frisoir: A tool of the metalcrafter, especially those working in pewter (q.v.). This is a chisel-like tool with a dull point, usually made of steel and used in burnishing (q.v.).

frit: In the ceramic crafts, frit refers to any melted or fluxed glaze with or without color. Used by the ancient Egyptians to get their blue color, known as Egyptian Blue (q.v.). It was made by melting copper and other metallic salts together. The above type is considered a pigment when used in the paint crafts.

front matter: In the printing and bookbinding crafts. The front matter precedes the actual printed matter of a book. The pages are usually numbered with Roman numerals; includes the introduction, table of contents.

frontispiece: A term in the printing and bookbinding crafts and illustration art. This is a picture or illustration in a book that faces the title page. In the early days of book making, this illustration usually was a portrait of the author.

frosted windows: As a temporary measure, to frost windows, beer and epsom salts can be used. See beer.

frottage: A technique of the artist and craftsman. A paper is placed on a surface, such as wood, stone or cloth. It is then rubbed with pencil, crayon or charcoal. This will result in a design (q.v.) on the paper that is the same as that on the object rubbed. This is done by coin collectors who make tracings of coins to send to other collectors or to others to identify.

fuchsin: A reddish purple color used by the artist, also known as magenta (q.v.).

full aspect: A term used in heraldry. See aspect.

full bound: This is a book that has a leather cover, made in one piece, which covers the book completely.

full leather: A bookbinding term, see full bound.

full stop: A term used in photography. Full stop means that the opening or aperture on the camera is wide open. Stopping down means that the lens opening is closed a set amount, thus cutting down on the amount of light admitted.

fuller's earth: This is a type of pigment, also known as diatomaceous earth (q.v.).

fundame: A lacquer technique. Powdered gold or silver is applied to the wet lacquer. This is polished until it is smooth, the result is a rich dull finish.

furniture: A term used by printers. These are blocks of wood or metal, the metal furniture is hollow to reduce weight. These blocks are used to fill out areas that have no type, known as white space (q.v.).

fused quartz: A type of pure crystal, melts at about 1,800 degrees C. Used in the making of flint glass (q.v.).

G

gadroon: Used in the metal and woodworking crafts, this is a group of curved lines that come from a common center area, this forms an oval.

gage knife: A type of knife used in leather working. This knife has a gage on one side and a sharp blade on the other side across from it. The knife may be set to a certain width and then a screw is set to hold the size. The knife is drawn toward the person doing the cutting, a long sweeping motion is used.

Galalith: A trade name for a plastic material made from formaldehyde-casein. Used as a substitute for ivory, bone, tortoise shell.

galena: A mineral of lead ore. Used in the making of pewter (q.v.). Also known as potter's ore (q.v.).

gallery work: This is a coarse variety of ceramics or pottery.

gallipot: This is a small container that is made to clamp on the artist's palette. Used for holding water or thinner or whatever medium is being used by the artist.

gallstone: This is an obsolete pigment made from oxgalls. Its color was pink.

Galvanotype: A trade name for a type of copperplate used in intaglio (q.v.).

gamboge: This is a type of resin from the trees in Siam. Gamboge can be used as a yellow glaze in ceramics. Gamboge has been in use from medieval times to the late nineteenth century. This is not a true paint pigment. It is rather transparent.

ganosis: A term used by sculptors to describe the process of toning down the shine or glare on a marble piece.

garden rugs: Rugs (q.v.) that are made with the designs of flowers and various types of shrubbery. All rugs of this type should have a crossed design of water with a pool depicted in the center.

garnet: Used in the jewelry and gem crafts. This is a

mineral with a red to brown color, crystal in shape. Used in the gem crafts for rings, etc.

garnet paper: Similar to sandpaper, but with the use of garnet sand.

garnish: In the metal crafts, especially pewter (q.v.), a garnish is a complete set of pewter ware, consisting of twelve cups, saucers, and twelve plates.

gas bells: A term used in photography. These are small bumps or bubbles that are caused by insufficient washing of a negative.

gash: This was an instrument used by the ancient Egyptian scribes. Made from a split reed, about ten inches long. One type had a sharp point and one type had a rough fuzzy point to make soft lines. The gash is also known as a writing reed (q.v.).

gassing: Used in several crafts, this is the burning or singeing of the small fibers that extend from cloth, applied to mercerized yarn. This gassing is also done in the printing crafts. A flame is placed in such a way that it drys the inked paper as it passes off the press.

gather: A term used in the glass-making and bookbinding crafts. Used in the making of stained glass. A small amount of clear glass is gathered on the blow pipe and is dipped into a color, when blown, this results in flashed glass (q.v.). Sometimes two colors are slightly stirred together and form a glass that is streaked. In the bookbinding crafts, gathering is done when a book is put together, each section piled in the correct order before it is bound.

gauge: In the metal crafts, a gauge is an important tool, made very carefully to a scale, to be used in measuring the thickness of wires, and thicknesses of various metals.

geat: This is the small hole that is left in a mold (q.v.). It is through this small hole that the material is poured to make the casting (q.v.).

gelatin: A substance made from the bones and connective tissue of animals. Used in photography, leather crafts.

gem: A term used in the jewelry and gem crafts. A gem is usually considered to be a mineral which is rather rare or sought after. A gem is cut and polished and can be set in a ring or other type of holder. Examples are an emerald, diamond, ruby, etc.

gemmary: A box or other container for gems (q.v.). This term is applied to all gems in general.

genius: A term used in the arts and crafts, meant to mean a person who has an abnormally high intelligence or who can do some task that is difficult for others in a way not yet thought of. A special talent.

gentleman: A term used in several crafts. This is a table with an iron or other metal top. This top revolves. An object such as is made of clay is placed on the surface and then it is spun. A device is used to shape the piece as it is turned. This differs from a banding wheel (q.v.).

German silver: This is an alloy (q.v.). Made from nickel, zinc and copper. This is a white metal. Used in the jewelry crafts.

gesso: This is a mixture of chalk, whiting or slaked plaster of Paris along with a mixture of water and glue or casein. This is used to cover a surface to be painted. When mixed rather thick it may be molded, carved and built up to form a relief. Used on picture frames to make pleasing designs. See mâché.

gesso panel: This is a board that has been prepared with gesso (q.v.), usually on both sides. Used by artists who paint in several types of mediums.

giallo antico: A yellow marble, found mainly in Algeria. Used by sculptors.

gilder's knife: A flexible steel knife, a tool of the gold craftsman. Used to cut and to lay on gold leaf (q.v.).

gilding: A process by which certain objects are covered with a thin layer of gold leaf (q.v.).

gilding burnisher: A hard stone, usually agate (q.v.), used to rub or polish gold leaf (q.v.) after it has been laid.

gilt: A term used to describe the application of gold to the edge of a page of a book . . . gilt edge.

gimp: *Braid* (q.v.).

girasol: A variety of opal (q.v.) used in the jewelry and gem crafts.

girdle: The girdle is the widest part of the diamond. This term is used in the jewelry and gem crafts.

glacure: A thin glaze done on fine ceramics (q.v.).

gladiolus: The blooms from this plant can be used in the making of corsages (q.v.). When picked, place the stems in strong vinegar water and let soak. The blooms should last two or three days.

glair: This is a term to describe a process of applying gold leaf to leather; this is done by the application of the white of egg and then applying the gold leaf (q.v.).

glass: Made mainly of silica, soda and lime. Made by melting under great heat. Made into many shapes and forms. Glass is brittle and has been made as far back as 2400 B.C. in Egypt.

glass blowing: This is a technique of the glass maker or the science of vitrics (q.v.). A lump is taken out of the melting pot on the end of the tube and either by mechanical means or by the human breath it is blown. The glass is kept at a rather liquid state so that it will be workable.

glass enamel: A type of glass that is used in making the shades for lamps, etc. Made with the addition of binoxide of tin, which gives it a milky opaque look.

glass flux: A flux when used in the making of glass is composed mainly of silicates. Flux is used as a binder. When it melts, as in glass or in the making of ceramics (q.v.), it fuses together and thus binds the material.

glass metallics: See flitters.

glass paddle: A tool of the glass maker. The glass paddle is a scoop shaped device used at the end of a long handle to stir molten glass.

glass painting: This is an art and a craft. Glass may be painted with a stain which is then heated and thus becomes a part of the glass. It may also be colored by small chips or cut pieces of glass, which are laid on a glass surface in such a way that they form designs or pictures; these are fastened in place with metal strips. Known as leaded glass. Glass may also be painted directly with oil paints or enamel paints. Used in this way for the making of shadow pictures or for special effects, such as in a museum background scene.

glass pencil: See china marking pencil. This is a pencil with rather thick waxy lead, used for marking on china, porcelain or other surface that would repel regular pencil or ink marks.

glaze: See glazing.

glaze gum: A gum mixed with the glaze in firing (q.q.v.). This gum helps strengthen the glaze and is burned away when it is fired.

glazing: As used in the craft of leather working, glazing is a method of living leather a shine or luster. This is done by friction, a glass roller being used.

Glazing is done in the ceramics crafts (q.v.). A piece is painted with slip (q.v.) and then fired (q.v.). The glaze is colored or clear and gives a ceramic (q.v.) a finish.

glitter: Used in the eggshell crafts and also in special sign effects. This is usually applied on a surface that has been coated with glue. These are small particles of metals, mica, glass and other materials, ground to a powder.

glory circle: A term used in heraldry. This is a form of crown that is shown with rays extending from it. This is applied to a shield or escutcheon (q.q.v.).

gloss: This term is used in the arts to denote the degree of reflection from a surface.

gloss glaze: A type of glaze that is applied with a brush; this glaze continues to run for awhile even during the firing and so results in a smooth very glossy finish.

glue: A substance, made of many materials such as bones, skins, intestines of animals and the well-known fish glue. Used for many arts and crafts. Some glues can be used cold, others have to be heated and then used. Some glues are powdered.

glycerin: This liquid can be used in many ways; with formalin it is used to preserve lichen for model making. Glycerin is the by-product of soap, fats and oils and from the making of candles. It is classed chemically as an alcohol. Used in the leather crafts as a softener.

glyphic art: A term applied to that branch of arts and crafts which is concerned mainly with the modeling in plastics.

glyptography: This is the knowledge and process of engraving on precious stones, such as on a gem stone in a ring. This differs from hyalography (q.v.).

gnomon: When making a sundial, this is one of the three parts that make up the sundial. The gnomon is the part that casts the shadow. This part is triangular in shape. The angle of this part is determined by the latitude of the location of the sundial. The angle of the gnomon has the same number of degrees as the latitude.

goatskin: A term used in the leather crafts. Also known as morocco grain (q.v.). Made from the skin of goats, used in making laces, etc.

gofun: A white chalk wash. Used in Japan as a ground (q.v.).

gogatsu bina: These are special Japanese dolls that are used at a boys' festival. This festival is celebrated on the fifth of May. The dolls represent soldiers and Japanese warriors.

gold: A mineral found in quartz rock. Gold bearing ore is found all over the world. Gold has a value in this country of $35 an ounce. This price is fixed by an Act of Congress. Pure gold is 24 Karat (q.v.). Pure gold melts at 1950° F. Gold has been in use for hundreds of years. It is the most malleable of the metals. Gold is not affected by sulphur or oxygen. It can be dissolved in a solution of aqua regia (q.v.).

gold beater: This term is used in the craft of making gold leaf (q.v.). A gold beater is a person who beats gold, a process of forming gold into thin sheets.

gold beating: The process of making gold leaf (q.v.), an exacting and ancient craft.

gold filled: This type of metal consists of a base metal on which a layer of gold alloy has been welded. The karat amount tells the exact amount of gold that is in the alloy.

gold leaf: Gold leaf has to be made by hand. This is a very ancient craft. The making of gold leaf was done in ancient Egypt. The methods have not changed since ancient times. Leaves of vellum (q.v.) are dusted with chalk. In between each sheet of vellum, a leaf of gold is placed. This is done until there are twenty-five leaves. This is known as a kutch (q.v.). This is then beaten by hand with a seventeen-pound hammer for exactly thirty minutes. Next, the shoder (q.v.) is beaten with a nine-pound hammer. This is done for two hours. Next the shoder is beaten for four hours with a seven-pound hammer. This will make about twelve hundred gold leaves which are about 254,000 of an inch thick.

gold size: This is a pigment used on various surfaces. It is applied prior to the application of gold leaf (q.v.), known as bole (q.v.). See gilding.

gold thread: This plant, Coptis trifolia, was used by the

Ojibwa Indians of the Great Lakes region of Canada and the United States. The root of this plant was used to make a yellow dye. Used by these Indians to dye porcupine quills yellow.

gong metal: A type of metal made in the Orient. Used for the making of metal gongs. This metal is an alloy of 25% tin and 75% copper.

goose feathers: Goose feathers are used for feathering arrows. The primary or wing feathers are used. The vanes should be cut from three matching feathers. These are cut and glued just below the nock (q.v.).

gooseberry stone: This is a type of yellow garnet. Used in the jewelry and gem crafts.

gouge: A tool used in the block printing crafts (q.v.). A gouge usually cuts a wide surface and has a beveled point. The cut made by a gouge is similar to a parenthesis. A chisel (q.v.) is also used.

gourd rattles: Gourds are the seed pods of a plant. When dried they can be cleaned out and several small stones or shells can be placed in the inside. The hole may be filled or a stick handle can be inserted through the gourd. This is then shaken. These rattles are also known by the name of maraccas.

graffito: This technique was used in early Italy. The process is simple; a coat of plaster, white or colored, is covered while it is still wet with a coat of another color. Both coats should be rather thin. They can then be scratched and the under coat thus exposed. The cuts should not be too deep as they will then catch dust and dirt. This method is also used in the ceramics crafts.

grain: This term, when applied to the leather crafts, refers to the hair side of the leather. The grain is the pattern that is left when the hair is removed.

grain split: When leather is split, or cut to various thicknesses, this is called split. Grain split refers to a split on the hair side of the leather. See "flesh split."

granite: A rock composed of orthoclase and quartz; sometimes mica is present. This hard grained rock is used for the carving of monuments and for buildings.

graph paper: A type of paper with a system of squares, usually of the same size. Used in the arts and crafts for making accurate drawings or sketches. Also used as a means of enlargement of a photograph or sketch. Such a graph paper with half inch squares could equal a half an inch to a foot.

graphite: When used in the crafts, graphite is used in polishes, pencils, as a lubricant. It is a greyish black mineral, a result of changes in the earth, formerly was plant life. In metal crafts, graphite is used in the making of crucibles (q.v.). Graphite is a type of carbon.

grater: A metal crafts tool. Used to make the first rough shape of a metal object; this differs from a burnisher (q.v.).

graver: A graver is a tool used in the craft of wood cutting. The graver differs from block cutting tools such as the chisel (q.v.) and the gouge (q.v.). A graver is not hollow or curved, but solid. The tool handle is flat on one side so that when a cut is made in the wood it will not go too deep, but instead move with a glide over the surface of the block. Gravers come in various sizes and shapes, the lozenge (q.v.), square graver (q.v.), half round (q.v.), round pointed graver (q.v.), bull-sticker (q.v.), spitsticker (q.v.), halftone tool (q.v.), and the tint tool (q.v.).

gravers: These are tools used in metal crafts. They are used to scratch metal and work on it, such as an engraver would.

green earth: This is a clay, used as a pigment in paints. Used in water colors and in the ceramic crafts as a glaze. In Europe, this pigment is also known by the names of: Bohemian, which is a pure green color, Cyprian, which has a yellow tinge, Verona, which has a blue tinge. There is another type known as Tyrolean, the latter is somewhat like Verona, only with a dull finish. In the making of dyes, green earth is very good because of its ability to absorb and its permanency.

green ivory: A type of fine African ivory, also known as Pangani (q.v.).

green ware: Any clay piece that is still damp, or un-fired and still requires drying.

greenhouse: A building warmed slightly, used for the drying of green or unfired pottery or ceramics. This dries the objects slowly.

Greiner: This name is used in the craft of doll making. Ludwig Greiner was a German doll maker who came to America. In the year 1858, he patented a type of doll head. Dolls that are made by his method can be identified by the label which can be found on the doll's back between its shoulders which says, "Greiner Patent Heads." The head was made hollow of papier mâché (q.v.) and then reenforced with thin strips of cloth.

grey cameo painting: A method of painting on the surface of glass with various shades and tones of grey. The result is a monochrome illustration.

griffin: A strange beast of heraldry. This animal is shown with the legs, body and tail of a lion, the head of an eagle, wings and long sharp claws. Placed on the shield and escutcheon (q.v.).

grinding: A process done in many ways in many arts and crafts. The object of grinding is to produce a fine powder or pigment in the paints. The finer the grind, the better the mixture will be. Many mechanical devices have been made for grinding.

grog: A term used in ceramics (q.v.). Grog is fired clay that has been broken or made useless in other ways. This is ground to a powder and mixed with fresh un-fired clay. When this is used, it results in rather coarse textured pieces. This use of grog helps to prevent crazing (q.v.).

gros: This is a term used in paint pigments. Gros denotes that a color is rather strong or bright.

gros point: This is a term used in needlepoint (q.v.). Gros point is done with a rather large needle and so the design is rather thick. This differs from petit point (q.v.).

ground: This is the coating that is applied to the surface of a plate in the etching crafts (q.q.v.). When the surface is cut in any way this admits the acid which bites the plate (q.q.v.). Ground is also applied to other crafts where a first surface coat or base is applied.

ground block: This is a flat block used in printing. This is used to print a block of color, a light tint. This is later used as an area to print type or other illustrations.

ground coat: Used in the painting crafts. A ground was used on a surface so that a mural (q.v.) or painting could be fastened to it. Usually made from chalk, whiting and glue.

ground glass: Glass that has been sand-blasted or rubbed with sandpaper. This produces a rough surface that is opaque and has a frosted appearance.

guilloche: A design that resembles twisted rope. Made with bands on the cover of a book. Used in the leather crafts and the bookbinding crafts.

guillotine cutter: This is a rather large machine that is used by printers and those who bind books. This machine cuts the fore edge (q.v.) of a book. A flat and sharp carpenter's chisel can be used in place of the guillotine cutter. Use care to clamp the book tightly, start at one end and pound the chisel with a hammer along a line which you must draw and follow. This will cut the pages in the book in such a manner that the pages can be opened one after another.

gum arabic: A gum coming from certain trees found in Africa where the best grade is obtained; it is also found in Asia and in Australia. To dissolve gum arabic, it is necessary to mix it with water and let it stand for several hours; don't cook the mixture, but use boiling water to start, pour it over the gum and stir and let it cool. Mucilage is usually made from gum arabic with some type of preservative added.

gumdrop trees: A tree can be made for a party with a paper cup, a twig and gumdrops. Fill a small paper cup with plaster of Paris (q.v.). While the plaster is still wet, insert a small twig with many branches on it. When the plaster is hard it may be painted or left white and the tree is ready for use. For the foliage, use gumdrops, these are pushed on the ends of the twigs and can be pulled off and eaten. The tree can be saved for future use.

gusset: An angular piece inserted. For the end and edges of a bag, cigarette case, etc. a gusset is used; the leather folds and allows for expansion, sometimes has the corner notched out. Gussets are laced, cemented or cloutaged (q.v.).

gypsum: Gypsum is calcium sulphate; in pigments, used only as an adulterant. When it is used in paints, it becomes hard and brittle. See plaster of Paris.

H

haban: A type of ceramics (q.v.), made by the Anabaptists that settled in the Slovakian countries about the middle of the sixteenth century.

habitat group: This is a large, almost full size group or exhibit of an actual location or habitat. Usually seen in museums. These groups have a curved background usually painted in oils by an artist (q.v.). The foreground is copied exactly from nature, animals are mounted, plants and large rock work are made by hand by skilled craftsmen. A diorama (q.v.) is usually made first so that time and materials can be better judged.

hacking: A term used in the gem crafts. Hacking is a method of cutting the metal lap (q.v.), so that it will serve as a container for the abrasive powder.

hagi yaki: A type of ceramic (q.v.) made in Japan in the province of Nagato.

Hahai-i Wuuti: This is a type of Hopi Indian kachina. This kachina is seen in the Water Serpent Ceremony; she is considered to be the mother of the kachinas. This kachina (q.v.) wears a dress, sometimes wears white boots and is sometimes barefooted. She wears a fox skin around her neck. Her face is painted white with two red dots, one on each cheek.

haircloth: This is a type of cloth made from horsehair and cotton. The horsehair is used for the weft (q.v.) and the cotton or linen used for the warp.

Hakata Ningyo: These were clay dolls made in Japan in the early days, made by Hakata, a Japanese tile maker.

hakemei: This is a technique of painting done in Japan. Lacquer (q.v.) is used and the strokes of the brush are left as part of the design instead of brushing them away.

hakudo: This is a type of bronze alloy made from copper and nickel. This alloy is used mainly in Japan.

halation: This is a term used in photography. Halation is the result of reflected light on a film (q.v.). A halo appears on the film; this is seen when photographs are taken of direct sunlight, etc.

half binding: This is a term used in bookbinding. Refers to a book that has its corners and back covered with leather. The rest of the cover is of another material.

half brilliant: A term used in the jewelry and gem crafts. A half brilliant is a gem stone that is cut and polished in the simplest form. Usually this is done because of the size of the stone, which may be too small to cut all of the facets (q.v.).

half circles: A term used especially in Greek art. Used in ceramics (q.v.), half circles are designs that were made on the object to form decorations.

half facet: This term is used in the gem and jewelry crafts. The half facet is a method of arrangement of the facets (q.v.) on a brilliant (q.v.).

half pearls: These are pearls that are rather imperfect. They have bad spots which are cut off and the good side is then used in the making of jewelry of various types. These pearls absorb moisture through the cut edge and often become discolored.

half relief: This is a sculpture technique. A half relief is a design that is slightly raised from the surface upon which it rests.

half round graver: The half round graver is a tool used in the crafts of wood-engraving (q.v.). The point of this tool is made from steel; it has a round top surface and two straight sides which join to make a point.

Half Roxburghe: A term used in the bookbinding crafts. A Roxburghe is a binding that has the addition of leather on the corners.

half title: This is the short title found at the front on the first page of the text of a book, it may also be a division such as "part two," etc.

half-tone: A term used in printing and the intaglio (q.v.) crafts. A half tone is a type of plate (q.v.). The surface of the plate is sensitive to the etch and a fine glass screen is placed over the plate. An intense light is shone on the plate. The various size dots on the screen are left on the plate. These dots form various patterns and combinations which the eye tolerates and thus an image is formed. Examine a picture in a newspaper with a hand lens and you will see the many small dots which make up the half tone picture.

half-tone screen: This is a glass surface that is cross hatched with small lines or dots. When a picture is projected through this screen, a half tone (q.v.) print is the result.

half-tone vignette: A term used in the intaglio crafts. This is a half tone which has a background that gradually fades away.

half-tone tool: This is a tool used in the craft of wood-engraving. This tool, made of steel, is square in shape, three of the four sides being smooth, one surface cut to form sharp teeth, which when drawn over the wood block, leave a series of evenly shaped grooves, such as a rake would make.

halved joint: A term used in woodworking. A halved joint is a joint where two pieces of wood are joined together at right angles, each piece cut so that half fits with the second half.

halveflossa: This is a weaving technic used in Sweden. The yarn is made into knots or tufts, these are woven into the fabric in such a manner that they will form a design in themselves.

hammerhead: A term used in the metalcrafts, especially in pewter work (q.v.). This is a type of thumb-knop (q.v.) made around the seventeenth century.

hammerman: This is the name first used in Scotland for a pewterer. So called because the early methods of pewter (q.v.) work involved much hammering. This name is little used any more because of the different techniques now used in the working of pewter.

han lin: This is an art term. Used when talking about a type of painting done in China. This term is used to denote trees that are painted without leaves, also known as a cold forest (q.v.).

hanap: A special pewter (q.v.) cup made in the early days. This cup or goblet was used for the guest of honor at special dinners.

hand: A term used in the weaving and sewing crafts. This is the texture or feel of the cloth, when it is felt with the hand.

hand wiped print: This term is used in the etching and intaglio (q.v.) crafts. When the plate (q.v.) is inked, it is wiped clean, only the ink in the etched lines remains. See wiping.

handcrafts: See handicrafts, woodcrafts, crafts.

handicraft: A term that seems to combine arts (q.v.) and crafts (q.v.). The term generally implies the use of the hands in creating some work of art or supplying some need, such as a table or chair while out camping. Handicrafts are not usually done with machines but rather with hand tools which at times may even be made themselves by hand. See woodcraft.

handling: A term used by artists (q.v.). Has several meanings; to some, it refers to the methods used, pigments, preparation of canvas, etc. To others the term is used to describe the method the artist used to portray his painting.

hanging creepers: An art term, used in Chinese painting. This is a technique of brush work, used in painting tree trunks, rocks and other natural materials.

hansa yellow: This is a paint pigment, made from a synthetic dye. Many types of fine green are made from a base of hansa yellow. Also a trade name for a pigment used in dye making.

harbor: A term used in the glass making crafts. The harbor is a large container that is used to mix all of the ingredients used in the making of glass. This is done in a harbor just before it is melted or fused together.

hard paste: Used in the making of porcelains (q.v.). A hard paste is usually used. The hard paste is composed of kaolin (q.v.). The finest porcelains of the Orient are made with hard paste.

hard porcelain: This term is applied to any ceramic that has a hard surface and cannot be cut or scratched with a sharp tool. This type of porcelain (q.v.) is made with kaolin (q.v.). It has a metallic glaze (q.v.).

hard solder: This solder is an alloy of silver, copper and zinc. It is used on very fine work and takes a red heat to melt.

hardening kiln: A term used in the ceramics (q.v.) crafts. The hardening kiln is a low heat kiln, used to drive out moisture and oils from a piece that has a design painted on it.

hardening on: A ceramics term, used to denote the technique or process by which the first glaze (q.v.) or other decoration is first applied and baked on in a hardening kiln (q.v.).

hardness: A term used in the arts and in photography. Hardness is a term used to define the contrast between colors or light and dark in a painting or photograph.

hare's fur glaze: A type of glaze (q.v.) seen on certain types of ceramics (q.v.) made in the Sung dynasty of China.

haricot: This is a material (red copper oxide), used in the ceramics (q.v.) crafts. Usually used as a background color.

harmony in color: A term used by the artist to describe colors that go well together and are pleasing to the eye.

harness: A device used in weaving. Used to hold the heddles.

Harrison red: A strong paint pigment, also used as a tinting pigment by artists.

hat box: A simple drum can be made from old hat boxes. Glue a tough paper over the open end of the box, this will form the head of the drum.

hashira: This is a type of print (q.v.) made in Japan, used mainly to hang in narrow places. This type of print or painting is about five inches wide and about thirty inches long.

hatch lines: These are lines made on maps and other types of drawings, used in cartography (q.v.).

hatchment: A term used in heraldry. At the time of death, the complete coat-of-arms is shown in black and is hung on the outside of the house of the deceased.

hau ch'i: When lacquer (q.v.) is used in any type of ceramics (q.v.) or painting in China, this term is used to describe the process.

hawksbill: This is a rather large pewter pitcher, also known as a ewer (q.v.). Also made of ceramic (q.v.).

hawthorn: A type of wood (Crataegus) used for carving and inlay (q.v.). The wood is rather light in color with a straight grain and smooth texture.

hawthorn design: A design that is seen on some types of blue and white ceramics (q.v.), made in China. The design represents the plum however.

hazel: The inner bark of this tree was used by the Ojibwa Indians of the Great Lakes region of Canada and the United States. This dye was made by mixing green hazel burs and bur oak (q.v.) and butternut (q.v.). The resulting dye was black. The Indians of this area used this dye on the rush from which they made baskets.

head: Used in the bookbinding crafts, the head is the top edge of the cover case (q.v.).

head hoops: See hoops.

headband: This is the inner part of a book, the part that is glued or sewn, just between the pages and the back (q.v.) of a book. This is a bookbinding term.

heddle: In a loom the heddle is the vertical device, usually made of wires and used to guide the warp threads.

He-e-e: This is a type of Hopi Indian kachina (q.v.). This is a male kachina dressed in woman's clothes. The face of this figure is black and has a beard, the hair is short on one side and on the other the hair is hanging down. The figure holds a quiver with arrows and a rattle. The story of this kachina is interesting; on Second Mesa, the figure represents the figure of a young man who, while changing clothes with his bride in a corn field, saw enemy raiders approaching his village; he ran to the village and warned the village. Because he was changing clothes and hair style when he saw the enemy, he didn't have time to finish, so the result was the He-e-e kachina.

Heheya: The figure of this kachina is painted red and has yellow shoulders. It has a face painted green and sometimes yellow and a nose painted in the form of a T. This kachina wears a neck piece made of fir, and green shoes. This kachina (q.v.) is usually found in pairs.

helmet: Used in heraldry. The helmet is situated on the shield or escutcheon (q.q.v.) just below the crest (q.v.).

hemachate: A light colored stone of the agate (q.v.) family, used in the jewelry crafts; used mostly for costume jewelry.

hematite: A mineral that is used to make a fine red paint pigment. The stone itself is used as a surface for the making of gold leaf (q.v.).

hemlock: A red dye was made from the inner bark of this tree. The bark was mixed with some rock powder to set the color. The Ojibwa Indians of the Great Lakes region of Canada and the United States used the dye to color porcupine quills and also their rush mats. The color was red.

hemp: A tall plant (Cannabis sativa), used for the making of rope and cord. Used in China for the making of a type of paper.

hemp oil: Oil pressed from the seeds of hemp has been used since very early times. Hemp oil is inferior to poppy oil (q.v.).

heraldry: The art of heraldry goes back to the 12th century. The art developed when the helmet of a soldier covered the complete face. It became necessary to paint a design on the helmet for identification in battle. Heraldry includes the designing of the coats-of-arms, also the history, records and rules for heralds. This is written or told in a special heraldic language and terms.

heroic: A sculpture (q.v.) term. A figure that is carved to represent a figure of a man or animals is considered to be heroic because of its size; figures are larger than life by a foot or two.

herringbone: A type of weaving. The effect is somewhat like a zig zag pattern. The design is usually run at about a forty-five degree angle.

hexagonal knop: A term used in the metal crafts. This knop (q.v.) is found on spoons made around the sixteenth century.

hexamine: This is a white, rather crystalline substance used to harden certain resins (q.v.) used on the surfaces of paintings.

hickory: A type of wood used in the woodworking crafts. This wood has a straight grain and a rather coarse texture. Used for the carving of parts of musical instruments, the making of canes, etc.

hiding power: A paint pigment that has a good hiding power is a pigment or paint that will cover the surface underneath very well or completely. In certain types of art work this is desirable, others wish the color beneath to show through.

high: A term used in the arts. High refers to the gloss (q.v.) or shine on a painted surface.

high key: High key is a term used in photography to denote a rather light picture, light shadows, and other dark areas that are rather light.

high relief: A term used in sculpturing (q.v.). High relief is a term that describes a figure or design that stands out boldly from its base or surface.

high warp: Used in the arts, the high warp refers to a painting that is hung so that the warp (q.v.) is hung straight up.

highlight: A term used in several crafts to denote the bright areas, such as the reflection of the sun, bright spots such as lights, light or bright colors.

hill jar: A type of Oriental ceramics (q.v.). The lids of these jars have pointed tops, the tops representing mountains. These jars are often decorated with the figures of animals and hunters.

hilliers: This is a cap that is placed over delicate objects that are being fired (q.v.) in a kiln (q.v.) in the ceramics (q.v.) crafts. See sagger.

Himalayan cedar: A type of wood from India used in carving. This wood has a straight grain and a smooth even texture; the wood is rather oily. Sometimes known as deodar (q.v.).

Hina Matsuri: This is a doll that is used in a special festival for girls in Japan. The custom is celebrated on March third of each year. Little girls arrange their dolls on shelves or steps in a traditional way and stories are told about them. They tend to show little girls the meaning of loyalty and about being good mothers, etc.

hinnokogi yaki: A home variety of Oriental pottery made in the Yamashiro province of Japan.

hinoki: A type of cypress wood found in Japan, used for carving of figures.

hirado yaki: A type of home ceramics (q.v.) made in Japan in the province of Hizen.

hitsui: A term used in art, especially in Japan, generally means the brush stroke.

Hizen yaki: A type of well known ceramic (q.v.). Made in the Hizen province of Japan.

hofa fiber: A synthetic fiber. A rather coarse fiber, can be used in place of hemp (q.v.).

Hogarth: This is a term used in the corsage (q.v.) crafts. The Hogarth is a form (q.v.) used to make a corsage. The form is shaped to form a graceful S, sometimes this form is reversed. The large blooms are usually placed in the center of the corsage and the smaller flowers or buds are placed out from the center of this corsage.

hogback: A term used in connection with a style of painting done in China. These are painting strokes made with a brush done to represent jagged rocks and cracks in rocks, usually painted white and not outlined.

hollow relief: A technique of the sculptor (q.v.). The design or figure is cut into the surface in such a way that it is reversed. When viewed, it appears to be in high relief (q.v.). Actually it is an optical illusion. This type of carving has been used in advertising, when a face is done in this manner, it appears to turn as you walk past it.

hollow ware: A term used in ceramics (q.v.), usually applied to objects that are hollow, such as a vase, bowls, pitchers. This differs from flatware (q.v.).

hollowing: A term used in sculpturing (q.v.). Hollowing is the cutting away or hollowing of a sculptured piece so that the shadows will be accented, rather than painting in shadows.

holly: A type of wood used for fine carving and inlay work (Ilex acquifolium). The wood has a rather irregular grain and a fine texture.

hollyhock: The flowers of this plant work in well in the crafts of corsage (q.v.) making. The stems should be scorched or dipped in boiling water before use. The blooms will last about two days.

holster lacing: A rather heavy cowhide lace, used in the leather crafts for the lacing of holsters, luggage and other leather objects that will have hard or heavy use.

homespun: A term used to describe cloth or clothes that have been made at home. Homespun cloth is rather coarse and loose, the colors are not usually uniform in homespun cloth or yarn. Wool is mainly used.

homogenous glass: A type of glass that is uniform throughout; this differs from cased glass (q.v.).

honing: The process of sharpening a knife or other craft tool on a whetstone.

honey: Used with tempera paint (q.v.), honey produces a matte finish (q.v.).

Hong Kong grass: A type of grass from China found growing in water. It is a woven product which resembles rope, woven under water. It is used mostly for chair seats because of its strength and long lengths, which is an asset for this use. Hong Kong grass is sold by the pound, with about three hundred feet to the pound. Its natural color is a yellow tan. It may be purchased in other colors and these may be worked together for rather pleasing effects.

Honiton lace: This is a type of lace (q.v.) made in Honiton, England. Well known for its beauty of design and workmanship.

honor point: A term used in heraldry (q.v.). This is the upper center section of the escutcheon (q.v.). It is in this section that the armorial bearings (q.v.) of the owner are displayed.

hooked rug: A rug made on burlap (q.v.). Long narrow strips of material are pulled through the burlap in such a manner as to leave little loops, this is done with a hook. When the design is complete, the little hooks or loops are cut with a shears so that the design has a rather soft appearance.

Hooker's green: This is a type of pigment named for the artist that first used the combination of the pigments, phthalocyanine (q.v.), with green and cadmium orange (q.v.). Can also be a mixture of Prussian blue and gamboge (q.v.). The pigment is olive in tone, this is not a permanent pigment however.

hoop pine: From the tree Araucaria cunninghamii, a rather straight grained soft wood used for picture frames and carvings. It has a yellowish brown color. Also known as kauri pine (q.v.).

hoops: Usually made of iron. A hoop is a part of a barrel. A barrel usually needs from four to six hoops, two head hoops, two quarter hoops and to check the swelling of the barrel, two bilge hoops are needed.

horn chips: Chips left over from the horner (q.v.) are used to make artificial flowers.

hornbeam: A type of wood (Carpinus betulus), used for carving and inlay (q.v.). This wood is sometimes dyed black so that it will look like ebony (q.v.).

horned head-dress: A type of knop (q.v.). Made to resemble the helmets of early Scandinavian soldiers. Made of pewter (q.v.).

horner: A rather unusual craftsman. A person who makes objects from animal horns, such articles as combs, boxes, spoons, knife handles, horns to blow, powder horns, etc.

horns: The horns of rams, cows and the buffalo or bison are used by the horner (q.v.) in making various objects.

horse chestnut: This is a type of wood used in the carving crafts. A wavy grain and a smooth fine texture.

horsehair artificial: Horsehair can be made from rayon (q.v.) in any lengths desired. Used for the bows of violins and similar instruments.

horse hoof knop: A type of knop (q.v.), used in the sixteenth century. Found on the handles of spoons, especially pewter (q.v.).

hoshino yaki: A decorated type of ceramics (q.v.) made in the Chikugo province of Japan.

hoso: A print that is hung only vertically. About six by twelve inches, made in Japan.

hot cast porcelain: A term used in the glass making crafts. Also known as opaline (q.v.).

hot colors: This term is used in the arts to describe the colors of red and yellow and the various shades of each. These are also known as warm colors.

hothouse: A ceramics (q.v.) term. The hothouse is a heated room that is used to dry out the clay before it is fired (q.v.).

housed joint: A term used in woodworking crafts. A housed joint is a type of cut made in a joint that is grooved and forms a socket.

hovel: A large round dome-shaped building in which there is a large kiln (q.v.) or several small kilns. Used in the making of pottery and porcelain (q.v.).

howell: The upper part of a porcelain (q.v.) kiln (q.v.).

hsiang: A term in Chinese painting, denotes the painting of a portrait of a single person. This does not cover the complete field of portrait painting.

hsieh i: A term used in Chinese art that refers to a free hand sketch, without much detail.

hsiung huang: A yellow paint pigment, prepared from realgar (q.v.). Used in paintings made in China. When used with gold, the resulting color is black.

hsüan chih: A white paper made from bamboo. Made in China, this paper is used for calligraphy (q.v.). The paper is not always sized (q.v.).

hua ch'i: This is a blue pigment used in China as a base on a painting, resembles the color of indigo (q.v.).

hua chüan: This is a prepared silk. Used in China for the purpose of painting. The silk is especially sized (q.v.). Fine paintings are done directly on the silk.

Hungary blue: A type of blue pigment. Made from cobalt (q.v.).

hutch table: This is a type of chair and table combined. This was made of rough wood in early America. The top of the table was hinged to the back of the chair. When this was open and straight it became a back on the chair. When the surface was closed, it formed a flat table top or a wide bench-like table.

hyacinth: Red and sometimes brown, this variety of zircon (q.v.) is used in the jewelry crafts.

hyaline quartz: This is a type quartz used in the gem and jewelry crafts. This type of quartz has a rather blue color and is used in costume jewelry.

hyalite: A type of opal (q.v.) used in the gem and jewelry crafts, somewhat resembles a drop of melted glass.

hyalography: This is the art of engraving (q.v.) on glass, either with acids or with some cutting instrument such as an emery wheel.

hybrid porcelain: This is an imitation of the original porcelain (q.v.) made in the Orient. It does, however, contain some kaolin (q.v.). This is a rather soft type of porcelain, however.

hydrangea: Used in the corsage (q.v.) crafts. This bloom can be used in many ways. Soak the complete bloom in cool water, the blooms will last about three days. The blooms may be dried and used as they are.

hydro-plastic: A hydro-plastic is any type of plastic material that comes in a paste form. This can be made into any shape desired. This plastic becomes hard when it is exposed to the air. Hydro-plastics come in any color.

hydrofluoric acid: This is a liquid compound used for the etching of glass.

hydrophane: This is a type of gem stone used in the gem and jewelry crafts. When this stone is immersed in water, it becomes almost invisible. This stone is a variety of opal (q.v.).

hydroquinone: This is a chemical of needle-like crystals used in photography for the developing of pictures.

Hydroresin: A trade name for a liquid that is practically non-drying. Used as a substitute for gum Arabic (q.v.).

Hydrostone: A trade name for a type of plaster. This is one of the hardest and strongest known types of plaster, used for sculpturing (q.v.) and casting.

hyomon: A technique of lacquer (q.v.) work done in Japan. It consists of the placing of thin gold strips on a lacquered surface.

hyperfocal distance: Used in photography, this is a distance beyond which objects are in clear focus on a film in a camera. This is known as infinity (q.v.).

hypericum red: A red dye made from the plant hypericum.

I

I tung pi hua: This is a type of mural (q.v.). This type of mural is done in China. They are done on fabric and are placed in temples. They are not permanent and are taken down and folded.

ice snow paper: This is a type of ground that is applied to paper for use in calligraphy (q.v.). This is done in China.

Ichima Ningyo: This is a type of Japanese doll that is bought without clothes. It is carried by young Japanese girls; it may be a boy or girl doll. When she is old enough to marry, the girl makes clothes for this doll and sends it to the house of her future husband.

ichi-mai: This is a type of Japanese wood block print (q.v.).

icon: A term used in art. This usually means some representation of a saint or other holy being. The paintings or objects were generally revered because of their holy resemblance.

idiochromatic: A term used in the gem crafts. This is used to denote certain gem stones and minerals that are colored due to their own special make-up.

Iga yaki: This is a practical type of ceramic (q.v.) made in the Iga province of Japan.

igeta yaki: This is a type of undecorated pottery or ceramic (q.v.) made in the province of Tanba in Japan.

igneous rock: This is a type of rock such as granite. Igneous rock is rock that has been molten at one time. This type of rock is used in sculpture (q.v.).

ihia: This is a small lacquered (q.v.) tablet made in Japan. The ihia is placed in a shrine and has the name of a deceased person on it.

ikake-ji: This is a technique of painting on a ground of gold. This is a lacquer technique done in Japan.

ikat: A technique of tie dyeing (q.v.) done in Java. The yarn was first tie dyed and then woven into a fabric.

ikebana: This is the art of flower arrangement as done in Japan. Any group of flowers that are used for decoration.

illuminate: An art term. Pages, etc., are decorated with gold or silver or color. Sometimes a combination of two colors.

illumination: This is applied to the bookbinding crafts. It refers to the ornamental gold or color that is applied to books. This is usually applied to vellum (q.v.).

illustrate: An art term. This means that a story or explanation is made through the use of drawings, models or photographs.

illustration board: Illustration board consists of a high grade of paper which is mounted on a cardboard in such a way that it will not warp. There are a variety of types and thicknesses. Used for pen and ink, wash drawings, water colors, etc.

imagiers: These were French craftsmen of the fifteenth century who made only statues and figures of sacred figures. They worked in ivory, wood and stone.

imarki yaki: This is a fine grade of Japanese ceramic (q.v.). Made in the province of Hizen, Japan.

imbition: This is a term used in the field of photography. This is a dye transfer process used in color work.

imbrex: This is a type of ceramic (q.v.) tile. This tile is curved.

imbuya: A type of wood from Brazil, sometimes called Brazilian walnut. This wood has a brown color with a figured grain, used in carving.

imitation art paper: This is a type paper made with a glossy finish. The finish is produced by the addition of a certain mineral ingredient to the pulp when it is being made into paper.

imitation Russia: This is a term used in the bookbinding crafts. This refers to the type of leather used on the cover of a book, made to imitate Russian leather.

imitative arts: These are art forms that tend to re-create paintings or sculptured pieces already in existence.

impalpable: This is a term used in the ceramics (q.v.) crafts. The term impalpable refers to the surface of a ceramic; it means that it is so smooth that no texture or surface grit can be felt to the touch.

impastation: This is a term used in the ceramics crafts. This term denotes a combination of materials that are baked together with a type of cement, such as porcelain (q.v.)

impasto: This is a painting technique. The process consists of painting with thick paint. The paint is applied to the surface with a palette knife (q.v.).

imperial yellow porcelain: This is a type of yellow porcelain (q.v.) made in China. Originally this was made only for the imperial family and other special court members. This type of porcelain is a collector's item today.

impression: A term used in the publishing of a book. This is the number of copies printed at one setting of the type.

impression: In the printing crafts, this term is used to describe the design that is left on a paper or other surface after it has been inked. In the etching (q.v.) crafts, an impression is usually recorded so that a person can tell at a glance just what impression he has of an etching. Such as, 14/50. This would indicate that the etching with that number was the 14th impression of a set of 50. It is usual for the artist to then destroy the plate (q.v.) so that no more can be made of that design.

imprint: A term used in the printing crafts. The imprint is the name and the address of the publisher. This is found at the bottom of the title page.

in print: A term used in the printing crafts. In print means that a book or publication is printed and is available for use.

in the round: A term used in sculpture. Denotes a complete figure or object, not just half or in relief (q.v.).

inaurate: This is a term used in the arts. Inaurate denotes any object or surface that has a rather golden luster.

inbe yaki: This is a type of ceramic (q.v.). This pottery was made in the Hizen province of Japan.

inbound cover: This is a bookbinding term. When a book cover is rebound and the old cover is used as a base, this is known as an inbound cover.

incandescence: A term used in the metalcrafts. When a metal is heated until it becomes red or white hot, this is incandescence of the metal. This is done to make the metal easier to work.

incensed: A term used in heraldry. This is a term used to denote an animal that is shown with fire coming from its eyes.

incised ware: This is a type of ceramic (q.v.). The surface of the object has a design that is scratched into its surface. Somewhat like sgraffito (q.v.).

incrustation: This is a term used in art. This consists of inlaying (q.v.) one substance on another, such as lacquer (q.v.) on wood or stone.

incrusted enamel: This is a term used where enameled pieces of metals are inlaid (q.v.) on a larger plane. Such a technique is used sometimes when metal is chased (q.v.).

incunabula: This is a term used in the early printing crafts. The term was used to describe books made from the first movable type that was used.

India cut: This is a term used in the gem crafts. An India cut was a rather rough cut done on gem stones. The style somewhat resembled a brilliant (q.v.).

India ink: A type of ink made from lampblack and a glue binder.

India paper: This is a very fine type of paper. Originally made in China and Japan. The paper is very thin, an inch high pile will number almost a thousand sheets. The paper has linen content along with flax and hemp. This paper takes ink very well and is used mainly for the making of prints and fine engravings (q.v.).

Indian headdress: A simple Indian headdress can be made from an old felt hat and some turkey or large chicken feathers. Cut the brim off of the hat and sew the feathers around the edge of the hat. A felt strip can be sewn on the back and two rows of feathers may be sewn to this to form a long feather tail. The feathers may be colored (see feather dye).

Indian lake: This is a type of paint pigment made from an insect known as Coccus iacca. This was a pigment that resulted in a red dye.

Indian purple: This is a rather transparent paint pigment. This is made by mixing madder (q.v.) with ultramarine blue (q.v.). This is not a very lasting or brilliant color.

Indian red: This is a type of paint pigment. Made from red earth, usually iron oxides. The color is rather purple than a deep red.

Indian yellow: A pigment that is no longer in use; however it has had an interesting past. Made of euxanthic acid, a bright transparent yellow. Indian yellow comes from India and is made from the urine of cows fed on mango leaves. The method of manufacture was unknown for many years. Production of

Indian yellow in India was done on a small scale; the urine was heated. Since 1908, the production of true Indian yellow has been prohibited. The Indian yellow of today is made of coal tar products; they are not as lasting as the true Indian yellow.

indico: This is another spelling or term used for a dye known as indigo (q.v.), which is a blue dye.

indicolite: This is a variety of a mineral known as tourmaline. This stone is sometimes used in the jewelry crafts.

indienne: This is a term used in the sewing crafts. Indienne is another variety of chintz (q.v.).

indigo: A deep blue dye; it is rather transparent and does not stand up under light and therefore is not a permanent color. Indigo dye is made from a plant found in India. This type of dye can now be made from coal tar products.

indischgelb: This is a paint pigment. Orange-yellow in color. Known also as Indian yellow (q.v.).

indium: This is an alloy (q.v.) of silver, sixty per cent silver and forty per cent indium. This metal is used in the metal crafts and in the jewelry crafts. It is used as a substitute for sterling silver (q.v.). This alloy takes a high polish.

individualism: A term used in art. This denotes any individual who does not follow the set standards in art. A person who tries new ideas and techniques.

industrial jewels: These are rather imperfect gem stones, such as an imperfect diamond. These jewels can be used on bits and drills for certain tools such as glass cutters.

inert: When used as a painting term, inert is meant to apply to the bulk or filler used in a paint, such as chalk or clay.

inescutcheon: A term used in heraldry. An inescutcheon is a small escutcheon (q.v.) that is found inside the borders of the larger one.

infinity: A term used in photography. Infinity is considered to be over a hundred feet away from the camera.

ingrain: This is a term used in sewing or weaving. Ingrain yarn is yarn that has been dyed before it is made into a fabric. This type is used for special designs or effects.

initial spurt: An artist who has an all-fired interest or spurt of activity before settling down to a regular work schedule, is working under an initial spurt.

ink: There are many types and all colors of inks. Blacks and blue blacks get their color from organic iron compounds. See lampblack and India ink. Waterproof inks can be used to color and design the surfaces of leather.

ink knife: An ink knife is used by a printer. This is a rather flat pliable blade with a blunt end, somewhat like a palette knife (q.v.). The ink knife is used to place ink on rollers or box on a printing press. Also used to mix various shades and colors of thick inks used in printing.

ink splash: This was a 13th century Japanese painting technique. This was a rather simple technique of painting with inks. As few lines as possible were used to paint a picture, making rather a painting of suggested lines.

inking a block print: Linoleum block printing (q.v.) can be very rewarding when it is done correctly. The inking of the block is important and if not done correctly, can ruin the work done previously. The ink used is usually in a paste form, in cans or tubes, some have a water base, others have an oil base. The ink should be placed on a hard flat surface and then rolled out in several directions with the brayer (q.v.). When the ink is smoothed out and is free from lumps and the brayer has a sticky sound it is ready to be applied to the block. Roll the brayer smoothly over the block in several directions until all of the surfaces are coated; care should be used so that small cuts are not filled with ink. Also use care so that ink does not get in the cut away portions and thus start to smear the surface. The block should be inked after each impression is made. To do several colors with a block print requires several blocks, one for each color. As each color is printed it requires that extreme care be used so that the colors will print only in the space they are designed for and not overlap with each other.

inkstone: This is a fine grained stone used in the Orient. A small block of stick carbon and glue was rubbed in water on the ink stone. The resulting color was used by artists.

inlaid metal: See inlaying.

inlay: As used in the craft of leather, and in other crafts, to inlay is to cut out the design and set in other leathers, glueing them in place. Inlay work should be done with care and the parts put under a press or weight to hold them in place. The Koryaks of Siberia do some very fine work with inlay of leather, mostly of reindeer. Also used in the woodworking crafts. Inlay is done also in Arabia, known as kashi (q.v.)

insert: See corrigenda.

insert: An insert is a loose paper that is placed in a book to tell of some last-minute changes, or for advertising. This is not part of a book.

instability: A term used in the arts. This term is used to describe paint pigments or colors that do not last. Some fade, others change color with time due to other types of pigments that are mixed with them.

intaglio: This is the name given to the several ways of making a print from metal plates. Several types of intaglio such as line etching (q.v.) aquatint (q.v.), mezzotint (q.v.), drypoint (q.v.). The type of cutting varies but the intaglio process is somewhat the reverse of block printing (q.v.). The parts that are to be printed are cut or etched away. This leaves a slight line cut into the surface of the plate, which is usually copper (q.v.). When the design is completed, it is ready to be inked. The ink is rubbed or rolled over the surface of the plate. The ink fills the cut surfaces, the surplus ink is then wiped off. This will leave a clean surface with ink only in the etched part. The paper is placed on the plate surface and then pressed or rolled. This causes the paper to sink into the etched part and thus take up the ink. Designs that have been done by this method have clear sharp lines, these lines stand out somewhat from the surface of the paper. When the fingers are rubbed across the surface of the paper the design can be felt slightly. This is a simple method of testing a print to see if it is a real etching.

intense: A term used in art. This denotes any bright color, vivid or outstanding. This can also mean a highlight.

intense blue: This is a rather bright paint pigment made from refined indigo blue (q.v.).

interleaved: A term used in connection with the printing of books. Interleaved pages are pages that are left blank in a book. They are left to make notes or to do sketches as the reader progresses through the book itself. This differs from an insert (q.v.).

interlocked grain: This is a woodworking term. This is applied to wood that has a grain or fiber that goes in different directions. This type of wood is not good for hand carving. Machine work on this lumber will work fairly well.

iodine scarlet: A pigment made of mercury iodide, not a permanent color; when it fades it turns a pale yellow. This is a poisonous substance and is little used as a pigment in present day paints.

iris green: This is a rather rare and obsolete paint pigment made from the juice of the flowers of the iris plant. This dye was used in the 15th century. Also known as sap green.

iron brush: This was a form of calligraphy (q.v.) done in China. The carving was done on iron mainly. Also done on stone and wood.

iron man: This was a device used in the glass making crafts. This table on wheels supported the pontil (q.v.). It was used when the glass blower was working on large pieces, such as a window pane.

iron wire: A painting technique done in China. This consisted of a rather stiff vertical brush stroke. This was first done in the fifth century.

ironing bag: The need to wax a hot iron when it sticks to the material, especially when the cloth has a large amount of starch in it, can be solved by waxing the surface of the iron. Rather than the fire hazard of a piece of wax being rubbed on the iron surface, a simple method is this. Make a small bag five or six inches square. Fill this bag with bayberries (q.v.). Sew shut and you will have a safe, simple ironing bag that will last and give your clothes the fine scent of bayberries and at the same time wax the surface of your iron.

ishi yak: This is a general Japanese term that is applied to all stoneware (q.v.).

ishizuri: This is a type of printing technique. An impression is made from a stone or other surface that is cut or carved in relief (q.v.). Also known as rubbing (q.v.).

isinglass: This is a fish glue made from the inner layer of the bladders of fish. The best grade of isinglass is known as Russian isinglass and is made from the sturgeon.

Isle of Wight diamond: This is a type of quartz used in the jewelry crafts. This quartz is transparent.

isocephaly: A term used in art. This applies to the use of composition in a painting or other work of art. The natural proportion was distorted so that all things were made the same size. This was done in the early Greek period.

istrian marble: This is a type of marble with large grain that is quarried on the Dalmatian Islands. The marble is rather tan in color and is used by sculptors (q.v.) all over the world.

itajime: This is an interesting technique of dyeing fabrics. The design is laid over the fabric. The fabric is then clamped between two thin boards. The whole frame is then soaked in a colored dye. Only the part that is exposed in the design will take. The rest will remain blank. This is somewhat like a stencil (q.v.) method. Itajime is done in Japan particularly in the Suiko period. Also known as kyokechi.

Ito Bina: This is a type of doll which comes in pairs and is given when a girl is born within the year. These dolls have heads that are made of bunches of threads. These dolls come from Japan.

ivory: The tusks of various animals are used. Elephant, walrus and even prehistoric tusks are used, such as the mammoth. Ivory is carved and made into many objects such as knife handles, piano keys, etc.

ivory black: True ivory black is made by burning ivory scraps, which results in a black pigment of carbon. Also known as negro de marfil. Because it has the same properties as does bone black (q.v.), this in most cases is substituted for ivory black, although it is not as pure or as intense as ivory.

ivory porcelain: This is a type of porcelain (q.v.). This finish is secured by depolishing the glaze (q.v.).

ivorywood: This is a type of wood used for making engraving (q.v.) blocks, also used for inlay work (q.v.). The wood comes from the tree known as Siphonodon australe. The wood is rather white, fine grained and the texture is uniform and smooth.

iwakurayama: This is a rather heavy grade of earthenware (q.v.) made in Japan.

izumo yaki: This is a type of ceramics (q.v.) made in the Izumo province of Japan. Most of this type of ceramic wear is made for common household use.

J

jacinto: In the gem crafts, this is a transparent type of zircon (q.v.). Jacinto applies to any quartz (q.v.) with a dark red color.

jack loom: A weaving term. This is a type of loom that raises the harness by means of a jack.

jacket: In the book-making crafts, the jacket is a loose cover for a book or booklet. The jacket is usually well designed and an eye catcher. It is also a protective cover for the main cover of the book.

jacquard: This is a device used in the weaving crafts which forms an opening for the shuttle (q.v.). This opening is formed in the warp (q.v.) threads or cords.

jade: This is a mineral used in the jewelry crafts. The color of this mineral is usually green, there are variations from white to black however. Jade can be carved and much carving is done in the Orient. Jade was carved by the ancient Mayan people of Central America, and southern Mexico.

jade tablet paper: This was a type of un-sized paper used in the Orient, used for calligraphy (q.v.).

jamaica ebony: This is a type of wood used in inlay (q.v.) work.

jan: This is a Chinese term used when applying color in the background of sky and mountains. The technique should be such that no brush strokes can be seen.

Japan lac: This is a type of varnish made from the sap of a tree. This type of varnish is used by Japanese craftsmen.

Japan wax: A yellow rather soft type of wax. Japan wax comes from several species of sumac plant, found growing in India and China. The wax is a by-product of lacquer that is made from this plant. The melting point of this wax varies but is about 50 to 52° C.

Japanese vellum: This is a type of handmade paper. This paper is made from the pulp of the inner bark from certain mulberry trees found in the Orient.

Japanese walnut: This is a type of hardwood used in the woodworking crafts.

jasminum sambac: The blooms of this flower are used in the corsage (q.v.) crafts, also to make small floral jewelry. These blooms have a very fine scent. The bloom will last about two days.

jasper: A form of quartz, a semi-precious stone used in the jewelry and gem crafts.

jasper ware: This is a term in the ceramics crafts. Jasper ware is blue with the figures or designs on its surface in relief (q.v.).

jaune Indian: This is a type of yellow paint pigment.

jesse: A term used in heraldry (q.v.). A falcon shown on an escutcheon (q.v.) is known as a jessed bearing. This means that the bird is shown with a strap of silk or leather around its leg, to keep it from flying away.

jet: A type of black marble used in the jewelry crafts.

jewel: When used in gem crafts and the jewelry crafts this refers to the gem stone which is cut and polished. This is usually mounted, as in a ring or strung as on a necklace.

jewel point: This is a point on a tool used in the etching crafts (q.v.). The point is sharp and made from a diamond.

jeweler: The present conception of a jeweler covers many crafts and trades. A jeweler makes jewelry (q.v.). He may repair watches. He may sell silverware, glass ware and dishes. A jeweler may also do lapidary work (q.v.).

jeweler's red: A term used in the jewelry crafts. This is a material used as a polishing agent, also known as rouge (q.v.).

jeweler's tongs: The jeweler's tongs are used for the holding of a gem for examination or when cutting or polishing the stone. See tongs.

jewelry: Jewelry covers many types of ornaments, real and artificial. Jewelry usually refers to some form of adornment, such as earrings, rings, etc.

jigger: A term used in the ceramics crafts. This is a type of potter's wheel (q.v.). The jigger provides a means for turning out large numbers of the same type of pottery.

jiki: This is a term used in the ceramics crafts of Japan; this term applies to all types of Japanese porcelain.

jiku: The jiku is a term that is used in connection with

Japanese paintings. Jiku is a part of the stick that is used to roll a painting on; these are the knobs that are on the ends of the roll.

jingles: Jingles are the small discs that are placed around a tambourine; when shaken, they jingle or make a rattle-like noise. Jingles can be made from bottle caps. They may be strung around a tin pie plate or a paper plate.

joiner: This term is European, especially English. This is a craftsman who is known also as a carpenter.

joint: A term used in the bookbinding crafts. This applies to the hinge of the book. The joint also applies to any part of a book that has been repaired.

Jordan clay: A rather white and plastic clay used in the ceramics crafts. When fired, this clay turns to a tan to buff color.

ju chin: A Chinese method of painting with gold leaf. The leaf is rubbed under water in a circular motion until a paste is formed. This paste is used to make bright highlights on paintings. The brush work must follow the same direction as the rubbing.

ju yao: This is a rather heavy piece of pottery known in the ceramics crafts. The glaze of this pottery was blue and was made in China in the Sung Dynasty.

jug: A jug is a rather thick vessel usually made of clay; it has a small neck and a single or double handle.

jump weld: Used in the metal crafts. This is a type of weld that is done by hammering the ends together while a joint is being welded with heat.

juniper: A straight-grained wood used in the wood carving crafts.

justification: A term used in the printing crafts. Justification is the adjustment of lines of type so that they begin and end evenly on both sides of a column.

jute: This is a plant fiber. The plant is grown in India and the fibers are taken from under the bark. The most well-known use of jute is in the making of burlap (q.v.).

jute board: This is a type of material used in the bookbinding crafts. Jute board is usually used for the covers on books.

K

kabe: This is a type of painting done in Japan, equivalent to a mural (q.v.).

kachina: A kachina is a doll-like figure made by the Hopi Indians of the southwestern United States. These figures represented spirits and supernatural beings. A kachina is carved from soft wood, usually the cottonwood, which is considered to be sacred, or the pith of the yucca plant. The kachinas are used in ceremonial rain dances and then after the ceremony they are given to children of the tribe, who keep them and hold them in great reverence; they are not usually considered as a toy or doll for them to play with.

kakemonoe: This is a large block print (q.v.) done on wood. Made in Japan.

Kakiemon ware: This is a type of Japanese porcelain (q.v.). This type is named after a well-known Japanese potter, Kakiemon.

kalamkar: A textile craft from India. This is the rather colorful printing on cotton cloth.

Kamakura-bori: This is a type of wood that has been lacquered in red and black. This type of carving is done in Kamakura, Japan.

kami: This term applies to the type of paper used in Japan for calligraphy (q.v.), etc. It is also used for other purposes in art.

kan pi: This is a technique of painting that is taught in China; it is very similar to dry brush painting (q.v.).

kanagai: This is a type of Japanese lacquer work. The metal and mother of pearl (q.v.) are inlaid on a layer of lacquer.

kane stone: This is a type of rather soft limestone used by sculptors (q.v.). A light tan fine-grained stone. Used mainly for indoor work. Found mainly in France.

kanshitsu: Known in ancient times as soku (q.v.). This is a type of modeling done with cloth. The cloth is soaked in lacquer (q.v.) and then as it hardens, it is shaped over an armature (q.v.) or frame. This is a late eighth century craft of the Orient.

kaolin: A type of clay of fine texture, composed of decomposed granite rock. Kaolin derives its name from a mountain in China, Kao-ling. Kaolin is used to make porcelain (q.v.) and fine china.

karakul: This is a type of sheep; the lambs have a shiny black wool. Used in the weaving crafts. Coats are also made from the hides. The wool is short and curly.

karat: This is a term used in the jewelry crafts. A karat is used to indicate the amount of alloy (q.v.) in gold. 24 karat gold is pure gold. 14 karat gold is by weight 14/24 fine gold, the balance being an alloy. See carat.

karatsu yaki: This is a type of Japanese ceramic made in the Hizen province.

kashi: This is a type of tile work done in Arabia. This is the application of glazed tile inlay (q.v.) on bricks.

kata: This is a Tibetan type of fabric. Always white in color, it is a woven cloth and is usually given as a gift to someone. This cloth is about the size of a scarf.

kata-kiribori: This is a type of chisel work done in Japan. The lines are carved in such a way that they will look as if they are brush strokes.

kauri gum: This is a type of resin that comes from the kauri pine. This is used to make a hard varnish. Linseed oil is used to dissolve the gum, it is thinned with turpentine.

kauri pine: A type of tree used in the woodworking crafts, this wood has a fine texture and a straight grain. Also known as hoop pine (q.v.).

kayak: This is a type of canoe made by the Eskimo. Usually made of seal skin. Ribs are made from the ribs of animals, sometimes wood if it is available. The kayak is made to hold one person. The place left to hold the occupant is rather small so that when it is occupied the person acts as a cork in the canoe and thus keeps out water. A kayak is pointed at both ends and is usually paddled with a double paddle. The kayak is a man's canoe. The umiak (q.v.) is a woman's boat.

keep: When making a leather belt, the keep is a part of the belt that holds the buckle.

kenchi: This is an ivory carving tool. A type of pliers used to cut ivory into small sections. The handles of the kenchi are not the same length.

Kentucky coffee tree: This is a rather soft wood used in woodworking.

kermes: This is a red dye made from an insect Coccus ilicis which is found on the kermes oak. This is a well known dye used in ancient Egypt. There is a similar color made from the cochineal (q.v.) of Mexico.

kersey: This is a wool rather coarse cloth with ribs. Made in England.

kettle-stitch: The kettle-stitch is a stitch used in the bookbinding crafts. The kettle-stitch is used to tie three signatures (q.v.) together. It consists of looping the thread through itself and pulling tight. A knot is tied at the end of the stitch.

key plate: A term used in the etching (q.v.) crafts. Also used in aquatint (q.v.). This term applies to the blue or black plate when color is used.

key-block: This is a type of wood block that follows the contour of a print.

khatt: This is an Arabic term for the art of calligraphy (q.v.).

khilim: This is a rug, made with a flat stitch and the same on both sides. Made without a shuttle (q.v.) by the people of Turkey.

kiak: This is an Eskimo term. Another name for kayak (q.v.), an Eskimo canoe.

kickplate: This is usually a metal plate. It is fastened at the bottom of a door and is used to prevent wear and tear on a door which is kicked sometimes when it is opened. The kickplate is sometimes of polished brass.

kickwheel: Used in the ceramics crafts, the kickwheel is also known as a potter's wheel (q.v.). It is worked with the foot.

kieselguhr: This is a type of clay used in the ceramics (q.v.) crafts.

kiln: This is a device used in the ceramics crafts (q.v.). This is an oven-like affair that is capable of firing (q.v.) ceramics, bricks or enamel work. A kiln made from firebrick (q.v.) can be a small size for use in a craft room, or it may be large and built outdoors to do hundreds of pieces at once. See tunnel kiln, circular kiln, periodic kiln.

kiln eye: This is the opening at the bottom of a kiln (q.v.).

kiln hole: This is the mouth or opening of a kiln (q.v.).

kindling style: The kindling style is a type of painting done in China. This painting is done with a rather stiff brush, which makes a rather rough line.

king's yellow: This is a very old yellow paint pigment.

kingwood: A wood from South America, when carved it takes a fine polish. The wood varies in color from black to purple, and is streaked with light and dark yellows.

kinji: This is a type of lacquer work done in Japan. The color is applied directly to a gold surface.

kinkazan yaki: This is a type of pottery ware made in Japan in the province of Mino.

kinkled glass: This is a type of glass with many small knobs on its surface. The knobs are formed by blowing the glass into a mold that is made from a netting of wire. Also known as crinkled glass.

kip side: This is a term used in the leather crafts. This is applied to cowhide which has the characteristics of calfskin (q.v.).

kira: This is a type of wood block (q.v.) made in Japan. The background is usually sprinkled with flitters (q.v.).

kirikane: Used in Japan, this process of applying gold foil to paintings and fabrics is well known. Small sections and slivers are cut and applied to the design. This is also done in lacquer work.

kiyomizu yaki: This is a type of rather heavy ceramic (q.v.) made in Japan. Made mainly around Kyoto, Japan.

kiyose-ho: This is a type of sculpture that is done in Japan. Kiyose-ho consists of a carving that is done in pieces. Each piece is carved separately and then fitted together to form one piece.

knife file: This is a type of file used in the woodworking crafts. The blade of this file narrows to a rather thin blade at one end.

knit: Knitting is done by the interlocking of strips of cloth or yarn. This is done with knitting needles (q.v.).

knitted rugs: Knitted rugs are made from scrap cloth. The cloth is cut into narrow strips and sewed together and then knitted into rugs. See knit.

knitting needles: Used for the technique of knitting. Knitting needles are made from metal or plastic. They are long and slender with a rather blunt point.

knop: Used in the metal crafts, this term applies to the knob or bud design or decoration that is found mainly on tableware, such as the design on the handle of a spoon. Knop is a term generally associated with pewter (q.v.), also known as writhen knop (q.v.).

knot: A term used in rug-making. In this method the fibers are tied around the warp (q.v.) threads. The texture of the rug is determined by the size of the knots.

ko yao: A type of ceramic ware made in China in the Sung Dynasty.

kobaltgelb: This is a rather pure paint pigment. This is a yellow pigment.

koban: This is a small sized wooden block, used in printing.

koen: This is a term used in Japan by artists. Koen in a painting is meant to mean distance, especially from far below.

kogo: This is a lacquered box made from ceramic (q.v.). This box is used to hold incense.

koka-ryokugo: This is a Japanese lacquer technique. Several alternating coats of lacquer are applied to a surface, red and then green, until several layers are built up. When hard, the layers are carved away, this exposes the different colors and thus the design has several colors.

kokechi: Tie-dyeing (q.v.) is known the world over. This is the same thing as practiced in Japan.

kokko: This is a rather coarse hardwood. This wood is used in the woodcarving crafts. Used especially for carving.

kokosori: A type of Hopi kachina (q.v.). This kachina used in the Bean Dance. It has a black head with yellow, blue and red spots. The head is topped with white downy feathers. The body of this kachina is painted black with a dye made of corn smut. The figure is dressed only in a sash.

kolinsky: This is a mammal from Asia. The hair of this

mink is used to make fine artists' brushes. Also known as sable (q.v.).

kolophon: Sometimes spelled colophon, this is a type of rosin used on the strings of a violin and related instruments. Kolophon is made from the residue from the distillation of turpentine (q.v.).

kondo: Any object that has a bronze gilt finish is known as kondo. This term is used in metal crafts and in sculpture (q.v.).

kopol: This is a trade name for a synthetic resin. This resin is used in the manufacture of many types of paints, varnishes and enamels.

Korai: This is a type of ceramic (q.v.) made in Japan from 918 to 1392. Named from the Korai dynasty.

Korean ceramics: See ceramics and E-gorai ware.

Korin Bina: The Korin Bina was a Japanese doll, made from mustard seeds. These dolls were only one inch tall.

kosobe yaki: This is a type of ceramic (q.v.) made in Japan in the Settsu province.

kou chin: This is a technique of painting done in China. It consists of outlining a design, usually a landscape, with gold.

krater: This is a type of pitcher made in the ceramics crafts. It is a rather wide pitcher with a large mouth.

kremnitz white: This is a type of white lead used in the painting crafts. This is made by adding carbon dioxide to white lead and lead acetate.

ku chou: A painting term used in Chinese art. Ku chou refers to a painting that is hung by itself, rather than being hung in a group with others. Also known as a lonely scroll.

k'uan: This is a term in Chinese painting crafts. The k'uan is the signature of the artist and is considered as part of the painting. Because it is considered as part of the painting it is usually done with great care.

kuang chiao: This is a type of glue used as a base for painting. This technique is used in China. The glue has no color or odor.

kumbar: A type of rather coarse wood. This wood comes from India. It is used for cabinet making. The color is a rather light tan.

kunzite: This is a semi-precious stone used in the gem crafts. A pink mineral, sometimes seen as a light purple.

kutch: A term used in the craft of making gold leaf (q.v.). The kutch is the package of leaves made up from thin sheets of vellum (q.v.). The gold is then beaten in these packages.

kyack: See kayak.

kylix: This is a rather wide ceramic (q.v.) bowl used as a drinking cup in ancient Greece.

kyokechi: A type of Oriental fabric dyeing technique. Also known as itajime (q.v.).

L

lace: This is a fine fabric, woven in a net-like fashion. Usually made by hand although it is made by machine. Usually made from the fibers of flax, wool and hemp. Acuna wool is used in Peru for the making of lace. In Central and South America, the fibers of the maguey plant (q.v.) are used.

lacemaker: A person who makes lace (q.v.).

lacing: A term used in several crafts. In the bookbinding crafts, lacing refers to the cover or boards that are pierced and laced together through the back.

lacquer: This is a substance that comes from the Japanese lacquer tree, Rhus verniciflua. This is a poisonous plant and a native of China and Japan. Urshiol the poison is similar to poison ivy and poison sumac. Many people have been poisoned from contact with objects that have been lacquered. The methods of preparation of the lacquer have been well-kept secrets. This type of lacquer is unaffected by alcohol or acids.

lacquerware: A technique of painting on wood with lacquer (q.v.). Done mainly in the Orient.

lactoid: This is a plastic material made from casein (q.v.). Also known as erinoid (q.v.).

lam: A device used in weaving. The lam consists of a bar which causes several harnesses to be lowered at one time.

lamb's quarters: This small edible plant was used by the Ojibwa Indians of the Great Lakes region of Canada and the United States. The complete plant was used to make a green dye.

lamé: A type of fabric that has metal threads running through it.

lametta: A term used in the metal crafts. This is a thin sheet of gold, brass or silver. Also used to describe a thin wire of the same materials.

lamp house: A term used in photography. The lamp house is the part of a projector or enlarger that houses the bulb or lamp, usually is fitted with a ventilator. The lamp house can be removed to replace the lamp.

lampblack: This pigment is the result of collecting the soot that is left from the burning of oils and fats. Lampblack is a permanent pigment.

lanolin: A type of grease found in the wool of sheep.

lap: A lap is a wheel that is used to cut and polish gem stones and is used in the lapidary crafts (q.v.). The wheels wear away and some are charged with diamond dust and are used to cut slices and facets (q.v.) on a stone which is later polished.

lapidary: Lapidary is a term that denotes a craft that covers the cutting and polishing of gem stones from the raw or natural minerals. This is done on a lap (q.v.).

lapis lazuli: A rich blue solid stone, specked with white. Used in the gem crafts.

latent image: A term used in photography to describe the image that is recorded on a sensitized film. This image is brought out when the film is treated with certain chemicals.

latticinio: A term used in the glass-making crafts. This is a white opaque glass, used in the making of designs on an object.

laurel: A rather light-colored, fine-grained wood (Laurus nobilis). Used for inlay work, carving. Also known by the name of bay laurel (q.v.).

lavender: This is a term used in the arts and crafts to denote a shade of purple (q.v.).

lay: When used in the metal crafts, lay denotes an alloy (q.v.) of lead and tin. Used in the making of pewter (q.v.).

lazy squaw stitch: A type of stitch used in the basketry crafts. This stitch consists of a long and short loop. Used on the rings or coils of a grass or raffia basket.

leach: In the craft of leather working, to leach is to soak the hide in the tanning liquor, made of oak bark or other vegetable matter.

lead luster: A term used in ceramics (q.v.), this is a lead oxide that is used as a glaze (q.v.) for ceramics.

leaf leis: See lei.

leaf print ash tray: A simple leaf print ash tray can be made outdoors. Secure some clay from along a stream, work it until it's soft. Next pat it out flat and lay a leaf on the surface of the clay. Press the leaf vein side down so that it will leave an impression of the leaf. Next, take a sharp knife and carefully cut around the leaf. When you have gone this far you will have a leaf print on clay. The next step is simple, bend the clay leaf up at the edges until you have a slight depression, use the stem of the leaf for a handle. Next, peel away the leaf and let the clay dry thoroughly, until all of the moisture is out of the clay. This can then be fired (q.v.). You can fire it outdoors in an open fire or use a regular kiln (q.v.).

leather bookbinding: See leather crafts.

leather: The skins of various animals are used. Skins of the cow are used, also lizard, snake, kangaroo. Leather is tanned to preserve it. See tannin.

leather lap: A term used in the jewelry and gem crafts. This is a polishing wheel that is covered with leather. Used to polish gems. See lap.

Lee process: A term used in the metal crafts. The Lee process is a technique of forming or shaping metals. Also known as the extrusion process (q.v.). The metal is forced through a hole or mold to form a certain shape or to make a longer piece from a short thick piece.

leer: This is used in a process of annealing (q.v.) glass. The leer is the oven.

lei: Leis are usually made from flowers, but can be made from any number of materials, such as crepe paper (q.v.). To make a flower lei, secure a number of flower blossoms, such as the hollyhock. Use a long and rather strong colored cord and with a large needle, string the blossoms through the back of the flower. Make the lei about four feet long and then tie the end so that it can be worn around the neck. A variation of the flower lei can be made with the use of leaves which can be strung in the same manner.

lemaire pearl: This is an imitation pearl. The pearl is made of glass with a coating of varnish or hard wax.

leno: A term used in the weaving crafts. This is a technique of twisted pairs of warp threads (q.v.) being woven between the filling (q.v.).

lens: Used in the field of photography. The lens is a transparent part, usually of glass. It is cut and polished and placed in such a way that it focuses a clear image on a sensitive film surface, thus forming a latent image (q.v.).

lens coating: The lens (q.v.) in a camera is coated with magnesium fluoride. This is done to eliminate internal reflections in the camera.

letterpress: This is the process of printing from type that has to be set. This differs from printing done from plates (q.v.).

library corner: A method of putting a cover on a book. See casing-in. This is a type of fold used in libraries. It is folded in three steps. A corner of a page or sheet is folded in to form a small triangle. Next each side is folded in again so that each fold will meet and thus leave only one line showing.

lichen: This plant was used by the Ojibwa Indians of the Great Lakes region of Canada and the United States. The complete plant was used to make a yellow dye.

lichtdruck: See aquatone.

life mask: A mask made directly on the face of a living person. When this is done, care should be used to protect the eyes and nose. Any hair on the face should be covered with vaseline or oil. The nostrils should be fixed in such a way that the person can breathe. Rather thick plaster of Paris (q.v.) should be used so that it will harden quickly.

light metal: A term used in the metal crafts. Light metal is any metal or alloy (q.v.) that has a density less than five times the density of water.

lignite wax: A type of wax made from coal. Used in the leather crafts and in the painting crafts. Lignite wax is a dark brown; it is usually bleached white.

lily of the valley: Used in the corsage (q.v.) crafts. Pull the lily of the valley from the bulb, cut stem under water. Soak for about two hours in cold water and then tie in a bunch and hang upside down in a cool place, such as a refrigerator. The blooms will last about a week.

lime: Lime is made by burning limestone, or chalk, ground into a powder. Used in many crafts. Used in the painting of frescos (q.v.).

lime blue: This is a sky blue paint pigment. This is a rather weak pigment. Also known as mountain blue (q.v.) and neuwied blue (q.v.).

limp: A term used in the bookbinding crafts. This term is used to describe a pliable book cover made of leather. Also known as limp leather.

line cutter: A tool used in many arts and crafts. Used in the craft of silk screen (q.v.). Used in blockprinting (q.v.) and many other arts and crafts that require a sharp bladed steel tool.

line etching: An intaglio process (q.v.). A drawing is made on the surface of a metal plate. This is then cut into the surface with a stylus (q.v.). Nitric acid is used to bite (q.v.) into the exposed surfaces.

line work: When used in the intaglio (q.v.) crafts, this refers to the process of cutting the design with the etching tool (q.v.). This is done just hard enough to cut through the ground (q.v.) of the plate (q.v.). The nitric acid (q.v.) will do the rest.

linen: A fabric made from the flax plant. Used in the painting crafts as a painting surface. Used in the bookbinding crafts for the making of certain types of book covers.

lining: A process used in the arts. This is done to old or torn paintings. The back is lined with new canvas or linen (q.v.). Also known as relining.

linoleum: Linoleum is used in the block printing (q.v.) crafts. It was first invented in England in 1863. It is made from linseed oil, wood flour, resins and ground cork. The mixture is spread out on a flat surface and left to oxidize and then another layer is poured over this until the desired thickness is reached. This is then removed and again ground and made into a thick paste-like substance. This is then poured over burlap especially selected for this use and is then smoothed into a hard flat surface. Many designs can be placed on this surface, by machine or other methods. The best material for block printing is known as battleship linoleum (q.v.).

linoleum block print: When cutting a block print (q.v.) it is first necessary to place the design (q.v.) on the surface of the block. This may be accomplished in several ways. An indelible pencil may be used to draw the design, the surface of the block may be wet slightly with water and then the design placed face down on the block and smoothed out; the water will cause the indelible penciled drawing to bleed; when this

COLLEGE OF THE SEQUOIAS
LIBRARY

happens, the drawing will transfer itself to the block. Care should be used with this method so that the dye does not run and blur. Another simple method is to trace the design on the surface of the block with carbon paper (q.v.); care should be used with this method as it is an easy matter to forget to turn the letters around on the design and then when the block is completed, it will not print correctly. It is also simple to place the design on thin paper and with a water glue or paste, apply the design, paper and all, to the block. The block is then cut directly through the paper. When the block is finished, wash with water and remove any paper that is left. If you are rather advanced in the block print cutting, you may draw your design directly on the block, with pencil or India Ink (q.v.).

linotype: A machine used in the printing crafts. This device casts one complete line of type at a time. This differs from the monotype (q.v.).

linseed oil: This oil used in painting is made from the pressed seeds of the flax plant. Cold pressed seed is the best because it has less impurities and is used more by artists. Hot pressed seed has more of the seed extracts and thus is not as pure as the cold pressed seed. The fresh pressed seed oil is rather cloudy and to be used it has to be clear with all of the impurities removed.

lion knop: A figure of a lion is used on the knop (q.v.). Used in the metal crafts, especially in the making of pewter (q.v.).

lisbon cut: A term used in the jewelry and gem crafts. See double brilliant.

list mill: A term used in the jewelry and gem crafts. The list mill is a wheel covered with cloth, used to polish gems.

lithochromatics: The art of painting on stone. This is done with oils. This is also the technique of taking a print or impression on canvas.

lithoglyph: This is used in the gem crafts. A lithoglyph is a carving or engraving (q.v.) that is done on a gem stone, also known as glyptography (q.v.).

lithograph: A print or reproduction made by the process of lithography (q.v.).

lithograph pencil: This is a type of pencil used in the

lithograph crafts (q.v.). The pencil is soft and greasy, is usually black. This pencil is sometimes called a china marking pencil.

lithographic stone: A fine grained stone, mainly Belgian limestone. Used in the art of lithography (q.v.).

lithography: A process of printing. As a craft, it is done on a fine grained limestone, usually about three inches thick. The design is drawn on the smooth surface with a grease pencil. The surface is then coated with a weak acid solution. This is then washed off. The part that has been covered by the design will take the ink and the other surface repels the ink. Lithography as used in modern printing is done on metal plates and used on regular printing presses.

litmus: Blue litmus paper is made from a lichen. Used in making simple barometers and also to test the acidity of soil. Acid soil will change the paper to a red color.

lithophone: A type of white paint pigment. The pigment is not a permanent color and changes under light.

liver: When used in the painting crafts liver is a term that applies to paint pigments. Pigments in tube paints that form a gummy or rubber-like mass are said to liver. Pure pigments in high grade paints will not liver.

liver of sulphur: This is a sulphur compound used to oxidize metal.

locking up: A printing term, used to describe tightening the frame that holds the type and plates used in printing. This is done so that no parts will come loose while the printing process is going on.

locust: An uneven grained hardwood, known also as courbaril plum (q.v.). Copal gum (q.v.) is made from the product of this tree.

locust bean gum: A gum used as a size (q.v.) in the textile crafts. Obtained from the seeds of the Carob tree found in the Mediterranean area.

log drum: There are many types of drums made from hollow logs. A simple drum can be made from a round hollow tree. Rawhide (q.v.) can be stretched over both ends of the log and laced together, much as you would lace a shoe. When this is being done, the rawhide should be wet so that it will stretch. When the drum is dry, the head will be tight and hard. You can make one or a pair of simple drumsticks (q.v.).

lokweave: A type of weaving done in the making of carpets (q.v.). This material can be cut and fitted together so that the edge cannot be seen except from the back. Used for wall to wall carpeting.

long clay: A ceramics term. Used to describe any clay that is very plastic and easy to work.

loom: This is a device used in the process of weaving (q.v.). A loom can be handmade or a large mechanical machine. The general function of a loom is to hold the warp (q.v.) threads or cords while the weft (q.v.) cords are threaded back and forth. The hand loom is usually made of wood, fastened together with cords or other means.

looping: A weaving process. Several parts are woven separately and are then joined together with loops in such a way that they look as if they had been woven in one piece.

lost wax process: This is a casting process. The object to be cast is made in wax. This is then coated on the outside with a substance such as plaster. Next molten metal is poured on the wax. This forces out the wax in the mold and replaces it with the metal which is then hardened. The mold is finally broken away.

low key: A term used in photography. Low key refers to the dark picture, a type of picture that has an all-over dark appearance.

low relief: A term used in sculpturing (q.v.). Low relief is a type of carving that is done so that the figures are not bold but raised from the surface very little, almost flat. See bas-relief.

low warp loom: A weaving term. A low warp loom is a loom with the warp (q.v.) in a horizontal position. To work this loom, it is necessary for the operator to lean over the loom (q.v.).

lower case: A printing term. Lower case is used to describe the small letters, differing from upper case or capital letters. The term came into use because of the location of the type in the type case or job case.

lozenge: Used in the craft of wood-engraving (q.v.). The lozenge is a sharp diamond-shaped tool, made of hard steel, usually with a wooden handle, rounded, with one flat side.

lozenge: A term used in heraldry (q.v.). The lozenge shape was rather diamond in shape. This was the form of escutcheon that was used by unmarried women. A shield was considered to be for men and could not be used by unmarried women.

lucite: This is a commercial name for a plastic made from the acrylic resins (q.v.).

lucullite: A type of black marble, found in Egypt. Used by sculptors (q.v.).

lumbang oil: This oil is sometimes used as a substitute for linseed oil (q.v.). Also known as candlenut oil and comes mainly from the Philippines.

lumia: An art term used to describe the use of lights as a form of expression, such as on fountains, plays, etc., also known as the art of light (q.v.).

lumiprinting: A new type of art, whereby the artist (q.v.) paints or draws on glass with crayons or other mediums. The resulting design appears to look like a negative of a photograph.

lune: A term used in heraldry. This is the silver color used on steel or representing steel objects. Also known as argent (q.v.).

luster: A term used in many types of arts and crafts. When used in the gem crafts, it refers to the gloss or brilliance of a gem as it is looked at.

In the weaving crafts, refers to the gloss of a fabric, such as silk.

In the metal crafts, refers to the gloss or finish on metals.

In the painting crafts, refers to the finish that is applied to a painting, usually made with a varnish or with a type of enamel.

In the ceramics crafts, refers to a type of ceramic that is iridescent and reflects light. Known as luster or lustre ware. Made from a mixture of copper, silver and iron or sulphur, applied to the surface of the object and then fired, as a glaze (q.v.).

M

mâché: Used in many crafts. Made of several types of materials. Torn paper mixed with paste or flour can be used to make masks, bowls. Also a mixture of plaster four parts, two parts dextrine, one part whiting, three parts shredded asbestos; mix well dry and then add water to make the consistency needed. This becomes very hard and sticks well to most surfaces. Known as papier mâché.

mackintosh: A type of cloth—a popular name applied to a cloth that has been made waterproof. The cloth was first processed in 1823 by Charles Mackintosh.

madder lake: Made from the root of a plant Rubia tinctorum. Modern madder is now made of organic substances and known as alizarin (q.v.).

madras: A type of cotton fabric. This fabric is made with a leno weave (q.v.).

magenta: Used as a water color, this is a reddish purple color. Also made as an aniline dye (q.v.). Known also as fuchsin. See purple.

maguey: A variety of cactus, found in Mexico and Central America. The plant of a thousand uses. Used as a fiber, for lace making, cords, rope, paper, soap-making, industrial alcohol and the roots roasted and eaten. The spine in the end of the leaf is used with its attached fiber for a quick sewing job.

mahlstick: This is a tool of the artist and signpainter. It consists of a stick, light in weight, sometimes made of aluminum. One end has a knob or ball. The mahlstick or rest stick is used when lettering or other detail work is to be done. The artist holds one end while the ball or knob end is rested on the surface. This provides an arm or hand rest without placing the arm or hand on the surface being worked.

maidenhead: A type of knop (q.v.). Made in the middle fifteenth century. Used on English and Scotch pewter (q.v.).

maîtres de forge: A term used in the metalcrafts. Used to describe a craftsman who worked with pewter (q.v.) and who was able to make a bowl with only a hammer, starting from the alloy (q.v.) right through to the completed object.

malabar: Also known as ebony (q.v.), this is a variety of wood used in the woodworking crafts.

malacca: This is a variety of cane (q.v.); it is not quite round and has a slight rib on one side. This is a very heavy rattan and is used mainly for the making of walking sticks or "canes."

male die: This is a metal plate with a raised surface, this surface is made to fit into the depression in the female die. When used together they form an embossed surface on paper. An example is the seal of a Notary Public.

malleability: A term used in the jewelry and metalcrafts. This is the ability of a metal or alloy (q.v.), to be worked, stretched and thinned.

malleable: A metal that is malleable can be shaped by rolling or hammering. Examples are gold and lead.

malleate: In the metal crafts, this is used as a term to describe the making of thin sheets of metal, as in gold beating (q.v.).

mallet: A tool used in many arts and crafts. A mallet is usually made of leather or wood. This differs from a hammer of iron or steel.

Mälzel: This man, the inventor of the metronome, patented a type of doll that would say "mamma" or "papa," when it was squeezed. The talking doll patent was given in 1824.

mandarin porcelain: A type of fine porcelain (q.v.) made in China. The decorations are made to represent the figures of mandarins.

manikin: A figure, usually human, used by artists and craftsmen. Used in store windows where they are dressed to show styles of clothes. Used in museum work in the form of animals where they are made in exact measurements to fit a certain animal hide. Manikins are hollow and now are made of mâché (q.v.), plastics or other light materials.

manila copal: This resin comes from trees in the Philippines and Malay. Its principal use is as a substitute for shellac. Manila copal is also used as a fixative that is sprayed on charcoal and pastel drawings.

mandrel: A term used in the metal crafts. This device is a tapered piece of steel used to hold a piece while it is being turned on the gentleman (q.v.). Term used in the making of pewter (q.v.).

mantiger: A term used in heraldry (q.v.). This is a figure with a human face, the body of a lion or tiger and the tail of a scorpion. Shown on a shield or escutcheon (q.q.v.). The figure also has long spiral horns.

mantling: A term used in heraldry (q.v.). This is a twist of fabric on the helmet, used to keep the sun off the neck. See torse.

maori carving: A type of carving found in the south sea islands. The carving is symbolic, many representations of forms of nature are intricately carved. Often the figures have eyes made of paua shells.

maple: The rotted wood of this tree was used by the Ojibwa Indians of the Great Lakes region of Canada and the United States. A purple dye was made and used to dye porcupine quills.

marakihau: A representation of a sea monster, seen in the carvings of the Maori (q.v.).

marble: A crystalline form of limestone. Used by sculptors (q.v.). There are many variations and colors. Marble takes a high polish, is very durable and works well with the sculptor's tools.

marble dust: Mixed with lime and used by artists in the making of fresco paintings (q.v.). Also known as whiting (q.v.).

marble edges: A term used in the bookbinding crafts. This is the finish that is applied to the edges of a book, resembling marble in design.

marble glaze: A type of glaze (q.v.). Used in the ceramics crafts, this is a design applied to the outside of a piece that resembles the lines found in marble.

marbleizing: The process of duplicating the appearance of marble. This is done on a variety of surfaces, paper, plaster, wood, etc. For example, on paper: A flat pan of water is used, the surface of the water is covered with several drops of various colored paints; as they blend, the paper is laid on the surface and the result is a marble-like effect. A drinking glass may be held by the inside and slowly dipped and turned as it is submerged, its surface becomes coated with the paint that is floating on the surface of the water. This may also be done with ceramic pieces. Oil paint or enamel is used.

marbleized end sheet: In the craft of bookbinding it has been a custom to use a fancy sheet design. (See end sheet.) This can be done in various ways, one way is to marbleize the sheet. This can be done by mixing a rather dilute solution of oil printing ink. Place several drops of different colors in a flat pan in which there is an inch or two of water. The ink will float on the surface and will blend in many interesting ways. Slip the end sheet in under the water and gently lift it up under the inks. This will leave a surface which is marbleized (q.v.).

marbleized glass: A process of heating glass and then dipping it in water. The glass is then reheated and blown, the resulting cracks are then fused together and the result is glass that has internal streaks that resemble marble.

margin: The outer edge of an illustration or a page of type; sometimes the margin is decorated.

maroon: A deep red color, magenta (q.v.), has a tinge of blue.

martin: A term used in the stone crafts; this is a device used to polish the surface of stone, especially marble (q.v.).

marver: A hollow-shaped table, made of iron or marble. Used for the shaping of glass balls, etc. Used by the glass blower.

masking ink: A type of quick-drying ink, intense black, used on glossy surfaces. Used with brush or pen.

masking tape: A type of gummed paper that adheres to a surface and can be removed by peeling off. Used on surfaces to guide a painter, used to hold papers, etc., in place. Comes in rolls of varying widths.

masterpiece: A term used in arts and crafts. Denotes excellence at a high level, the best of an artist or craftsman.

mastic: A resin obtained from the Pistacia lentiscus, a kind of tree found along the Mediterranean. It is on the market in small pieces about ¼ inch in size. This mastic is also used in chewing gum and is known as Chios mastic. Mastic varnish is made, about seven pounds to a gallon of turpentine.

Mastof: This is a type of kachina (q.v.) used in the Second and Third Mesa of the Hopi Indians. Mastof represents the Spirit of the Earth God. He is used in initiation ceremonies.

mat: A stiff white paper, used for the mounting of drawings and illustrations. Usually has a pebbled surface.

mat finish: A dull, lusterless, finish on a work of art. The flat or glossy paints may be purchased ready for use. The addition of turpentine dulls the finish. Also matte finish.

matrix: A term used in the gem and jewelry crafts. The matrix is the material that a certain mineral is found in, the bed rock. Any crystallized mineral imbedded in rock.

matrix mold: A term used in the printing crafts. The matrix is a mold made of paper, made by pressing the paper on a bed of type, used on cylinder presses. Molten metal is forced against the mat and makes an exact impression which is used on the press.

matt glaze: A type of ceramic glaze (q.q.v.). The result is a dull finish on a piece after it has been fired (q.v.).

matte finish: A term used in several crafts to denote a flat or dull finish. A matte finish gives little or no reflection; tempera paints, unglazed ceramics (q.v.) are examples. A rather rough paper with a dull finish used in photography.

maulstick: A tool of the artist and letterer, see mahlstick.

Mayan blue: A blue pigment made from iron and copper, found in the Mayan murals (q.v.) and wall paintings.

mechlin lace: A type of lace made by the bobbin method (q.v.). This lace has a flat band around it.

Mellen Bray: A man who invented a method of fleshing (q.v.) hides. The method was mechanical, the hide was fastened on a frame and moved against a series of sharp blades which cut off the flesh from the hide.

merino: The wool from sheep that originally came from Spain. Now also comes from Australia and Africa. Cloth made from merino is also known as botany (q.v.).

metal crafts: The metal crafts are those crafts which deal with metals in all shapes and forms, from the raw material to the finished product.

Mexican silver: This is a name given to the silver used by Mexican and Indian craftsmen. The silver content varies and is usually below 90 per cent. When this silver is tested with nitric acid it usually turns black or very dark.

mezzotint: This term is used in the intaglio (q.v.) crafts. The surface of a copper (q.v.) plate is rocked with a mezzotint rocker (q.v.). The marks that are left on the surface are small impressions with a raised edge around them. When the surface has been completely covered, or a part, depending on the technique (q.v.), this surface can then be scraped in or out of the design, producing a grey tone. The dots that are thus scraped away will leave a flat black.

mezzotint rocker: This is a tool used in the craft of mezzotinting. The tool resembles a curved food chopper, the blade part has sharp teeth that are spaced a set distance apart and thus when this tool is rocked over the surface of a plate (q.v.), the surface is marred or punctured with many small dots.

midé bag: A midé bag was a special bag made by many American Indian tribes. These bags were used for special occasions. The Ojibwa Indians of the Great Lakes region of Canada and the United States used these bags. The bag was made from the whole animal such as a beaver, otter, or mink. The skin was turned inside out and cleaned. Next the skin was again reversed and filled with grass or straw. This was left to dry. Several ornaments might be added to the bag; these were fastened to the feet and tail. The midé bag was used to hold special herbs, shells and other articles that were regarded as having special powers.

milk carton: Used for the making of doll furniture, flower pots, and other articles. Used also as a mold for the making of tall wax candles.

milk glass: This is a type of glass that has a milky color, also known as opaline glass (q.v.).

milkweed: The floss of this plant is used in textiles; its seeds produce an oil used in paints and also used in certain plastics.

millefiori: A type of glass made by fusing together several different colored rods of glass and enamels. This mass is then cut and imbedded in clear glass and made into the well-known paper weights made of glass.

mineral oil: When the crude petroleum has been changed and the kerosene, gasoline and other parts have been distilled away, the resulting oil is further refined to make mineral oil. Mineral oil has many uses in plastics and polishes. It is also used in cosmetics, medicine.

minium red lead: This is a fine grade of red oxide. Used in the middle ages, mixed with cinnabar, the result was a cheaper variety of cinnabar.

mobiles: This term is used when referring to the type of objects or designs that are made of all sorts of materials and usually hang; they are free forms which combine arts and mechanics and are supposed to be pleasing to the eye.

mold: A mold is an impression or a copy, usually in reverse, of some object. A mold can be made of many types of materials, plastic, plaster, metal, wax, clay, etc. The process is known as casting (q.v.).

molding compounds: See plaster, sand, lucite, acrylic, resin.

molding sand: A sand, mixed with a small part of clay. Used to make metal molds for casting, such as manhole covers.

monograms: A pleasing arrangement of initials. Done in such a way as to make them distinctive. Used for decoration or on seals.

monotype: A term used in the printing and graphic arts. A monotype is a machine that is used to set type; this is done by individual letters and differs from a linotype (q.v.). In the graphic arts, a monotype print is a print made by inking the surface and then placing the paper on the plate and rubbing the back of the paper, thus making a single impression or proof. The surface has to be inked each time. A monotype print done in this manner will not be the same each time and will vary in color and density.

montage: The cutting and grouping together of many pictures to form a new picture. Such a picture is usually made up of related subjects, such as an assortment of sporting pictures, cut and fitted together to form a montage of sports. When this is done with photographs, it is known as a photomontage.

montan wax: A type of wax made from lignite, a variety of coal. A black or dark brown wax, usually bleached white. Used in the making of adhesives, paints and leather finishes.

montre: A term used in the ceramics crafts (q.v.). This is an opening in the wall of a kiln (q.v.). Used to look into the kiln to make an inspection of the insides.

moonstone: A type of mineral used in the gem crafts. Moonstone is cut in the cabochon shape (q.v.).

moose hair embroidery: Moose hair was used by several

American Indian tribes. It was used in a similar fashion to quill embroidery (q.v.).

mordant: This is a term used in many crafts where material has to be dyed (q.v.). The mordant is a material used to make the dye permanent or to "fix" it. Alum is an example of an ordinary mordant. Use about three ounces of alum to one quart of water. Soft water, such as rain water, is the best to use for dye purposes.

morocco leather: Made from goatskin, this is a fine leather from France, Switzerland and Turkey. Used in the bookbinding crafts. A dye made from barberry roots is used along with an alkali to produce a brown dye, used in finishing this leather.

mosaic: A decoration on a surface made up of small pieces, glued or fastened together to form a design.

mother-of-pearl: A lustrous part of a shell used in inlay work on wood.

motto: A term used in heraldry (q.v.). The motto was the result of the yells and battle cries of early days. Now a slogan or sentiment of the owner of the shield or escutcheon (q.q.v.).

mountain blue: This is a paint pigment. The color is sky blue. This is a rather weak pigment. Also known as neuwied blue (q.v.) and lime blue (q.v.).

mounting: The process of mounting is done with works of art, drawings and photographs, done to enhance the piece. Sometimes glued on the surface, fastened to a board under pressure and heated.

mousseline glass: Also known as muslin (q.v.). This fine thin glass is blown in such a manner that it will look lace-like in design. This type of glass is used to make wine glasses.

Mpongwe: An African tribe, known for its fine wood carving. This tribe also makes fine musical instruments, the type common in Africa.

muffle: This is a small kiln (q.v.), used in ceramics (q.v.). The muffle is used for special firing (q.v.). The temperature of a muffle kiln does not go as high as a regular kiln.

muffle painting: This is a type of painting, such as might be done on porcelain (q.v.). The painting is then baked or fired (q.v.) directly on the surface of the object. This is done in a muffle kiln (q.v.).

muller glass: Used in the jewelry and lapidary crafts. This is a type of opal (q.v.). This stone is colorless and is used in costume jewelry and other types of work using such small stones.

mural: This is usually a large wall or ceiling decoration. Murals usually depict a story or theme. They are not supposed to be just a large painting on a wall but should tell a story, a large composite illustration.

muslin: This is a rather plain soft cotton fabric. One variety is known as organdy (q.v.).

muslin glass: This is a fine type of glass, also known as mousseline (q.v.).

N

nachayama yaki: This is a type of ceramic (q.v.). This household pottery is made in Japan in the Tosa province.

Nagasaki ware: This is a type of ceramics (q.v.) made in Japan in the city of Nagasaki. The designs were applied to the glazed (q.v.) ceramic.

naif: This is a term applied to the natural luster that is found in many gem stones, such as a diamond in the rough.

nakiachop kachina: This is a type of kachina (q.v.) of the Hopi Indians of the United States. This kachina has a triangular shaped mouth. It has a green head, sometimes the cloud symbol is painted on the cheeks. This kachina is seen in the Bean Dance and sometimes in the Water Serpent Ceremony. This is also known as the silent kachina.

nana: A term used in the woodworking crafts. Also known as benteak (q.v.).

nankin porcelain: This is a type of ceramic (q.v.) made in China. The background of the pottery is a deep blue.

nap: A term used in the textile crafts. The nap on cloth is a brushed surface rather than being made of small points of cloth on the surface. This differs from pile (q.v.).

naphtha: A coal tar product. Special types of benzine are sometimes called naphtha. Naphtha is used as a solvent.

naphthol dye: A dye used mainly for the scarlet and red colors. This dye is used to dye cloth.

Naples yellow: This is a yellow-orange paint pigment. Made from lead antimoniate. The pigment has been found on the tiles of ancient Babylonia in the fifteenth century. The color has been imitated by other pigments such as zinc oxide, cadmium yellow and yellow ochre. This material has been used in the ceramics crafts also as a glaze (q.v.).

Napoleon blue: This is a blue paint pigment, sometimes known as a variety of Prussian blue (q.v.). This term is generally used when the dye is employed on silk.

napped: See nap.

nashiji: This is a technique in lacquer crafts (q.v.). Nashiji is done in Japan. The technique consists of sprinkling gold dust on a tacky lacquered surface. When this is dry, it is rubbed. The rubbing produces a flakelike surface.

nata-aska: This kachina (q.v.) has a black face, marked with a green crowfoot on its forehead. It also has large movable jaws, wears a buckskin (q.v.) shirt, red buckskin leggings. Usually carries a bow and arrows and a saw. This kachina helps Soyoko (q.v.).

native paraffin: This is a natural material. It is wax-like and is sometimes used in place of beeswax (q.v.). Native paraffin is also known as ozokerite (q.v.).

natural: A term used in the painting crafts. This term formerly was called carnation. This term is usually applied to the skin color of the person or persons in a painting.

naviform: An art term, naviform is used to denote a boat-like shape.

Navajo rug: This type of cloth is made by the Navajo Indians of the Southwestern United States. The rugs are usually heavy, bright colored and well made. Wool is generally used to weave the rug. In the early days, these so-called rugs were used as a robe for a person to wear.

Navajo silver work: The Navajo Indians of the United States learned to work with silver around the year 1868.

navel: A term used in heraldry (q.v.). The navel is the lower center of an escutcheon (q.v.).

necklace: A term used in ceramics (q.v.). Necklace is a term that applies to the design that is around the upper part of a jar or vase.

necktie crafts: Old neckties can be used for many things. Covers for ear muffs, covers for glasses case. Mittens can be brightened with the cut designs from a tie. The tie can be cut and one end filled with beans to make a fine bean bag (q.v.).

needle: This is a tool used in the etching crafts (q.v.). The needle is also used in drypoint (q.v.).

needle file: This is a fine file used in the gem crafts. This is also known as a Dutch file (q.v.).

needlepoint: This is a type of embroidery (q.v.). This sewing is done with rather heavy threads. Used in upholstery and furniture fabrics.

needlework: A term generally used to describe any craft that is done with a needle, such as sewing, embroidery, petit point.

negative: A term used in photography. A negative is the result of a picture that has been taken on a film (q.v.). The image is just the opposite of the actual scene or object. A positive (q.v.) is made from a negative.

negative carving: This is a type of carving that is done in reverse. The design is carved into a block. This is used to make smaller objects, such as coins and medals. The block is cut in low relief.

negro azulado: This is a black paint pigment. This pigment is made from the waste from wine, grape vines, twigs. This is also known as nero bleustro (q.v.).

negro de marfil: This is a type of black pigment. This pigment is made from charred chips of ivory. Also known as ivory black (q.v.).

negro de nueso: This is a paint pigment that is similar to bone black (q.v.) and negro de marfil (q.v.). This particular pigment is made from bone and ivory chips. This is not a permanent pigment, however.

nero bleustro: This is another name for the paint pigment known as negro azulado (q.v.).

nero d'avoiro: This is a black paint pigment. Made from the charred chips of ivory. Also known as ivory black (q.v.).

nest saucers: These are small dishes or trays used to hold small amounts of paint. Called nest saucers because they fit together when they are stacked.

nettlewood: This is a rather coarse hardwood. This wood is used for carving such things as the handles of guns and tools. The wood is a rather yellowish color.

neutral color: A neutral color absorbs the colors around it. This color causes the colors around it to blend with each other.

neuwied blue: This is a paint pigment. The color is sky blue. Also known as mountain blue (q.v.).

newspaper dolls: Many interesting and simple dolls can be made from old newspapers. Arms and legs can be made from tightly rolled newspapers, the head can be made from a ball of newspaper. The outside of the doll's head can be wrapped in a paper towel so that you will have a clear surface to paint the features on. A flaired skirt can be made from a large sheet of newspaper; pleat the paper for variety.

newsprint: A rather cheap grade of paper used to print newspapers on. Used in many of the arts and crafts as paper for practice sketching such as would be done with charcoal (q.v.).

Newton rings: These are colored light reflections that are seen around a convex lens (q.v.).

nichrome: This is a type of metal used in the ceramics crafts. Nichrome is used because it can withstand the heat used in firing (q.v.) a ceramic (q.v.). There are times when metal is needed as part of an object, such as jewelry, armatures (q.v.).

nick: A nick is a part of a piece of type. The nick is a groove or nick that is cut in base of type. When the correct type is used this nick will form an even groove across a line without a break. Incorrect type family will show because the nick will be in a different location.

nickel: This is a metal used in many crafts and trades. This metal is very hard and magnetic. Used in electrotyping (q.v.).

nickel silver: A type of metal used in the jewelry crafts. Somewhat resembles German silver (q.v.) but it contains more nickel.

niello: This is a process used in the metal crafts. The design is engraved (q.v.) on the surface, this is then filled with an alloy (q.v.). The effect is a design of two colors. This was first done in Italy.

niggling: A term used in art work and in many crafts. Niggling means that much detail work is done, great care to the smallest detail of the design or drawing being given.

night blue: A term used in art or painting. Night blue is a blue that has no tinge of violet. This is a true blue shade.

night piece: A term used in art. This is applied to any painting that represents a night scene.

nipocer: A trade name for a synthetic wax. This wax is used to coat the surface of paintings and other works of art.

nise: This is a term used in Japan and applies to any type of portrait painting.

nishiki: A weaving term. This denotes a rich brocade (q.v.) that is done in Japan.

nitratine: This is a transparent crystal used as a flux (q.v.) in the making of glass.

nitric acid: This acid is used in the etching (q.v.) crafts. The acid comes in glass stoppered bottles. Acids are sold not by liquid but by weight and so are purchased by the pound. The acid should be mixed with water, one part acid to two parts water. Care should be used when mixing, doing this slowly. Do not let the acid come into contact with your eyes or skin. When the plate (q.v.) has been soaked in this bath it will gradually change to a blue color. When this happens, a fresh bath should be used as this is a sign that the acid has absorbed all of the copper plate that it can.

noble: A term used in the jewelry and gem crafts and lapidary crafts. This denotes purity or superior quality.

noble metals: These are metals that are not readily tarnished or affected by acids. Metals such as silver, gold and platinum.

noble opal: This is a rather changeable opal; the colors vary from green to red and yellow. Used in the jewelry and gem crafts.

noble serpentine: This is a rather rare mineral. It is translucent and takes a high polish. The color is a dark green. Used by the sculpture crafts.

nock: This is a part of an arrow or stele (q.v.). The nock is on the end of the arrow nearest the feathers, it has a groove which fits the string on the bow.

noir belge: This is a type of black marble. This marble is a solid black without veins. It takes a fine polish. It is rather difficult to work with, however, because it fractures very easily.

noir d'ivorie: This is a black paint pigment. Made from the charred chips of ivory. Also known as ivory black (q.v.).

noire famille: A term applied to a type of Chinese porcelain (q.v.). The pattern or design is usually floral in this case and the dominant color is black.

nolan vase: A type of ancient Greek vase. Made of ceramic (q.v.), this vase has a long thin neck. Also known as amphora (q.v.).

nombril: This is a term used in heraldry. Similar to the term navel (q.v.).

non-actinic: A term used in photography. This term is applied to certain colors that do not affect certain light-sensitive emulsions (q.v.).

non-creep: This is a type of liquid that is added to various substances to make them flow smoothly on a surface. Used on smooth surfaces, such as a glazed or waxed surface.

non-halation: This is a term in photography. This is a coating that is used to prevent reflection from the back of a film (q.v.). See halation.

nonpareil: A term used in the printing crafts for a size of type.

normal butyric: This is a colorless liquid used in the making of lacquers.

Norway spruce: A type of timber used in woodworking. This type of wood is used in the making of musical instruments.

nose hole: A term in glass-making. This is a small hole through which the glass was blown in the early days; this formed a circular shaped glass known as crown glass (q.v.). This blown glass was distorted and was known as having a bullion (q.v.) in the center of it.

nosing: A term used in the woodworking crafts. Nosing is the part of a step that extends out over the riser (q.v.).

notan: A term used in Japanese art. Notan denotes the effect of light and shade on paintings.

note: An art term. A note is a rough sketch made by an artist in preparation for the rendering of an oil painting. This also applies to a sketch of a small part or detail of a painting.

nuance: An art term. Nuance is the study of color as it changes through its various shades from dark to light.

nui-haku: This is a fabric that is decorated with gold-leaf (q.v.) and painting. This type of cloth is sometimes also decorated with embroidery (q.v.). This technique is done in Japan.

Numidian marble: This is a rather general term that is given to several types of marble. This marble is found chiefly in the northern part of Africa. The name is rather misleading as the marble comes from Mauritania.

nunome: A textile term that is applied to a fabric that has a mesh texture. Nunome, when used in the painting and ceramics (q.v.) crafts, is a style somewhat similar to the design in the mesh texture used in fabrics.

Nuremberg pottery: This is a name given to any ceramics (q.v.) that are made in Nuremberg, Bavaria. This is an art center for the ceramics arts and crafts. The colors are usually dark green or brown, sometimes yellow.

nurimono: This is a term that is applied to ceramics a variety of that which is made in Japan. This term applies to all types of Japanese lacquer-ware.

nurtunja: This is an art form of the aboriginal Australian. Banners were made of feathers. Sometimes attached to the body of the owner as a headdress.

nutwood: This is a type of timber used in art. Nutwood is used in the making of painting panels (q.v.).

nylon: This is a synthetic fiber, also made into other forms. This is a thermoplastic (q.v.). Nylon is used in place of the silk threads that were found in American paper money. Nylon is a trade name.

O

oban: This is a type of large print made in Japan; the print measures about ten by fifteen inches.

occidental diamond: This is a term used in the jewelry crafts. An occidental diamond is a type of rock crystal used in making jewelry.

occult lines: These are lines that are made in a sketch or painting. The lines, however, are erased or painted out during the drawing or painting process.

ochre: This is a type of clay. It has a wide range of colors. The best grades come from France. This is a permanent pigment. Ochre has been in use since prehistoric times.

octavo: Octavo is a term used in the bookbinding crafts. This is the result of folding the paper three times to form sixteen pages.

odd folio: This is a method of numbering in the book crafts. The odd folio is used to denote the right hand pages of a book, or recto, all those that have an odd number. The left hand page is known as the verso (q.v.).

odo yaki: This is a type of ceramic (q.v.) made in Japan. This is a household variety. Made in the Tosa province of Japan.

offset: This is a type of printing. This is an impression that is made from a wet print. A paper is laid on a wet print and pressed. The design will then be transferred.

ofuke yaki: This is a rather coarse type of oriental ceramic (q.v.) ware made mainly in the Owari province of Japan.

oil of ants: A liquid added to varnishes, surface films, etc., to produce a soft hue on the surface of an oil painting. This is due to the make-up of the various paints and varnishes that are used.

oil paint: When oil paints are used by artists, they usually come all prepared in tubes. They are made by certain standards, the mixtures are rolled on steel rollers and mixed to the consistency of peanut butter. Oil paints can be mixed by the artist, ground by hand, etc. Hand mixed paints cannot be compared with commercial mixed paint.

oil painting: Oil paintings are done usually on canvas (q.v.). These are representations made of landscapes, people or other objects. They are painted by an artist (q.v.). Oil paintings are made with oil paint (q.v.).

oil varnish: This is a type of coating that is applied to a surface. Made of oil and resins.

oiled paper: Oiled paper has several uses. It is oiled so that it can be used to see through and thus be used for tracing. It is also oiled to make it waterproof.

oiling out: This is a painting technique. The surface of a painting that is to be touched up or repaired is first rubbed with a coat of drying oil. The slight oily film that is left prepares the surface of the painting so that it will take the new paint more readily.

oils: Oils are known and used all over the world. When used in painting mainly vegetable oils are used, such as poppy seed oil, and linseed. Oils for painting have been known and used since the fifteenth century. Too little use of oil in a painting renders the paint rather brittle, too much may turn the painting rather yellow in a short time.

oilstone: This is a type of smooth stone used for polishing and for sharpening knives. Several drops of oil are put on the stone so that the polishing will be done evenly and smoothly.

oiticica oil: This type of oil, used in the painting crafts, comes from Brazil and is used as a drier in paints.

Oki-Agari: This is the common name for the doll known as Daruma (q.v.) or tumbling doll. The Oki-Agari was a doll that when knocked over, would stand right up; if the doll failed to stand, it was considered to be bad luck and was discarded.

old masters: The old masters is a term given to the artists (q.v.) of the Low Countries and Italy. These masters are considered to have done their work from the thirteenth century to the sixteenth century. This term is also applied to the actual paintings.

oleic acid: These are crystals that can be dissolved in benzene or ether. They are used as a dryer in oil paints. Also used in the textile crafts as a water-proof agent.

oleoresin: This is a type of turpentine, also known as Venice turpentine. This oleoresin is obtained from the sap of certain coniferous trees.

olive: This is a fine even-textured wood used for carving. Also used for inlay (q.v.) work.

olive pit technique: This is an Oriental painting technique. The brush strokes are such that they are rather pointed and thicker in the middle and then tapering off to a point. A large stiff brush is used.

olla: A type of Mexican ceramics (q.v.). The olla is used in tropical countries. It is a large earthenware (q.v.) jar. Used to store and cool liquids through evaporation.

olpe: This is a small vase with no neck, but a wide mouth. Used for dipping liquids. It has a rather even rim.

oltremare: This is a well-known type of blue paint pigment. Also known by the name of ultramarine (q.v.).

omnibus: This is a sheet iron cover used in the furnace or leer (q.v.). A term used in the glassmaking crafts.

omnibus volume: This term is used in the book crafts. An omnibus volume is a book that has several volumes combined into one book. This type of book usually has very thin paper for its pages.

ondoyant glass: This is a variety of glass. The surface of this glass is rippled and the glass is tinted. This window glass is used to simulate the early stained glass windows.

ondule: This is a form of twisted French yarn. This yarn has an irregular twist or loop.

ongchoma: This is a Hopi Indian kachina. The body of this kachina (q.v.) is painted red, one shoulder is painted green and the other shoulder is painted yellow. The head is painted green. The neck is covered with a fox skin. Ongchoma is a kachina used in the Bean Dance; this kachina sympathizes with the children who are to be whipped by the Tungwup kachina (q.v.). He makes them tough so that they will not feel the whip.

onicolo: This is a type of onyx. This stone is used in the making of certain forms of cameos (q.v.). It has a slight bluish tinge.

onohara yaki: This is a type of ceramic (q.v.) made in the Tanba province of Japan.

onto yaki: A type of common ceramic (q.v.). Made in the Ise province, Japan.

onychite: This is a type of alabaster (q.v.) used in the early days for the carving of vases and other objects.

ooze leather: This is a type of leather used in the bookbinding crafts. The leather is thin and the tanning liquor is forced through the pores of the leather mechanically. This leather is generally used with the flesh side out. Used mainly on small books.

opal: This is a gem stone used in the jewelry crafts. There are several kinds of opals. Some are considered lucky and others unlucky. The precious or noble opal has a reflection of several colors, blue, green, yellow and red. The fire opal gives only a red reflection.

opalescence: A term used in photography. This term is used to describe the whitish appearance of the emulsion (q.v.) on the negative (q.v.). This is usually caused by the use of alcohol which has been used to hasten the drying of an incorrectly washed negative.

opaline: A term in glassmaking, known also as hot-cast porcelain. This is a type of milky glass. See milk glass.

opalized wood: This is a type of petrified wood (q.v.). This means that the actual wood has been replaced by some mineral that is in the sand or mud of prehistoric times. The color is similar to opal (q.v.).

opaque white: This is a white liquid that will cover other colors. Such a liquid is used to cover India ink (q.v.) and other dark colors. When the surface has been covered with opaque white, it will be ready to receive another color over it. This fluid is used to make corrections in lettering and for photo offset work (q.v.).

opened: A term used in the book arts and crafts. This term refers to the pages in a book that have been cut open with a knife.

orange: This is a color. Orange comes between red and yellow in the spectrum (q.v.). The color can be made by mixing red and yellow.

ordinary: A term used in heraldry. This is a charge (q.v.). There are nine in number: bend, chevron, chief, cross, fess, pale, pile, quarter and saltire.

ordonnance: A term used in the arts. Ordonnance refers to the arrangement or the composition of a painting. The relation of the parts of a painting to the whole with regard to balance and harmony.

oreala: This is a type of clay used in British Guiana. The clay is found locally and is used by the natives of Guiana to make ceramics (q.v.).

organdy: This is a type of fine cotton fabric. It is a type of muslin (q.v.). Organdy comes in plain and flowered patterns.

organic colors: This term includes all types of pigments that are derived from vegetable and animal dyes. Used in the arts.

oribe yaki: A type of Japanese ceramic (q.v.). This type of ceramic is made in the Owari province of Japan.

orichalc: This was an ancient type of alloy (q.v.) made in Rome. This alloy was made from copper and zinc and resembled gold in color.

orient: This is a term used in the gem crafts. The term is used to describe certain characteristics of a pearl (q.v.).

oriental agate: This is a type of agate, valuable and used in the jewelry crafts.

oriental amethyst: This is a type of sapphire (q.v.). The term is used in the jewelry crafts and applies to any amethyst of exceptional beauty.

oriental garnet: This type of garnet is considered by the jewelry craftsmen as a precious stone. The garnet is rather clear.

oriental sapphire: This is a gem stone used in the lapidary arts.

original boards: This is a term used in the bookbinding crafts. The original boards are considered to be the first covers of a book, back and front. This term is also used to describe the condition of a book.

orlon: This is a trade name for a fabric. Orlon is made from a liquid which is passed through small holes and hardens into thread. Orlon is made from a chemical mixture of carbon, hydrogen and nitrogen.

ormolu: This is a material made to imitate gold. It is an alloy (q.v.) made from zinc and copper. Used to gild picture frames.

ornament: This is an esthetic addition to an object or work of art. Ornamentation is done by an artist or craftsman. An ornament is not a basic part of an object but a form of addition to make it more pleasing to the eye.

ornamental brick: A type of brick. Usually used on the front of a building. It is usually of a different style or color. Used for decoration or to make a design or letters.

oroide: This is an alloy used in the metalcrafts. Made from copper, zinc and sometimes tin. The color resembles gold. This alloy is mainly used in the making of jewelry.

orpiment: This is a paint pigment, also known as king's yellow (q.v.). This is a natural yellow sulphide of arsenic. Found mainly in Central Asia.

Orr's white: This is a type of white paint pigment. Used mostly in commercial art. This pigment is also known as lithopone (q.v.).

orthochromatic: In photography, this is a type of film that is sensitive to color.

orthochromatic: This is a term used to denote the colors used in painting that are representations of the colors found in nature, such as green, etc.

orthoclase: When used in the ceramics crafts, this term refers to one of the feldspars, potassium aluminum silicate. This is used in the making of fine porcelains (q.v.).

orthographic projection: A term used in mechanical drawing. This is a mechanical type of drawing which shows all sides of an object. It is drawn as if the object was clear enough to see through. Usually dotted lines are used to depict the surfaces that actually can't be seen.

oryctology: This name is applied to the study of paleontology, geology, petrology and mineralogy.

ostraka: This is a thin slab of white limestone, used in ancient Egypt about 1400 B.C. The ostraka was used to write on. Used for government decrees and other legal documents. Another form, a wooden tablet (q.v.), was used in some cases.

oulopholite: This is a variety of gypsum found in certain caves in the United States. Usually in the shapes of various flowers.

out of print: A term used in the printing crafts. Out of print means that a book or publication is no longer available for sale and can only be found in libraries or collections.

out of register: A printing term. Out of register means that the impression is not placed exactly where it should be in the printing process. This is sometimes noticed in color printing. One color is slightly off or out of register.

outil plat: A tool used in the craft of making pewter (q.v.). Somewhat resembles a chisel.

outremer: Used in the arts. This is another name for the well-known blue pigment, known as ultramarine blue (q.v.).

overcast: This is a type of stitch used in the bookbinding crafts. The overcast stitch is rather simple. The top cover or sheet is pierced and the cord is passed through the book, out the back cover and then out around the back and into the top again, sometimes known as oversewn (q.v.).

overdevelopment: A term used in photography. This is used to describe what has happened to a film that has been placed in the developer too long and has usually become too dark.

overexposure: A term used in the photography arts and crafts. This term is used to describe what has happened when a film is exposed to the light for too long a time; the result is a washed-out or cloudy picture.

overfired: This term is used in the ceramics crafts. Overfired ceramics (q.v.) are pieces that have been left too long in the kiln (q.v.) or have been subjected to heat too intense. The result may be a melting of the material or a change in color.

overglaze: A ceramics (q.v.) term. The overglaze is applied to the surface of a piece already glazed sometimes for a special effect, or to cover up a crack or other defect.

overglaze painting: This is a type of painting that is done on ceramics (q.v.) either before or after firing. The painting is done directly on the glazed surface.

overrun: A term used in the printing crafts. This term is used to denote an extra amount of printing that is done over and above the number that is ordered.

oversewn: A term used in the bookbinding crafts. The same as overcast.

oxalic acid: When used as a solution in the craft of leather working, oxalic acid cleans leathers which are to be stained later on.

oxford ocher: This is a type of yellow paint pigment. Found in England.

oxgall: A yellow powder that is added to paints and inks to give them a clinging quality. It helps to prevent bubbles.

oxidizing flame: This is a flame having total combustion; a term used in ceramics (q.v.).

oxybaphon: A type of wide-mouthed vase. Made in ancient Greece. Usually decorated with scenes of combat.

oyster white: A type of paint pigment. Also used with lime to make a sort of plaster used as a base for fresco (q.v.) painting.

ozalid printing: This printing is similar to blueprint printing (q.v.). Ozalid paper can be cut to a size that can be easily handled. First prepare a frame from a pane of glass and a cardboard. See blueprint printing. To develop an ozalid print is a rather simple matter. Place the print in an airtight container, a jar or box. Next add some plain household ammonia. The fumes from the ammonia will develop the print; when completed the design will be purple.

ozokerite: This substance is used as a substitute for beeswax (q.v.). This wax-like material has a rather greasy feel when touched.

P

Pachavu Hú: The body of this Hopi kachina (q.v.) is painted white. The head is painted black and has white spots under the eyes. The head is adorned with a pair of horns. The fox skin is used as a muff on the neck. The feet of this kachina are red. Used in the Bean Dance only and also used in the initiation years. This kachina also guards the bean plants.

Pachavuin Mana: The head of this kachina is painted orange. The figure is dressed in a woman's or a maiden's dress. The hands hold a tray of bean sprouts. This is a kachina (q.v.) of the Hopi Indians of America.

packing box play houses: Many pieces of furniture come in large boxes, some made of wood, others made of cardboard. These can be made into play houses for children. Doors and windows can be cut in them, shelves, window boxes and many extra things such as curtains can be added. Instead of throwing the box away, make this use of it first. It costs nothing to make and will provide many happy hours for a small child, either in some corner of a room or on a porch, or outside in the yard if it is a wooden box.

padded leather: A term used in the bookbinding crafts. Padded leather is leather that has been applied over a padding of wool or cotton. This is placed on the covers of the book, thus giving it a soft padded look and feel.

paddle: A bat or flat paddle used in the ceramics (q.v.) crafts. Used to mix fresh clay.

paddle and anvil: The paddle and anvil method is a technique used in the making of objects of clay.

Paduasoy: This is a type of strong silk. The name is derived from the place it originally came from, Padua, Italy.

pagination: A printing term, also in the bookbinding crafts. Pagination refers to the number of pages in a book. See odd folio and even folio.

pagoda stone: This is a type of fossil limestone found in

China. Called pagoda stone because when cut, the fossils leave a shape somewhat like that of a pagoda.

pagodite: Also known as pinite or agalmatolite. A rather soft stone used in China and the Orient for the carving of small pagodas and other small figures.

paine's grey: This is a mixture of pigments, used as a water color. Paine's grey is made from black, ochre (q.v.) and ultramarine.

paint: Paint is usually applied in a liquid; it can be sprayed or applied with a palette knife (q.v.). Paint is a combination of pigments of one or many colors. It is spread on any surface where color or decoration is desired. It is usually applied in a very thin coat. Oil paints are usually mixed with linseed oil (q.v.) and turpentine (q.v.) as a drier.

paint mill: A small device used by artists to mix paints or pigments. Mineral substances are ground in a paint mill and are made into pigments.

paint remover: There are many commercial paint removers on the market. They usually contain paraffin or wax to slow down evaporation. Sometimes a blowtorch is used to burn off the excess paint on a surface.

painter: A painter is one who applies paint (q.v.) to a surface. A painter is also sometimes considered to be an artist who creates a picture or painting on a surface. A painter can be an amateur or a professional.

painter stainer: A term used in heraldry, used to describe the artist that does only coats of arms.

painter's etching: This is a term used to apply to an etching (q.v.) that is done completely by one artist, from start to finish. Not an etching that has been designed by one person and then the plate made by another, etc.

painting in oil: There are many techniques and methods of painting with oils. The use the painting will get should be considered, length of time the painting is expected to last and where it will be placed. Oil painting in museum exhibits is an example; color is exposed in exhibits for some twenty years or so and such painting as a sky must be done with care; some paints change color when mixed with other pigments, light ones fade, others darken with age. The three coats that are applied to walls and houses by painters is a good guide, the same principle applies to canvas panels. Porous woods, etc., should be given a prime coat of paint or a thin coat of shellac. The idea is to keep moisture out of the back of the painting. Smooth surfaces should be roughened a bit with steel wool or a rough brush so that the paint will take.

painting modeling clay: To paint modeling clay with oil paints, first coat the object to be painted with shellac. If the object is to be painted with poster paints (q.v.), first paint the object with a coat of thick soap suds, this will cut the oil and thus enable the poster paints to be applied to the surface evenly.

painting panels: Before the 17th century most paintings were done on wooden panels. These panels were known generally as nutwood (q.v.). The wood, however, was usually pine, oak, and willow, or nutwood from Italy. The panels were made in sections, the wood was fastened with dowels (q.v.).

paint-out: An art term used when an artist tests a color or pigment. A small dab is painted on a surface to test it before the actual painting is done.

palapore: This is a type of wall hanging usually made of cotton. This type of designed cloth was popular in the eighteenth century.

Palembang: Named after a port in Sumatra. A variety of cane (q.v.), somewhat dark in color. Used in making baskets and hampers. The finer grades are used in the making of chair seats.

paleography: This is the science of writing, the use of symbols to convey messages, etc.

palette: A tool of the artist. This consists of a thin board of wood or other material used by an artist (q.v.) for the mixing of small amounts of paint while the artist is actually at work. A palette is curved or of many other shapes, usually has a thumb hole so that the artist can hold the palette and have the fingers free to hold brushes, etc. See arm palette.

palette knife: This is a tool used in painting. A palette knife is rather flat, with a rounded end and rather flexible. This is used to apply paint to a surface. Used in the technique known as impasto (q.v.).

palette knife work: This is a painting technique. Thick

paint is used and applied to the surface of a canvas. Also known as impasto (q.v.).

palimpsest: This term is used when reference is made to parchment (q.v.) that has been used over again. This happens when faded parchment is used over or when the previous writing or design has been removed from the parchment surface.

palissy ware: Types of ceramics that were made in France. The surface of the objects were enameled in high relief, the designs were usually of animals and flowers.

palladium: A member of the platinum family, sometimes used as a substitute for platinum. It has a melting point of 2831° F.

pamphlet: A term in the printing crafts; usually means a small book of less than sixty pages. Not bound nor with a stiff cover, has stitched pages.

panama hat: A hat made in tropical South America. Made from the leaves of the Cardulavia palmata tree.

panathenaic vase: A Greek ceramic (q.v.) vase. Made in ancient Greece, decorated with the warrior goddess, Athena. Given as a reward in contests.

panchromatic film: Used in photography, this film is sensitive to all colors, including red.

pane: A type of hammer used in the metal crafts. Used to hammer the metal surface to give it a rough finish. Also known as a ball peen hammer (q.v.).

panel: A term used in rug weaving. The panel is the outer edge of a rug.

pangani: A type of fine ivory from the east coast area of Africa. Used for the making of fine ivory carved objects.

pannetiers green: This is a brilliant green paint pigment used by artists.

panoramic camera: This is a type of camera that can take a picture of a large group of people at one time. The camera has a device that turns it slowly in an arc, at the same time, film is unwound at the same rate of speed.

pantile: A type of tile made of ceramic (q.v.). This tile is used in buildings and has the shape of a slightly bent S.

pantins: Pantins were animated paper dolls, made in France in the town of Pantin in 1746. To make a pantin became a fad that lasted for over ten years. The doll was drawn or printed on thin paper which was then pasted to a stiff card and then cut out. Each part was cut so that a string could be attached to it and then run through the back. When all of the parts were connected with a string, a loop was left in the back so that the index finger could pull and thus move the arms, legs and head.

pantograph: This is a device used in art or drawing. The shape is somewhat in the form of a double X. This tool of the artist is used for duplicating a drawing or design. It can be adjusted so that it will enlarge a design. One point is used to follow the design, while the other end has a pen or pencil which traces on another surface.

pantomime puppets: These are simple puppets to make. They were made in China and have since been copied in many countries. The puppet is flat and is made from bits of colored paper and cellophane of various colors. This is done so that the light will show through from the back. Sometimes the arms and legs can be moved. Usually the puppet is worked from the bottom and is fastened to a short stick and moved back and forth as a story is told.

papa: A type of clay used by the Maori people. This bluish clay is rubbed on the surface and into the designs that are carved in wood.

paper: Paper is made in various thicknesses. It is a substance made from wood pulp, rags or other fibers. It differs from parchment (q.v.). See chih, papyrus and tchama.

paper box animals: Many interesting toy animals can be made from all sorts of discarded paper boxes. Turtles from flat boxes, dogs and cats from round and long boxes. Simple ears can be cut from paper and pasted or glued on for the head. Broom straws for whiskers and tails can be used. Buttons make fine eyes. The boxes can be painted to represent the animal colors.

paper cup crafts: Many toys and party favors can be made from various sized paper cups. Bells can be made for the Christmas tree; flower pots, dolls and animals can be made also. Old ping pong balls and rubber balls can be used to make a fine head for a doll made from a paper cup, eyes, nose and mouth painted on the head.

paper marks: This is a pattern or design that can be seen on paper when it is held up to a light. Paper marks are also known as watermarks (q.v.).

paper size: Sized paper is treated so that it will absorb less ink when it is printed. This also stiffens paper.

papier-mâché: Made from various materials; see mâché.

papyrus: This is a paper made along the Nile river in Egypt. Made from the plant Cyperus papyrus. Strips of the reed were cut and laid flat and others were laid across the bottom layer. This was then soaked and pounded until it became a pulp. This was then sun dried and used as a form of paper.

paradise wood: This is a fine grade of wood used for inlay wood. Sometimes called aloes wood (q.v.).

paraffin: This wax is a refined petroleum product. It is used in candle making and also to seal jars in canning. The melting point of paraffin is from 50 to 60° C.

parallax: In photography, this refers to the part of an object that is seen by the lens of the camera. This is not what is actually seen in the viewfinder.

parallel pliers: These pliers are used in metal working. They are so constructed that they will always open with the jaws of the pliers parallel with each other.

parallelism: This term describes what appears to be an independent development of some art or craft or method of doing something, in different places, such as the Mayan pyramids and the Egyptian pyramids. Built in a somewhat similar manner and design and yet there is no apparent connection between the peoples of the two hemispheres.

parathymia: This term is used to describe an artist who isn't in the "mood" to paint or create. A frustration of the artist brought on by the thoughts of the artist himself.

parchment: This is a type of leather, made from the skin of sheep or goats. Parchment was used when books were written by hand.

parchment paper: A high grade of paper made to resemble parchment (q.v.). This is a thin rather transparent paper, used in the making of lampshades.

pardo Vandyck: This is a full brown paint pigment. Used in oil painting.

parfleche bag: This was a type of bag made of rather heavy rawhide (q.v.). These bags were used much as we would use a suitcase or other bag. The parfleche was made by the American Indian. Found mostly in the Western United States.

Parian biscuit: A term used in ceramics (q.v.). This is a type of porcelain (q.v.). Glazed in such a manner that it appears like marble.

Parian marble: This is a type of marble used by sculptors (q.v.). Used by the ancient Greeks for special statues. This marble was quarried on the island of Paros, the marble reflects light and is suited for rather lively carved pieces.

Parian ware: A type of ceramic (q.v.) made in the state of Vermont. It resembles the famed Parian marble that is quarried on the Greek Island of Paros.

Paris green: Used as a pigment, it is called emerald green (q.v.). It also has a use as an insecticide.

Paris white: This is a natural substance, white in color used as an amorphous (q.v.) powder; used in painting and many crafts, see whiting.

paste: There are many kinds of paste used in crafts. Common paste is made by mixing starch or flour with water, cooking and stirring until it becomes thick. A paste that works very well can be made from wheat flour 20%, alum 1%, 1% formalin and 78% water. This should be mixed until all of the lumps are gone and then cooked in a double boiler until it has become thick.

paste: This is a type of clay mixture used in the ceramics crafts. Hard paste is clay that takes a higher heat than a soft paste. The surface is tougher on ceramics made with hard paste.

paste for linoleum: Special commercial pastes are made to fasten linoleum to blocks for use in blockprinting. Nails are not used because they interfere with the cutting of the block.

pasteboard: Used in the bookbinding crafts and many other crafts. Pasteboard is so named because it is pasted together in layers. The number of ply is determined by the number of sheets that are pasted together.

pastel: Pastels, as they are used today, are in the forms of sticks about the size of regular chalks, in many colors. Pastels are not mixed on a palette (q.v.) as are oil or water colors, but are mixed directly on the surface of the paper or other surface. When a pastel drawing is completed it is necessary to fix (q.v.) the drawing; this is done with a spray, either mechanical or a simple blower.

patina: In metal working, this refers to the film that forms on the surface of the metal. This is a result of age and exposure, such as the darkening of silver.

pavilion: A term used in the jewelry and gem crafts. The pavilion is the part of a diamond that extends down from the girdle (q.v.). This is also known as the base (q.v.).

payon: A trade name for water soluble crayons.

peachblow: A pinkish purple glaze (q.v.) seen on certain ceramic pieces.

pear: A type of hardwood, used in carving. The wood is fine textured and is a light reddish brown. The wood is used for inlay (q.v.) and other fine woodworking needs.

pearl: Pearls are used in the jewelry crafts. Natural pearls are found in oysters and mussels. A pearl is the result of an irritation inside the shell of an oyster or mussel, such as a grain of sand or other particle. The animal deposits layer after layer of substance over this speck, and after about a year has produced what we know as a pearl. Cultured pearls are made by placing a foreign particle inside the shell and replacing the oyster or mussel in the water. Simulated pearls are made by dipping glass beads in various types of mixtures; one solution is made from fish scales.

pearl color: A term used in heraldry; this is the silver white color used on weapons.

pearl essence: Made from fish scales, this lustrous material is used in the making of artificial pearls.

peasant jewelry: This term is usually applied to jewelry made in the rural areas of Europe. They have a decorative design and are sometimes set with pearls or garnets.

pearl white: This is a paint pigment. White in color. This is also known as cosmetic bismuth (q.v.). Used sometimes in the making of artificial pearls.

peau d'orange: This is a type of finish that is applied to certain types of ceramics (q.v.). The result is a rather rough surface that resembles an orange.

pebble: This is a term used to denote an agate (q.v.). Used in the jewelry crafts.

pedlar doll: This doll was a type made in England and

France at the end of the eighteenth century. These dolls were made in pairs, a man and a woman. They were made to represent vendors. Each doll carried a basket which was full of small objects, watches, knives, needles and thread, kitchen ware and many other articles; some dolls had over a hundred articles. The pedlar dolls were also known as English hawker dolls.

peen: A type of hammer used in the metal crafts. The head is rounded and sometimes crosshatched to give special effects. Also used by sculptors (q.v.).

pen: Originally from Europe, this is a device used to draw, write or design with the use of ink as a medium. Pens have been made from split reeds, bamboo, quill made from bird feathers.

pencil: A device used by artists and craftsmen. Consists of a cylinder of wood with a center of graphite, usually varies in thickness and in grades from very hard to very soft. Considered to be any writing instrument that does not use ink.

pencil diamond: A device in the shape of a pencil with a diamond chip for a point. Used for the cutting of glass.

percale: A type of smoothly woven fabric, made of cotton. Used in place of calico (q.v.).

perchloride of iron: When etching on copper (q.v.), it is sometimes desirable to use perchloride of iron instead of nitric acid (q.v.). The yellow lumps of perchloride of iron can be mixed with water and used to etch copper, much in the same way as nitric acid.

perclose: A term used in heraldry (q.v.). This is a design placed on a shield or escutcheon (q.q.v.). Shown as a lower half of a circle. It represents the lower part of a garter with a buckle.

perilla oil: Many crafts that require enamels and varnishes find that the use of perilla oil will make the paint tough and hard. Perilla oil comes from a plant grown in Manchuria, India and Japan.

periodic kiln: This is a kiln (q.v.). This type of kiln has to be cooled and then unloaded or loaded. This led to the development of the tunnel kiln and the circular kiln (q.q.v.).

permalba: This is a trade name for white paint, used by artists.

pernetti: These are the supports for ceramic pieces in a kiln; they can be made of iron or bits of fired ceramics. The marks left on the bottoms of a piece are known as pernetti marks.

petit point: This term is used in embroidery (q.v.). Petit point consists of small stitches. It is done with a fine needle. This type of design is usually done on silk.

petrified wood: This is wood that has changed through a long geological period of time. This is wood that has been replaced, cell by cell, by some type of mineral. This is known as agatized wood and also as opalized wood (q.v.).

pewter: This metal was first made in Roman times. Pewter is an alloy (q.v.), being made from tin and lead; sometimes other metals are added to give it strength such as copper, zinc and bismuth. Pewter is made into objects by casting it in molds, or by hammering it into shape. Pewter can be enameled as well as inlaid (q.v.).

photo-gelatin: A process used in printing; see aquatone.

photo-offset: A term used in the printing crafts. A page is set in type, and pictures can be pasted in place. This is then photographed. The negative (q.v.) is then projected on a metal plate that is sensitive to light; this may be enlarged or reduced from the original. The image is formed on the plate, which is then etched (q.v.). The resulting plate is used for printing.

photomontage: See montage.

phthalein: This is a type of dye made from phthalic acid and types of phenols. When the water is removed from these substances the result is a series of very good dyes. Some of these dyes are fluorescent.

phthalocyanine: A blue pigment used by artists. This name is used for several of the pigments of other colors, green and other shades of blue. A strong color.

pica: A term used in the printing crafts. A pica is a unit of measure for type. An inch consists of six picas. Each pica is divided into twelve equal parts, called points. Six points make a half a pica or a nonpareil.

pick: This is a single strand of yarn that stretches the width of the cloth along the weft (q.v.).

pick glass: A calibrated magnifying glass used to measure the number of threads or yarns in the warp (q.v.) of a fabric.

picking: A weaving term; picking is the placing of weft threads between the warp threads (q.v.).

picture bread: In the thirteenth century picture bread was forbidden by the Christian Church. Picture bread was the forerunner of our well-known animal crackers and gingerbread figures. In the seventeenth century and on into the eighteenth century the making of picture bread became popular. Molds to cook these figures were made by hand and were carved from wood, no two molds being exactly alike. The figures were made to represent various saints, kings, queens. These figures were exchanged on certain days. The early American settlers that came to this country brought with them the craft of making cooky molds and cooky cutters. Most of these early molds and cutters are now collectors' pieces.

pigment: There must be a pigment in every paint. A pigment may be animal, vegetable or mineral. There are hundreds of pigments used in every country of the world. Pigment is usually ground into a powder. When used in the arts it is usually mixed with linseed oil for a binder, turpentine as a thinner, and a dryer or siccative (q.v.).

pile: Used in the textile crafts, pile denotes small points or projections on the surface. These points are made as a result of the knots that are tied around the warp (q.v.) cords. This term differs from the term nap (q.v.).

pillow method: A technique of making lace (q.v.) also known as the bobbin method (q.v.).

pin grain: Pin grain is the name given to the fine tanned skins of young seals. Pin grain can be duplicated on sheepskin and calfskin; the real sealskin can be identified by its softness.

pinchbeck: An alloy (q.v.), one part zinc and five parts copper; resembles gold.

pincher: A tool of the glass maker, used to shape the necks of glass bottles.

pinching tongs: Used in the glass making crafts. These are tongs the ends of which form a small mold. Used to form glass pendants; a sharp point is a part of the mold and forms the eyelet in the glass.

pine needle dolls: The needles of the long leaf pine can be used to make a quaint doll. The needles can be used while fresh; they are first braided (q.v.) and then fastened together to form the arms and legs. Several braided pieces fastened together can form the body of the doll. Raffia (q.v.) can also be used to make dolls of this type.

pineapple stitch: A sewing term; this is an oval stitch, usually done on a knitted fabric.

ping pong balls: Used in the paper cup crafts (q.v.).

pinhole camera: A simple type of camera, made of a box. A small pinhole in one end and the film in the other end form the camera.

pins: Pins are small pieces of fired ceramics used to hold the clay pieces in a sagger (q.v.).

pipe cleaner: A soft wire covered with a fiber used in many crafts for the making of figures, puppets.

pique: A type of cotton cloth, the raised cords running lengthwise. First made in France.

pitcher molding: In the ceramics crafts it is necessary to make hollow rather thin objects. The technique is to pour the slip into the mold and then out again. This is done until the required thickness is built up.

plaiting: This is the technique of knitting two fabrics together so that one becomes the face and the other the back of the fabric.

planigraph: A device used to reduce or enlarge an illustration. Similar to a pantograph (q.v.).

planish: A technique used in the metal crafts. This is done by pounding the metal. This toughens the metal. Also denotes the surface texture that results from the tapping with a ball peen hammer or other tool.

plaques: These are illustrations or designs made in relief (q.v.), usually having some means to enable them to be hung on a wall.

plaster of Paris: A substance, also known as gypsum (q.v.). Named Plaster of Paris because it was first found in the quarries of Montmartre, near Paris. Quick setting when mixed with water; used in casting (q.v.), for walls, making artificial fruit, molds, etc.

plastics: Plastics can be organic or synthetic. These materials can be shaped, molded or melted. Used in many crafts, in place of wood, metals, etc.

plastigraph: This is a substance that is used in place of linoleum blocks (q.v.). It is a thermo-plastic. This means that the substance is warmed slightly until it pours. It is poured on a flat surface, such as wood or metal; the liquid will seek its own level. When plastigraph is cool it can be cut with rather dull tools, such as a bobby pin. After it has set several months, regular block printing (q.v.) tools will have to be used. Plastigraph is a recent American product and has many advantages, such as being able to re-use the scraps or the complete material when the block is no longer needed. Plastigraph may be poured on any size block and will take any ink that can be used on other types of printing mediums.

plasti-print: A plasti-print is similar to a block print (q.v.). It is known as a plasti-print because of the material, known as plastigraph, which is used as the surface from which the print is made.

plate: This term, when used in the intaglio (q.v.) crafts, refers to the material or surface that is to be used, such as copper (q.v.). Plates can be made in many sizes and the thickness of the copper or zinc (q.v.) plate depends on its use. When plates are to be used by a printer and many impressions (q.v.) are to be made, a thicker plate is necessary.

plate glass: A variety of glass. The surface of plate glass is highly polished and ground. Known also as polished plate glass.

plate mark: In the metalcrafts, this is the mark that is applied to show the manufacturer, and fineness of the metal.

plate oil: Plate oil is a type of oil used to thin the inks used in the intaglio (q.v.) crafts. This oil is used in very small amounts. It is made from linseed oil which has been heated until it is burnt. This oil should be well mixed into the ink before use.

plater: A person who plates metals. This is done mainly by electrical techniques and chemicals.

platinum: A valuable ore, greyish white in color. Platinum melts at 3224° F. This is an ideal metal for rings because of its strength and color.

play garden: A small child can make his own play garden from a few simple materials. A cardboard box is first turned upside down. This box serves as the base in which to "plant" the garden. Next cut out the colored flowers that can be found in seed catalogues. Stems can be made from tongue depressors or used ice cream pop sticks. Glue or paste the flower on the stick and then insert one end into the box. Cut out a picket fence and place around your "garden."

play houses: Interesting play houses for children can be made from packing boxes (q.v.).

plucky: A term used in the jewelry and gem crafts. This is a gem stone that breaks into conchoidal chips when it is being cut.

plush: A type of fabric made from wool, cotton or silk, similar in looks to velvet but with longer threads or pile (q.v.).

ply yarn: This is a weaving term; the ply is the number of yarns that are twisted together, such as three ply yarn, made of three yarns twisted together, etc.

plywood: Plywood is formed by gluing several layers of thin pieces of wood. These panels are used in building, making furniture, etc. Plywood is very strong. It is usually cut into panels four by eight feet.

poinsettia: This plant may be used in the crafts of corsage (q.v.) making. To best preserve the plant after cutting, dip the stem in boiling water. As a corsage, it will last about one day.

point appliqué: A sewing term, used to describe a technique of lace making. The design is made and then applied to the surface of the net or lace.

pointed cross: A term used in heraldry; this is a cross that is shown with the points of the cross with sharp endings.

pointillé: A term used in the metalcrafts, especially in the making of pewter (q.v.). This is a technique of pricking the surface of the metal with a sharp tool to form a design or surface texture.

Polish egg decorating: Many people in Poland decorate eggs. The egg is first blown; this can be done in the following manner, punch a hole in each end of the egg and blow in one end. This will empty the egg. The egg can now be used. Cut a design that will unfold when cut, this can be glued around the egg in a contrasting color. Many interesting designs can be made. Care must be used so that the egg will not be crushed and also the design should lie flat on the egg.

polishing mill: Used in the jewelry and gem crafts. This is a polishing wheel that is covered with leather, used to polish gems.

pomander: A mixture of aromatic substances. An interesting project can be found in the making of a pomander. You will need a stout cord, a needle or some object that you can use to thread the cord through an orange. Push the cord into the orange and out the other end, next loop the cork back into the orange and out so that you can tie it and thus be able to hang the orange. Next, secure a box of whole cloves. Push the cloves into the orange until all of the surface is covered. This pomander can now be hung in a closet and will give a fine spicy smell for many months.

pontil: This is a type of iron rod used in the glass-making crafts. This rod was used in the making of such pieces of glass as a pane for windows. The pontil was used to hold hot glass that could be worked.

poona: This is a rather snub-nosed brush used in the stencil crafts (q.v.). The brush has stiff bristles. Also known as a dabber (q.v.).

poppy oil: Poppy oil is a pale yellow color. This type of oil is used in paints; it dries rather slowly and when it ages it cracks. Poppy oil is obtained by grinding and pressing poppy seeds.

porcelain: Made in China since 206 B.C., porcelain is made from kaolin (q.v.). This is the finest type of pottery made; it is hard, white and unaffected by acids.

porcupine quills: The quills of the porcupine were used by the Indians of Canada and the United States. The quills are rather short, white and tipped with brown. They were used as is and also dyed, flattened and woven into designs.

porringer: A small metal dish with a handle on either one or both sides, used for the holding of porridge or cereals. Usually made of pewter.

port-crayon: A tool of the artist. This is a holder for pastels, crayons or chalk. It is shaped somewhat like a tube that is split at both ends. The chalk is inserted in one end and a small ring is forced down over the end, thus holding the chalk in place. To release the chalk, just slip the ring away from the chalk.

portfolio: This is a container used to hold loose sheets.

Used by artists. The portfolio is tied with a cord on one side and hinged on the other.

porto marble: A dense black marble with yellow veins, used by sculptors (q.v.).

portrait: This is a term used in the arts. A portrait is considered to be a representation of a human. Usually from the neck up. This can be done in any medium such as oils, water colors, charcoal, etc. A portrait is done from life usually.

positive: This term is used in the photography arts and crafts. The positive is the print made from the negative (q.v.). The positive is a copy of the scene or object that has been printed through a photographic process. This may be in color or in black and white.

poster: In the arts and crafts, a poster is a hand drawn illustration done with poster paints (q.v.).

poster paint: A name that has commonly come to mean a type of paint that can be thinned and mixed with water. Illustrations done with this type of paint are known as posters (q.v.).

poster painting on glass: Poster paint (q.v.) can be painted on glass as a temporary measure. First paint the glass with a thick coat of plain soap and water.

potato dolls: In the 1900's many dolls were made from potatoes. Burnt matches were used for eyes, cloth was fastened over the potato and tied in such a way as to form arms and legs; these were then filled with sand.

potato printing: Slice a potato in half, using care so that it will have a clean cut surface that is flat. Next, cut a design as you would a blockprint (q.v.). Ink the potato design with poster paint or regular printing ink and print on paper, cloth, etc.

potter's ore: This is a mineral, known as galena (q.v.), a compound of lead with a silvery appearance, used in the making of a green glaze.

potter's wheel: This is a wheel that can be turned by hand, foot or powered by some other means. The potter's wheel turns at various speeds. As the wheel is turned, it is possible to form bowls, dishes, etc. with the hands. The clay has been wedged (q.v.) and is soft and easily worked. The potter's wheel is used in the ceramics crafts.

pounce: To pounce a design, a small bag of powder is pounced or patted over a design that has been cut with a pounce wheel (q.v.) making a perforated pattern. This leaves an exact copy of a design or lettering on the surface beneath. This method is used on truck lettering, etc.

pounce wheel: A pounce wheel is a wheel with sharp teeth. This is attached to a handle. The wheel is rolled over the surface of paper. Small holes are punched or pounced in the paper. The wheel is rolled along a design. The result is similar to the Ojibwa Indian bitten pattern (q.v.). The pattern is then pounced and through this technique the exact design is transferred to the surface directly under the paper.

Powamui: The Powamui kachina appears in the Hopi Indian Bean Dance. His body is red, he wears flowers in his hair. The face of this kachina (q.v.) is also red. These kachinas appear in groups.

Pozzuoli: The blue and red pigments that come from earth or clay found in Pozzuoli, Italy.

primitive colors: When mixing pigments, the colors red, yellow and blue are considered to be primitive colors because most other colors can be made from them in various combinations.

Princeton yellow: This is a bright yellow paint pigment. Made from a mineral that is reddish in its natural state, when ground it results in a yellow pigment. Used mainly in the Orient.

print: This term is used in the arts and crafts in many ways. In photography, a print is a picture that is an exact duplicate of the image on the negative (q.v.). A print is made when a plate (q.v.) is used, or type in printing. Anything that leaves a printed impression on one surface from another surface.

printed linen: Linen can be given a hand-printed look by a method of printing on the fabric. The design is rolled with wooden rollers and the cloth is backed with some soft material or padding.

printing: Printing is an art or technique of making impressions on a surface with type, either metal or wood or other material. The printing is done with a printing press or with a simple block print (q.v.).

printing a linoleum block: Simple printing with a block print (q.v.) can be done, without any mechanical press. When the block has been cut and inked, it may be placed, inked side down, on the paper that is to receive the impression; this is then placed on the floor on which a small pile of folded newspapers or other soft material has been placed. Now stand on the block. The weight of your body will be enough to print the design. It is best to use care when doing this, do not twist or turn the block as this will cause the print to be blurred. The old stand-by, a rolling pin, can be used. Lay the inked block on a hard surface, inked side up, lay the paper to be printed on the block and on top of this, lay two or three sheets of paper, now roll over the surface with a smooth even motion, as you would roll out dough. Use care so that you will not cause the paper to slide or slip to one side and thus blur the design that is to be printed.

printing face: A printing term; this is the impression side of type, the part that causes an impression to be left on a page. Also refers to the size of type or the style, such as bold face, light face, etc.

printing size: This is a rather sticky substance which is used as an ink which is printed the same as regular printer's ink. Next the surface is dusted with a powder, gold, silver, etc. This causes the letters to look as if they are metallic.

process plates: Color plates used in photoengraving. When printing colored illustrations several printing plates must be used, one for each color. They are printed one over another; the result should be a natural color.

proper charge: A term used in heraldry (q.v.). A proper charge is a charge (q.v.) that is the original charge, copied from the original owner or knight.

Prussian blue: Also known as Milori blue and Chinese blue. This pigment is made from ferric ferrocyanide; it has a deep greenish blue color.

puccoon (Lithospermum carolinense): This plant was used by the Ojibwa Indians of the Great Lakes region of Canada and the United States. The dried root of this plant made a dye which was used as face paint and also to dye porcupine quills red.

pug mill: A mechanical device used to grind and mix clay, used in the ceramics crafts (q.v.).

pugging: A process used in the ceramics crafts; this is the wedging (q.v.) of clay in a pug mill (q.v.).

pull: A printing term. Used to describe the process of making a print or impression on a surface with a printing press.

pulp board: Used in the bookbinding crafts. This is a rather cheap heavy paper used in the making of book covers. This differs from pasteboard (q.v.).

pumice: This is a material from a volcano. It is light and spongy in texture, used as an abrasive (q.v.) or as a fine polish. It can often be found on the beach along oceans where it has floated thousands of miles.

punch: This is a tool used to make a hole in a surface, sometimes made as a single tool and sometimes several punches are made on a wheel that can be turned and adjusted to various sizes.

punic wax: An ancient type of wax. This wax was made by spreading out beeswax in the air, and then boiling it in sea water and also potassium carbonate. This was then poured into cold water and again exposed to the air and sunlight. This method bleached the wax.

purl stitch: Also known as link and link, this is a stitch done in knitting. It consists of loops running crosswise and with loops on both sides.

purple: Also known as violet, lavender, magenta. The color is made of various mixtures of blue and red.

putty: The term as used in the jewelry crafts, is a mixture made from lead oxide and tin oxide. Used to bring gems and other metals to a high luster. Also used in the ceramics (q.v.) crafts in the making of a glaze (q.v.). Putty is used also by glaziers to fasten windows in their frames, then made of white lead.

putz: A type of diorama (q.v.) or crib (q.v.). Made by the early Moravian colonists in Pennsylvania. A putz is made with papier-mâché (q.v.), moss and bark; usually shows snow-capped mountains and a cave where the Holy Family was shown.

pyrographic pen: This is a type of pen used in bookbinding crafts. It is usually electric and is used to place gold or silver on books. It is also used to decorate cloth and leathers.

pyrometric cones: Also known by the name cone (q.v.). These are small cone or pyramid-shaped pieces of clay. Used to test the heat of a kiln (q.v.). This is done prior to stacking the kiln for the actual firing (q.v.).

pyropyllite: A type of aluminum silicate, sometimes used in place of flint in the making of fine glass and porcelain.

Q

qalavi: The body of this American Indian Hopi kachina is painted black with corn smut. The face has two green lines, these run across the face between the eyes. The only clothing that this kachina (q.v.) has is a green copper belt around the waist. Qalavi carries a whip made of the yucca leaf. This figure holds children who are to be whipped.

qaletaqa: This is a type of kachina (q.v.) used on the First Mesa of the Hopi Indians. Used with the Ahulani kachina in the solstice ceremony of the First Mesa.

qochaf: This is a type of kachina (q.v.), the body is painted white and is barefooted; there is a black band across the eyes. The figure is dressed in women's clothes. This Hopi Indian kachina has as its special duty the job of purifying everyone present at the Bean Dance.

qoqlo: This is a type of Hopi kachina usually found in pairs and is used four nights before the Bean Dance. This kachina (q.v.) is a prophet kachina and predicts good crops.

quads: This is a term used in the printing crafts. A quad is a piece of metal that is used to fill out a line of type. Quads have no letters but are blank.

quaich: This is a term used in the metal crafts. A quaich is a type of drinking vessel made in Scotland. This was usually made from pewter (q.v.).

quarter: A term used in heraldry, known also as the franc-quartier. This is placed in one quarter of the escutcheon (q.v.), in the part known as the dexter chief (q.v.).

quarter hoops: Used in barrel making, see hoops.

quarter-binding: This is a term used in the bookbinding crafts. A book that is quarter-bound is a book that has a back (q.v.) of one material, such as leather, and the side covers of another material. This term is generally applied to books with leather or cloth backs.

quaternary alloy: This is a term in metalcrafts. This means

199

that an alloy (q.v.) of metal is composed of four metals or elements.

quarto: A term used in the bookbinding crafts. A quarto is a book made of sheets folded to make eight pages.

quartz: A mineral used in the gem crafts. Usually colorless, but sometimes colored with small amounts of impurities.

Quebec birch: This is a type of wood used in the woodworking crafts.

queen closer: A brick used in building. This brick is only half the width of standard bricks. The length and thickness are the same as regular bricks.

queen conch: This is a type of conch or shell. This conch is used for the carving of cameos.

queen's ware: This is a type of English ceramic. This pottery has a creamy color.

Queensland maple: Not a true maple. This hardwood is used in the woodworking crafts. It has a rather coarse texture.

quenching: This is a term used in the metal crafts. The process of quenching is done by plunging the red hot metal into a bath of oil or water. The result of this process is to make the metal very hard and brittle.

Quercitron lake: This is a type of paint pigment made from the inner bark of a plant called Quercus tinctoria. This is a yellow pigment.

quilate: This is a term used in the jewelry crafts. It refers to the purity of gold. See carat.

quill embroidery: This is a type of embroidery (q.v.) done with the quills of the porcupine. The Ojibwa Indians used three types of stitches in their quill work, loop stitch, spot stitch and the back stitch. The stitching was done only through the surface of the skin and not completely through it. Sinew (q.v.) was used for thread. The quills were washed first and then flattened with the teeth or with a quill flattener (q.v.). A loop was made and then the quill slipped under the loop and bent over. In this way, the stitches could not be seen. The sinew was not threaded through the quill, this would cause it to split.

quill flattener: A quill flattener was used by the Ojibwa Indians of the Great Lakes region of Canada and the United States. This tool was also used by the Western Sioux. This was made from a flat bone or piece of antler. The porcupine quill was made flat by pressure. It was then used in quill embroidery (q.v.).

quill on birch: Porcupine quills are woven on the surface of many containers made of birch bark. The quills are soaked until soft. The design is first drawn or pressed with a blunt tool on the surface of the birch bark. The quills are pushed into the holes that have been punched and then out again. They are tucked in and out in such a fashion that there are no ends showing. As the quills dry they become hard again and the birch bark shrinks slightly around the holes that hold the quill. The early Ojibwa Indians of the Great Lakes region of Canada and the United States did not draw the designs on the bark containers, but worked directly on the surface.

quill pen: A pen using ink. Made from a large bird feather, the pointed end was cut at a slight angle to form the writing point.

quilting: Quilting is an old European craft. A quilt is used like a blanket and consists of three layers of cloth. The two outside layers are usually sewn on the cloth in some design, such as triangles, squares, etc. A quilt can have its design made up of many small pieces of cloth that are sewn together to form a design. The designs can be packed with cotton to make them raised or in relief. The edge of the quilt can be bound with some type of cloth tape.

quirk: This is a term used in the woodworking crafts. This is a type of molding which has a sharp design cut in it, an extreme angle.

quivering brush: This is a painting technique. The quivering brush is used to give the effect of the motion of waves in oceans, etc. This technique is done in China.

quoin: This is a term used in the gem crafts. A quoin refers to one of the facets (q.v.) that has been cut on a gem stone.

R

rabbit skin blankets: The Ojibwa Indians of the Great Lakes region of the United States and Canada make blankets of rabbit skin. There are several methods used. Sometimes the whole rabbit skin is sewn together with other skins until the size blanket desired is reached. Sometimes, the skin is cut in strips. These strips are hung on a pole to dry; the loose hair is blown away in the wind. The strips are then sewn together. Sometimes the skin is cut in a circle; this results in a long thin strip. The skins are also sewn so that they form a loop. When a loop method is used, the result is a robe with fur on both sides.

raffia: A material used in the making of baskets, mats and other objects of that type. Raffia is the leaves of several of the types of palms found on Madagascar and other islands of that area, cut in long, rather coarse, fibers. It is a very durable and inexpensive material to use; a large needle is about the only tool needed to work with it. This makes it an ideal material for children to work with. This material does not come in different sizes as does rattan (q.v.), but the strands can be split to the desired size. It is a very easy matter to dye (q.v.) raffia. It can be worked wet or dry.

rag doll: These dolls are made in much the same way as the bean bag doll (q.v.). Made from rags and odds and ends of cloth, they are stuffed with cotton, straw, or sawdust.

rag rug: A rug made from rags which are braided together. The long strips of braided rags are sewn together to make a rug. Also known as a braided rug.

raguly: A term used in heraldry. This is a type of representation of a cross with its extremities covered with small bumps or projections.

ramie: A fiber made from an Oriental plant, also known as China grass. This fiber resembles cotton and is used in the making of velvets.

rampant: A term used in heraldry. This is a position of a

202

beast of prey such as a lion, shown on its hind legs with its front feet in a position of pawing the air. The animal should face the dexter side (q.v.).

rangier: A term used in heraldry. This is a scythe that is shown on a shield or escutcheon (q.q.v.).

rape: A term used in the metal crafts. This is a process of preparing the surface of metals with a rasp (q.v.).

rapin: A term used in heraldry. This is a design on a shield or escutcheon (q.q.v.) showing a bird or beast eating another animal.

rasp: A tool of the metal craftsman. The surface of the rasp is made like a punched surface rather than a chisel-like surface.

rattan: In the craft of basketry, this is a natural product that has many uses. Rattan is a long climbing vine that grows mostly in Malay. It is cut in various lengths and sizes, the outside being used for chair cane work. The inside or pulp is used for baskets and for the frames. The cane ranges from the very small sizes 00 to 1, used for fine basket work, through to the larger sizes 6 to 10 used to make the handles and spokes of the larger and more heavy baskets.

raw linseed oil: Linseed oil which has not been refined. Linseed oil (q.v.) has to be aged and also filtered; this is done over a long period of time; sometimes the oil stands in vats from one to two years. When the raw linseed oil is ready, it should have a pale yellow color.

raw sienna: A pigment made from a clay found in Italy; it contains iron and manganese. This is a permanent pigment.

raw umber: A dark brown. Found in Italy. The best grades come from Cyprus; this is known as Turkey umber. This pigment is very permanent.

rawhide: This is the untanned skin of an animal, used for making laces, drum heads, whips, etc.

rawhide mallet: This is a mallet or hammer made of rawhide, a type of leather. The leather is rolled into a hard piece with a handle. This rawhide mallet is used in the metal crafts and in woodworking.

rayon: A fiber made from cellulose and other substances. Made into a variety of materials and products.

realgar: An orange-red paint pigment well-known in the Far East in very early times. It is a poisonous pigment made of an arsenic disulphide. This pigment is now obsolete and has been replaced by the cadmiums.

reamer: A tool used in metal working to enlarge a hole that has been punched or drilled.

rebus: As used in heraldry, this is a pictorial design suggestive of the owner's name.

reconstructed turquoise: This can be made by mixing copper and finely powdered ivory. This is mixed, dried and fired (q.v.). Used in much the same way as the real material. The difference can be seen under a microscope; it appears rather granular.

rectangle: This is a form (q.v.) used in the corsage (q.v.) crafts. The rectangle is used for long shoulder corsages.

recto: A term used in the book crafts. This denotes the right hand side of a book and all of the pages on that side. All of these pages are uneven in number. See odd folio.

red cedar: The Ojibwa Indians of the Great Lakes region of Canada and the United States used the inner bark of the red cedar to make a red dye. This was used to color mats.

red lead: This pigment was used by the early Greeks and Romans. Made from lead monoxide and lead peroxide, a bright red. No longer used as a pigment for fine painting. Used now as a prime color or coat for steel and other metals that are exposed to the elements.

reed: A weaving device made of wood or metal. Has many holes or dents along its surface. Used to space the warp threads evenly.

register: A term in printing. This denotes that the type or cut (q.v.) is printing or leaving a perfect impression with no light spots or areas that are not printing. When several colors are used in printing, it is necessary to be careful so that the colors do not overlap or run together in any way. This requires an exact print each time. When color printing is done with a block print (q.v.) it is necessary to mark the block so that each impression (q.v.) is made in an exact spot. A block must be cut for each color used.

relief: A term used in sculpturing (q.v.). This is a technique in which the design is raised from the surface it is placed on or carved from. This differs from in the round.

relief carving knife: This is a short handled knife with a chisel like blade. Used to cut wood in the technique of relief (q.v.) carving.

relief printing: This is a printing term used where type is used or another raised surface. This differs from the intaglio (q.v.) techniques. This is also known as cameo printing (q.v.).

repoussé: Used in the crafts of leather working and metal crafts. See embossing.

resin: This is the hardened sap from trees. Resins are insoluble in water but can be dissolved in alcohol, turpentine, and oils. Those from living trees are known as recent resins, those which are dug from the earth are known as fossil resins. Many resins have the names of the places in which they are found. See rosin.

respectant: A term used in heraldry (q.v.). This is a representation of two animals such as lions, shown in an upright position, facing each other.

retorted: A term used in heraldry. This is a design showing entwined serpents. The design is placed on the shield or escutcheon (q.q.v.).

retroussage: An aquatint process. This is done by wiping the ink from the plate surface in such a way that a small amount of ink is left on the plate surface. This is done to achieve special textures.

rhinestone: A synthetic gem-stone. It is made of glass.

rhinoceros cup: A cup carved from the horn of the rhinoceros. Used supposedly to test a liquid for poison.

rifflers: Various shaped files with sharp points used in the jewelry and gem crafts.

ripsaw: A type of saw with chisel-like teeth, used to cut along the grain of wood.

riser: The riser is the vertical part of a step or staircase.

rocker vat: A large vat used in the tanning of leathers. The vats contain the tanning liquids, the hide is hung above the vat and the vat rocks back and forth, this swirls the tanning liquids in and around the hide for a more complete soaking.

rolled glass: A type of glass that is run through rollers while it is in a semi-liquid state. This makes a long rather thin sheet.

Roman rag doll: Children's dolls were made of rags as are many present day dolls. Dolls were made in ancient Rome in the third century A.D.

rose: A term used in heraldry. This is a design showing an opened rose on a shield or escutcheon (q.q.v.).

rose point: A type of lace with raised flowers in its design.

rose quartz: This is a variety of rose-pink quartz, color in this quartz due likely to a small amount of titanium. Strong light can fade this stone.

rosin: This is a type of resin obtained from pine trees found in the southern United States. It is used as an adulterant in cheap paints and varnishes; there are some fifteen grades of this rosin. This type of rosin forms when turpentine is made and the residue that is left in the tanks is known as rosin. One use other than in paints that is better known is in the music world; it is used on violin bows. Its meaning comes from the Greek, and means "sound glue." See resin.

rotogravure: A type of intaglio printing (q.v.). The printing is done from an etched copper plate.

rouge: This artificial red oxide of iron in its less pure grades, is used as a polishing agent. This powder is not suited for use in paint as a pigment.

rough cut: When applied to lumber, this means that the wood has been sawed into rough cut timbers, these pieces show saw marks and have many fibers on their surface. Rough cut wood is then dressed (q.v.).

round pointed graver: A tool used in the craft of wood engraving. The blade of this tool is rounded on one side and has two sharp edges which are joined in a point. This tool is somewhat like the half round graver (q.v.) but more narrow in shape.

roxburghe binding: This is a type of binding done in the bookbinding crafts. This refers to a book that has the back covered with leather and the sides covered with paper or cloth. The cover is usually plain except for some lettering on the back.

rubber cement: Produced under a variety of trade names. Used for the mounting of illustrations which may have to be removed at a later date. Prevents wrinkles and the excess may be rubbed away with the fingers.

rubbing: This is a technique of taking an impression from a raised surface. This may be done from such objects as a coin. A thin paper is laid on the surface and is then rubbed with the finger, crayon or other type of pencil. The result will be a duplicate of the design that is in relief (q.v.).

rubbing block: This is a rather coarse block used to smooth the surface of other blocks of stone such as marble. Also known as a rubbing brick (q.v.).

rubbing brick: A type of block used to smooth other blocks of stone. Also known as a rubbing block (q.v.).

ruby glass: A type of glass, usually found in the dark rooms of photographic laboratories. This glass is colored by the adding of cassius purple (q.v.) or through the use of copper.

ruddle: A red ochre used to make industrial chalk, used in many industries and crafts.

rug: This is a floor covering, square or oblong, made in one piece. It is placed loosely on the floor and is not fastened in place as is a carpet (q.v.). Rugs are woven and made of many materials, such as wool, cotton, grasses, etc. See hooked rugs.

rug field: The center or the main part of the rug that has the design.

rugmaking: This is the process of making a rug (q.v.).

rummer: A term used in glass-making crafts. This describes any glass vessel in the shape of a long-stemmed goblet.

running head: A term used in the book crafts. This is the short heading which appears at the top of each page, usually on the left page.

rush: A plant that is grown in the Northern Hemisphere, popularly known as cattail and flag. Found growing in marshes and along fresh water streams; there is also a salt water rush grown in Holland. Rushes are cut when green in about the month of August or when the tips of the leaves start to turn brown. Rush work is an old craft and goes back several thousand years. Leaves are used for chair seats and come in six- to eight-foot lengths.

Russia leather: A type of leather used in the bookbinding crafts. Russia leather has a characteristic odor. The leather is usually a brownish-red. This type of leather is supposed to be tanned with willow bark, dyed with sandalwood and softened with birch oil.

S

sable: A small mink whose hair is used for artists' brushes. See kolinsky. Sable is also a term in heraldry (q.v.). A term that is used to denote a bearing on an escutcheon (q.v.). Term used for a bearing in black on a silver or other colored ground.

saddle soap: A type of soap and leather preserver, used on saddles and other leathers. It softens the leather.

safflower: A red paint pigment, made from the petals of the plant safflower. The petals are dried and ground into a powder.

safflower oil: A siccative (q.v.) for use in the paints of artists (q.v.). Soluble in turpentine and is a rapid dryer. The oil is obtained from the seeds of Carthamus tinctorius, a plant growing in East Africa and North Africa. It has been used as a substitute for linseed oil (q.v.). See carthame.

saffron: This paint pigment is made from the petals of Crocus sativus, which are dried and ground into a powder, making an orange color. This pigment is not used as commonly as in the very early days; it was a favorite color in ancient Rome.

saga ningyo: These are portrait dolls, carved of wood and made in Japan.

sagger: A term used in the ceramics (q.v.) crafts. The sagger is a device that is placed over and under delicate objects that are being fired (q.v.) so that they will be somewhat protected from the great heat of the kiln (q.v.).

sago dextrin: A rather strong adhesive, known also as dextrin (q.v.).

salient: A term used in heraldry. This is any animal that is shown flying or leaping through the air in a forward direction on a shield or escutcheon (q.q.v.).

salt glaze: A technique used in ceramics. While a piece is being fired (q.v.) a small amount of common table salt is placed in the kiln (q.v.). The result on the partially fired piece is a different type of glaze (q.v.) on the surface.

sampler: A piece of cloth used to show a learner's skill in the various types of sewing and stitching. Sometimes done with verses or sayings as part of the design.

sand painting: A Southwestern American Indian technique. This is done with several colors of finely ground sand. The sands are held in the hands and are slowly dropped on the ground in set patterns to form certain designs, usually done for special ceremonies.

sanda yaki: A type of ceramic (q.v.). Made in the Settsu province of Japan.

sandarac: A resin (q.v.), from the Calitris quadrivalis, a tree found in North Africa. Sandarac is added to varnishes to harden them.

sandaraca: Since very early medieval times this term applied to a type of varnish resin. The ancient Greeks and Romans used the term when they applied it to the various red earths and cinnabar.

sanding: This is a process done in the ceramics crafts. After a piece has been fired (q.v.), the hardness of the surface is tested with sand and water.

sandpaper: Paper coated with various grades of sands, made of quartz, etc. Used for the smoothing of wood, metals, etc.

sandpaper printing: A technique of drawing on sandpaper with a crayon, and inking the drawing, which is then printed.

sap green: This pigment is made from crushed, unripe buckthorn berries. This is not a permanent pigment however and fades very rapidly.

sapphire: This is a valuable stone used since ancient times. The color of the sapphire is a rather transparent blue. It is next in hardness and value to the diamond. The best specimens come from Ceylon and Burma.

sarawak: A type of cane (q.v.) having a fine yellow color with a glossy surface. Used for furniture and for baskets. The best of the canes for use in hand weaving.

satin: A fabric that has a rather shiny surface and a dull reverse side.

satin white: In the manufacture of coated papers, this pigment is used. It is composed of alumina hydrate and gypsum.

scarlet lake: A semi-transparent pigment made of cochineal (q.v.) and also vermilion. The more modern scarlet lakes are made of aniline (q.v.) dyes; this is not a permanent pigment.

scauper: A tool of the engraving crafts, used to clean out the places between the lines in an engraving.

schamoying: The craft of leather working. See chamois.

sconce: A device usually made of metal used for holding candles. Also used in heraldry to refer to a helmet.

scoring: In metal crafts, this is done with a sharp tool. Scoring is done much the same as you would draw a line on paper as a guide for a design or to cut along.

Scotch tape: A trade name for a cellulose tape with one side coated with an adhesive. Used in many crafts.

scrap toys: Many interesting toys can be made for small children from odds and ends of wood. Wheels can be made from spools of various sizes. These toys are similar to the paper box animals (q.v.).

scratchboard: A type of paper used by artists. This paper has a special coating which is scratched away to make a black and white drawing.

scrimshaw: A craft of decorating shells and ivory with designs. Color is sometimes added to the design.

sculpstone: A rather soft stone used by sculptors (q.v.). This stone has a soft rather starch-like feel.

sculptor: A sculptor is one who does sculpturing. The result of his work is known as a piece of sculpture (q.v.).

sculpture: The term sculpture covers many types of arts and crafts, carving in wood, stone or metal or any other mediums. Usually sculpturing is considered to be three-dimensional, not flat as in a drawing or painting.

sculpturing châssis: A device with a revolving top. Used for holding the model used by a sculptor (q.v.). See gentleman.

sealing wax: Made in various ways, such as with beeswax and coloring pigment. Present day methods use rosin, shellac and turpentine. Used in the gem crafts and many other crafts.

section: Used in the book crafts. A section may be two or more signatures (q.v.). This is a group of pages ready to be sewn together.

seed craft: Seeds have been used the world over to make various types of ornaments for personal use. There are thousands of plants that have seeds that are suitable for stringing. A hot needle or ice pick can be used to pierce the seeds. A needle can be used for smaller seeds. Bracelets and necklaces can be made from seeds. They may also be glued on a base and used as a pin or clip.

sejant: A term used in heraldry (q.v.). This is a position in which an animal such as a lion is shown. The animal is sitting with its hind legs down and its top weight on the front legs which may be shown elevated.

selvage: This is the edge of a fabric that has been woven, a term used in the textile crafts. Selvage is often a narrow tape that forms a base that holds the woof (q.v.).

senegal gum: Also known as Arabic gum (q.v.). A vegetable powder used in the making of adhesives and inks.

sepia: This semi-transparent pigment is prepared from the "ink sacs" of the various cephalopods such as the cuttlefish. This pigment is used in water colors and also in inks. It sometimes fades under an excess of light.

sequins: Small bright colored spangles, used on dresses, hats and other decorations, sometimes made from thin slices of certain minerals.

serpentine: Used in the jewelry and gem crafts, this is a greenish, sometimes spotted mineral.

sewing bag: Used for holding sewing materials, needles, threads and unfinished pieces. Made from a variety of materials.

sexdecimo: This term is used in the bookbinding crafts. A sexdecimo is the result of folding paper four times; this will result in a book of thirty-two pages.

sgraffito: This is a type of technique used in art in Italy in the fifteenth century. The method was to coat a surface such as a wall with one color and coat of plaster. Next the same surface was coated with another color. While the second coat was still rather soft, this was incised (q.v.). This would reveal the undercoat. This is also done in the ceramics (q.v.) crafts. A piece is coated with a slip or glaze and then this is incised, thus revealing the undercoat.

shadow stitch: Used in the sewing crafts, this is a type of stitch.

shadowbox: A simple method of making a three dimensional picture. This is done in a shallow box. Glass is sometimes placed in front of the picture.

shark liver oil: A yellowish-brown oil from the shark's liver. Used in the leather crafts and in the making of certain paints. Soluble in benzine.

shasta daisy: The blooms of this flower can be used in corsage (q.v.) making. White in color, they will last about five days. When the flowers are cut, soak the stems in a mixture of one teaspoon of peppermint oil and one quart of water.

shed: A weaving term. This is formed when the heddle (q.v.) is raised. The shed is made up of the warp threads.

shell jewelry: A simple shell bracelet can be made from shells found on any beach. Punch a hole through the shell and string with a cord or bright ribbon. A knot tied between the shells will help hold them in place. There are hundreds of types of shells that can be used. Pins and ear rings can be made of the small shells, they may be glued to a clip. Various designs can be made with the shells. You may make flowers, etc.

shellac: Shellac comes from India; it is gathered from certain trees where it is deposited by insects which feed on the trees and exude the substance which is collected. When shellac is used on a painting, it has a tendency to flake or yellow with age. When applied to paintings it should be applied in a thin coat.

shield: A term used in heraldry (q.v.). The shield is an escutcheon usually shaped like a shield used in battle by knights. This is one of the main parts of a coat of arms (q.v.).

shigamine yaki: A type of earthenware (q.v.) made in the Hizen province of Japan. Usually for home use.

shigaraki yaki: A high grade of ceramics (q.v.) made in the Omi province of Japan. This ceramic is decorated with fine designs.

shim brass: Used by sculptors (q.v.), these are thin sheets of brass which are applied to a piece which is to be cast. This acts as a separator for the mold.

shoder: The shoder is a term used in the gold beating crafts. It is the term that is used when the gold leaf (q.v.) is in its second and third stages of the process.

short-fired: A term used in ceramics crafts, used to describe a piece that is underfired.

shot: A weaving term, this is another name for a row of weft cords.

shuttle: This is used in the weaving crafts. A shuttle is used to carry the thread or cord of the weft (q.v.). Usually pointed and smooth so that it will slip through the other cords.

shutter: A part of a camera. This device is used to open and close the opening in the front of a camera to admit or to keep out light.

siccative: This is a substance such as oleic acid (q.v.), used as a paint dryer. These siccatives are added after the regular drying oils.

siderography: The art of engraving on a steel plate; such as is done in the making of plates for the engraving of paper money; or the process of transferring an engraving from one plate to another.

sigillated ware: Any ceramic piece that has a decoration which has been stamped on its surface.

signature: A signature is a term used in the bookbinding crafts. A signature consists of the folded pages, which when bound together, form a book. A signature usually has sixteen pages and a book will have a number of pages that will be multiples of sixteen.

silica: When used in paints as a ground it gives them a holding power and is also used as an adulterant. Silica when used in the paint crafts is powdered quartz, silicon dioxide. This ingredient has no coloring power.

silk: A fabric, strong and lustrous. Made from the fine filament which is taken from a cocoon and twisted into a fine thread. The cocoon is made by a moth which feeds mainly on the leaves of certain mulberry trees.

silk screen: A method of printing. This is done by cutting a design or lettering on a thin coated surface that has been applied to a sheet of silk. The ink is squeezed through the silk in the areas that have been cut out, onto another material, such as glass, wood, cloth. This differs from stenciling, which limits the design because parts like the center of an O might fall out.

silver: The mineral silver is almost white in color. Sulphur and other compounds of sulphur tend to discolor it. Silver is usually alloyed with copper and then appears as sterling silver (q.v.), coin silver (q.v.), Mexican silver (q.v.), spring silver. Pure silver melts at 1762° F. Pure silver will stay a pure white after it has been heated to a light red.

silver paper: A thin paper, known also as tissue paper. Used for polishing and for the wrapping of delicate objects.

silver sand: A sharp variety of sand used on the surface of a lithograph stone (q.v.) to grind it smooth and clean.

silver solder: An alloy used for soldering parts of silver together.

silver white: This is not a specific name for a color, it is applied to many types of white paints. Such pigments as white lead, zinc white and other white mixtures are called silver white.

simulated stars: Here is a use for old black and white negatives that you may have and no longer need. Use a sharp needle and push into the negative so that you will have a series of small holes. Do this in the sky part of your negative. Next cut the negative down so that it can be mounted in a two by two slide mount. When this is projected on a wall or screen, you will have a dark landscape with bright simulated stars.

sinew: Sinew that comes from the tendon in the back of a deer or other large animal was used as a thread by the Ojibwa Indians of the Great Lakes region of Canada and the United States. The tendons were dried and cleaned and then separated into many thin parts. Sinew was used to sew porcupine quills to skins. See quill embroidery.

singeing: When weaving with reeds, there are many short fibres, which are unsightly and make the object rough to touch. A simple method to remove these fibres is to singe the fibres. This is done with a small flame, such as an alcohol lamp produces, or any type of blue flame; a yellow flame will color the reed a dark brown. To keep from scorching the reed, it is best to singe the reed while it is wet.

sinister side: A term used in heraldry. This is the left side of the shield or escutcheon (q.q.v.).

sinope: A name no longer in common use; applied to paint pigments, it covered all of the red iron oxides.

size: This term, when applied to oil painting on canvas, means a preparation applied to the canvas to fill the pores of the canvas. In this sense, it is not a glue but a preparation to prevent oil paint from being absorbed by the cloth, thus causing it to rot. There are many kinds of size; one useful example is about $1\frac{1}{2}$ oz. of rabbit glue to about a quart of water. Do not apply a size so thick that it becomes a coat, the idea is to seal the pores only. See printing, textile and paper size.

size, corsage: In the making of a corsage (q.v.), the size is important. The use of the corsage should be considered. The size of the person who will wear the corsage should also be considered. The types of blooms and their color are important when making a corsage.

skeletonized leaves: In the corsage (q.v.) crafts, the skeletonized leaf is sometimes used. To make a skeletonized leaf, boil some heavy leaf, such as from a magnolia or tulip tree. Boil in a mixture of strong soap to which a small amount of lye has been added. Boil slowly until the leaf has disappeared and only the ribs are left. Remove the leaf, rinse in cool water and then press dry between paper. These skeletonized leaves make unusual arrangements for corsages and shadowboxes (q.v.).

skiving knife: A sharp, short knife used in the leather crafts to trim the edge of leather. When lacing two pieces of leather together, a skiving knife is used to slice through the leather at the edge and cut away part of it, this will prevent a large bulge along the edge when two parts are laced together.

skin blankets: See rabbit skin blankets.

slate black: This paint pigment is made from powdered or ground shale or slate. The color is greyish black and is used in water paints.

sley: This is a weaving term, used to describe the threading of the warp threads through the reed (q.v.).

sling: A tight piece of wire used on a table for the cutting of clay that is being wedged (q.v.) in the ceramics crafts.

slip: This is a type of clay used in ceramic crafts (q.v.) for decorating pottery. Slip is made by mixing a large amount of water with the clay so that it is almost liquid. Slip is applied to ceramics in various ways, by brush, by dipping, etc.

slip kiln: A device used in a kiln (q.v.). Used to drive off excess moisture in the clay. This is done before firing, thus making the object firmer.

slopping: The process of kneading and wedging clay before it is used. A ceramics craft.

slur: A printing term, used to describe an impression that has not registered correctly and is blurred.

smalt: This is a pigment used in ceramics, also by sign-painters. Smalt is made by roasting cobalt ores (q.v.) with other ingredients. The name as it is used today dates from the middle of the seventeenth century, before that the name meant any ceramic glaze of any color. Known also as azure blue (q.v.). See zaffre.

smock: Used in many arts and crafts, this is a garment used to cover the person or his clothing while working. It is usually tied in the back or buttoned. Made mainly from cotton.

smoking a plate: In the etching crafts, it is necessary to provide a smooth flat surface to work with, one that can be used as well as seen. When you have a properly prepared plate that has a smooth ground (q.v.) it is ready to smoke. This process will give your plate a flat dull black finish. This surface can now be worked on with a graver (q.v.) or sharp needle. The surface must be smoked evenly; this can be done with a candle. Care should be used so that the ground will not be melted away. If this happens, the whole process should be done over because the acid will find any weak spots. Hold the plate rather closely over the flame, this will cause the soot to collect and deposit on the surface of the plate.

smooth calf: Used in the leather crafts and the bookbinding crafts. This is plain calf leather or binding that has no decoration.

smother kiln: A kiln in the ceramics crafts in which the smoke is prevented from escaping, thus giving the pieces inside a black color.

snake stick: Certain American Indian tribes made in the past, and still do, a simple stick game. This game used a stick that was carved to resemble a snake. This was thrown so that it skimmed over snow. The object was to make your stick go the longest distance. Also known as a snow stick. This can be done on sand and water.

snakewood: This wood comes from Dutch Guiana. The wood has spots in it which resemble snake markings, thus the name snakewood. Modeling tools and walking sticks are made from this wood.

snarling iron: This device, used in metal craft work, is used to put designs on the surfaces of metal containers. It consists of a bent piece of iron, bent in such a way that the points of the iron are facing each other. The iron is fastened in a vise and the object to be designed is placed between the two points of the iron, the iron is then struck with a sharp blow, the resulting vibrations raise the design on the container.

snow man: A use for old ping pong balls. . . . glue two together and glue one end on a flat round card so that they will stand. Paint a face on the top and place a few pieces of broom straw in the front to represent a broom. This can be used as a party favor.

snow stick: See snake stick.

soak: A term used in the ceramics crafts. This is the holding of the heat of a kiln at a certain temperature so that the heat will penetrate the object being fired.

soaking reed: When working with reed, cane, raffia, rush, Hong Kong Grass, it is necessary to soak the material in warm water before use. The soaking time, of course, varies with the material, it depends on size and coarseness. The time varies from ten minutes to a half an hour. When working the material, it is a good idea to work with a sponge so that the above materials will remain pliable.

soaking vat: A large vat in which hides are kept. This is the first step in the process of tanning hides. The vats are filled with water, the hides are kept in motion either by hand or by mechanical means for a week or less, depending on the type hide.

soapstone: Used in several crafts, this is a variety of talc. There is a rather soft slippery feeling to the surface of this stone.

sock doll: The craft of making dolls is as varied as its materials; many materials are thrown away by some. Others save them and turn them into dolls. Odd socks may be used to make a fine doll, or socks that have outlived their regular use may be used. The doll's head is formed by the toe, this is stuffed with cotton or sawdust; when the head size has been reached, a stout cord is tied around to form the neck; the sock may now be further filled and the top may be split to form the legs of the doll, these may be stuffed and sewn. Arms may be made from odd pieces of cloth, or by splitting another sock and then stuffing with the cotton or other material. The toe of the second sock will then become the hand of the doll. The face of the doll may be drawn with India ink (q.v.) or sewn on with bright thread or yarn.

soft pottery: This is unglazed pottery with a surface that can be easily scratched with a metal tool.

sohan: A tool of the ivory carver. Made in various grades, this is a file-like tool used for the roughing in of a carved piece of ivory.

soku: A type of ancient craft done in Japan. Now known as kanshitsu (q.v.).

soluble blue: This is a variety of Prussian blue (q.v.). This pigment is used as a laundry blue and also for inks used to rule the lines on paper. This pigment is water soluble.

solder: Any of many metal alloys (q.v.). Used to fuse two pieces together.

soy bean oil: This is a substitute for linseed oil (q.v.). Soy oil may be bleached to a pale yellow color but it requires a drier to be added when used with paints. Made from pressed soy beans. Used in the making of inks, paper coating.

soyal kachina: This is a type of kachina (q.v.). The Hopi Indians use this kachina; it is first used at the time of the winter solstice.

soyoko: This is a type of kachina (q.v.) of the Hopi Indians of America. Soyoko is an evil woman. She appears the night after the bean dance. She visits various houses to get children to work for her; she threatens to eat them if they don't help her. She has a black face with a wide mouth. She also has a beak and a tongue that hangs out.

spacing wheel: This is a tool used in leather crafts. The tool consists of a handle with a rotary wheel with spokes of varying widths; this is used as a marker along the edge of leather work. It marks the place for the punch so that lacing will be uniform along the edge.

spall: A term used by sculptors; this is a chip or flake that is worked off a sculptured piece.

Spanish black: This type of paint pigment is made from burned cork.

Spanish leather: This term is used to describe bright rather straight-grained leather. Used in the bookbinding and leather crafts.

Spanish white: This paint pigment is known also as Paris white when it is in lump form. Spanish white also meant bismuth white (q.v.); it is no longer in common use.

spatter prints: To make a spatter print is a rather simple matter when you know how. For example, let's make a spatter print of a leaf. You will need a bottle of India ink (q.v.), some coarse screen wire, an old toothbrush, paper to be used for the design and a leaf. Several pins will help if the leaf will not stay in place. Pin the leaf to the surface of the paper. Next, ink the toothbrush and take the small piece of screen wire and hold it over the leaf. Now brush the wire gently. This will cause many small drops or spatters to scatter over the leaf and the paper. When you have covered the outline of the leaf, re-move the leaf and you will have a white leaf or what-ever color the paper happens to be. The outline of the leaf will be left. This outline will be made up of many small dots or spatters. This can, of course, be varied with several leaves, etc.

spectrum: The series of colors into which a beam of light is broken when it passes through a prism. When a band of light is examined, it is found to be made up of many colors, starting with red, then orange, yellow, green, blue and violet. There are many shades between, but these are the main colors that are visible to the naked eye.

spermaceti: A very brittle wax found in the head cavities of the sperm whale. This is a clean white wax and rather translucent. The melting point of spermaceti wax is 41 to 44° C.

spine: This is a bookbinding term; the spine is the back of the cover of a bound book.

spinning: A process of twisting fibers together to form yarns or threads. This also includes synthetic and plastic fibers made of vegetable or mineral substances.

spitsticker: This is a tool used in the craft of wood-engraving. The shape of the blade is somewhat like a shield, flat on one surface and curving to a point on the other two sides. The blade is made of very hard steel.

split brilliant: This term is used to describe a brilliant (q.v.) that has been split, thus making two gems.

sponge rubber dolls: Dolls can be made from sponge rubber; they can be cut from one piece of rubber, or from several small pieces and then fastened together with cement or rubber glue. Sponge rubber dolls can be made from old rubber pads, cushions, etc.

spool dolls: Fine little dolls can be made from discarded spools.

A small spool for the doll head and large spool for the body of the doll; arms and legs of the doll can be made from small spools strung together. The body part of the doll, made from a large spool, must be drilled first, a hole must be drilled through the spool about a quarter of the way down; this is done so that the arms can be fastened on. The head, arms and legs may be fastened on with stout cord or with rubber bands. A face may be drawn on the top spool with India ink (q.v.) or any kind of paint or with colored nail polish.

spray gun: A device used to spray paint, shellac or other substances on a surface. The spray gun can be worked from compressed air or by blowing with the mouth.

spring back: This is the cover of a book that is not entirely fastened to the spine (q.v.). A cover of this type leaves a hollow space when the book is opened.

spring silver: This is a type of sterling silver that has been reduced by rolling and drawing. This type is used to make tie clips, buckles, cigarette cases and clips to hold money or other objects that have need of a spring-like action in their use.

spruce ocher: This is a term used to describe yellow ocher, sometimes also given to brown ocher.

spur marks: Spur marks are the remains of the little separators that are used under a piece of ceramic (q.v.). These are used in the kiln (q.v.). These sometimes adhere to the piece and have to be broken away; later they are filed off so that the base of the fired object will be smooth.

squabble: A term used in the printing crafts. This term is used to apply to any type that is twisted out of place.

square: The square is a type of form (q.v.) used in the

corsage crafts. When used in the craft of corsage (q.v.) making, the square is usually used for special corsages—not usually used for shoulder corsages.

square graver. The square graver is a tool used in the craft of wood-engraving (q.v.). The tool is made of steel. The point is square in shape, with all four corners very sharp. The handle of this tool is usually made of wood and is round, with one side flat.

stained glass: This type of glass is made in several ways. The color may be added to the molten glass by adding various metallic oxides. The surface may be coated with a colored glass which is later etched away; this is known as flashed glass (q.v.). The surface of the glass may be colored by applying enamels to the surface. Another method is to apply a silver solution to the surface of the glass; this is done while the glass is under fire, resulting in a glass with a yellow color. Stained glass windows are made by arranging the various shapes, colors and sizes in a pattern that will form a picture or design, this is then held together by lead strips.

staining the head: This is a bookbinding term. The head (q.v.) is stained with a color that will go with the color of the book cover. The stain is made with a thin solution of ink.

stand oil: When linseed oil (q.v.) is heated to 525° to 575° and held at that temperature a change takes place. The oil becomes heavy and thick, making stand oil. The change in color of stand oil is not as great as that of raw linseed oil. Stand oil dries with a hard smooth finish.

star chart: A simple star chart can be made from an old shoe box or hat box. Stars can be shown on a wall or screen by using a flashlight or a light on a cord. Place the light in the box and it will shine through the small holes in the box. The holes can be punched in the box with an ice pick or an awl (q.v.). Use a sky chart to make your electric star chart accurate.

statant: A term used in heraldry. This term is used to describe an animal that is shown standing, with both feet on the ground. The animal is shown on a shield or escutcheon (q.q.v.).

stave: This is part of a barrel. A stave is wider in the middle than it is at either end. The stave is beveled (q.v.) to fit the next stave.

St. Crispin: St. Crispin is the patron saint of the shoemaker. Crispin made shoes for the poor, because of his work and his efforts on behalf of the poor. This was done at the expense of others. Because of his Robin Hood-like methods, called in those days "Crispinades," Crispin was put to death and October 25th is now called St. Crispin's Day. St. Crispin lived in what is now the city of Soissons, France.

stearic acid: This substance is refined from animal fats, producing a waxy substance used in candle making. The melting point of stearic acid is 69 to 71° C.

steatite: A rather soft rock used by sculptors. Also known as soapstone (q.v.).

steerhide: This is a design that is impressed on cowhide, used in leather crafts.

stele: This is the body of an arrow without feathers or point.

stencil: A metal or cardboard cut in such a way that when the design is rubbed with ink or is sprayed, the design is reproduced on the surface of the paper or other material placed underneath.

stephanotis: The blooms of this flower are a favorite when making a corsage (q.v.). The flowers are bell shaped, have a fine scent and a wax-like texture. When correctly prepared, they will last about ten days.

stereotype: A term used in the printing crafts. This is a metal plate used in printing. It is made by pouring molten metal into a form which is prepared with a cardboard mat.

sterling silver: This is an alloy, 92½ per cent silver and 7½ per cent copper. This metal is used to make jewelry, flatware and other objects that call for sterling silver. To test for sterling silver, put a drop of nitric acid on a gash cut in the object to be tested. Sterling silver will turn a cloudy cream color. Sterling silver will melt at 1640° F. When sterling silver is heated to a light red and then cooled, it will turn black.

stick printing: A simple method of printing with soft sticks, cut into a design and used to print such things as wrapping paper, boxes, etc.

stilling: This is a stand used in the ceramics crafts, used for holding unfired pieces which are drying before firing (q.v.).

stillingia oil: Obtained from a tree that is grown in China.

Used when mixing vermilion (q.v.) in China which was used on the seals for their paintings. Also known as tallowseed oil.

stippling: When applied to the craft of leather working, this means to use a stippling tool or any blunt tool to press out the design; this will make the design stand out in relief.

stomp: Usually made of paper. This is a tightly rolled paper usually cut into a point. Used to blend or shade charcoal or pastels. The stomp does not leave any color itself.

stone lithography: Lithography (q.v.) can be done on several types of surfaces; one of the materials is stone. The stone comes from the Jura mountains of Bavaria. This is a smooth very fine textured limestone. This stone is cut into blocks that vary in size with a thickness of three or four inches. The design is drawn on the stone with a grease pencil (q.v.). When the stone is to be used over, the design can be removed by rubbing with a smaller stone in a circular motion, this will grind the surface until it is again smooth and clean.

stoneware: This is a type of ceramics (q.v.). It is made from clay and ground flint. This is mixed in water and then ground. Ordinary salt is used as a glaze (q.v.). This attaches itself to the object during firing.

straw angels: A craft from the country of Sweden and changed in many other countries is the straw crafts. Real straw should be used; if this is not available, plain drinking straws can be used. A bundle of straws can be used to make the body of the doll. Wings can be made by making a fan of straws. The straws can be tied with string or a dampened straw.

streamlines: There are various other names for this fault in painting, tears, runs, frilling, streaks. This is the result of painting a canvas on a slant and the paint or varnish was thin, as it ran down the surface it dried, resulting in the faults listed.

string crafts: For a free form (q.v.) in arts and crafts, a simple design can be made from string, a few tacks and a wood frame. Tacks should be placed in the back of the frame. Put the tacks in various spaced intervals so that they will make an interesting pattern. Next take a ball of string or several different colors and tie the string back and forth across the frame so that you will form many interesting and colorful designs.

stringer: An early craftsman who made strings for use on bows used in archery. The strings or cords were made by hand. They were made of hemp, flax, silk, etc.

strontium yellow: This pigment is a bright yellow with a greenish tinge. This is rather opaque and does not mix with water. Strontium yellow is a permanent pigment.

stuffers: A term used in rug weaving to describe the extra threads or cords which are added to a woven rug. Only used as a filler and do not add strength to the rug.

stylus: A tool of many artists and craftsmen. Used in the cutting of designs on the surface of clay, metal and on stencils used in mimeographing. The point varies in size and sharpness, depending on the surface that it is to be used on. Usually it has a rather fine point, sometimes rounded.

sublimed white lead: A lead sulphate combined with zinc; this forms a very dense white pigment.

suede: The flesh side of leather is buffed (q.v.) by machine. This method produces a soft surface on the leather from which the well-known suede shoes are made.

sulphuric acid: Used in the metal crafts. Used for the cleaning of metals—removes rust.

sumac (Rhus glabra): The inner bark and the pulp of this plant were used by the Ojibwa Indians of the Great Lakes region of Canada and the United States. A yellow dye resulted and was used for the dye used on porcupine quills and also for their rush mats.

sumac wax: A light yellow wax made from the fruit of a species of sumac. The fruit is boiled in water to secure the wax. Sumac wax is also known as Japan wax (q.v.). This type of wax is soluble in benzene and naphtha.

sumi: This is carbon and glue that is mixed and made into sticks. This is then rubbed in water and used as a paint medium. This is a Japanese method.

sunflower oil: The oil from sunflower seeds have somewhat the same properties as oil from the poppy seed (q.v.). Used more in Europe as a substitute for linseed oil (q.v.).

supporters: A term used in heraldry. The supporters are figures that are shown on either side of a shield and appear to be holding it up.

surimono: A type of Japanese wood brick print.

suzuri: A stone with a very fine grain, used to rub with water and the sumi (q.v.).

sweep: A term used in ceramics. This is a curved blade made of metal and is part of a pug mill (q.v.), used to force clay through the holes in the bottom of the mill.

sweet william: The blooms of this plant may be used in corsage (q.v.) making. When collected and prepared correctly, these blooms will last about five days.

synchronizer: A device used on a camera. This device is used to time a flash lamp and the opening on a camera so that they will work in conjunction with each other.

T

tabinet: A type of fabric made from silk and wool, used for furniture covering.

tabby weft: This is a plain weave formed by the thread as it is passed through the shed (q.v.).

table: A term used in several arts and crafts. When used in the lapidary crafts, the table refers to the flat surface of the gem, the un-faceted (q.v.) surface. There is no table on a gem with a cabochon cut (q.v.). The table is also a flat surface, made of iron, used in the glass-making crafts. The table is flat, with a raised edge, used for the making of panes of glass.

table cut: A term used in the jewelry and gem cutting crafts. The table cut is done by a gemmologist, usually done on precious stones such as emeralds and diamonds. The table cut is flat, the edges are beveled in various ways depending on the type of stone and cut.

table easel: Used by artists. A table easel does not stand on the floor but is designed to stand on a table or other raised surface.

Tachi Bina: These are special Japanese dolls; they were first used at bridal parties and are now a nationalistic doll. These dolls come in pairs, the female doll is decorated with wisteria and the male doll is decorated with a pine tree.

tacking iron: A device used by photographers to dry mount pictures or other illustrations. The illustration is pressed and heated at the same time, thus bonding the illustration to a stiff surface.

tacky: When the surface of a painted or inked surface is sticky and not yet dry it is said to be tacky. This is caused by slow drying of the paints or inks.

taffeta: This is a smooth lustrous fabric made of silk. Usually has a series of raised areas.

Tahaum Soyoko: This kachina of the Hopi Indians of America represents the uncle of Soyoko. This figure has a black face with horns. Usually has a fox skin around its neck, dressed with a white shirt and pants with red shoes. The figure carries a rattle and bow and arrows.

tail: The tail is the bottom part of the pages within the cover of a book. This term is used in the bookbinding crafts.

tail-piece: In the book crafts, this is a small illustration or vignette (q.v.). Placed on a page at the end of a chapter.

talc: Talc is magnesium silicate. When ground it is used for many purposes as a dryer, and a filler in paints. Used on plastigraph (q.v.) plates to retard stickiness when cutting a blockprint.

talc rock: A soft rock used by sculptors (q.v.). This rock is known better by the name soapstone (q.v.).

tallowseed oil: See stillingia oil.

talmi-gold: A type of brass used in the jewelry crafts. It resembles gold in color.

tambour: A term used in embroidery. This is a loop-shaped frame which can be stretched tight, thus forming the base for the needlework.

tambourine: How to make, see jingles.

Tanakwewa: The body of this kachina (q.v.) is painted white, including its head. The eyes and the mouth are extended. Its waist is adorned with turtle shells. This kachina is barefooted. It is seen in the Bean Dance.

tane: A type of Japanese block print; the main color of the prints from these block prints was tan.

tannin: Tannin is an essential vegetable substance needed to tan leather.

tanning leather: This process has been done since very ancient times. The first known tanner to come to America arrived in Plymouth on the ship "Ann" in the year 1623. An early process of tanning leather was to soak the hide in a large vat of lime and water. The hair was then scraped off and the hides were placed in boxes and layers of ground oak bark were placed on the hides. Next the box was filled with water and left to soak for about a half a year. The present method of tanning with chrome chemicals can do the tanning in several hours.

tapa cloth: This is a type cloth made mainly by the peoples of the Pacific islands. Made from the inner bark of certain mulberry trees. The bark is pounded under water until it is soft and matted. Decorations are done in brown on the surface; the color is derived from the juice of berries.

tape: See: Masking tape, Scotch tape.

taping: In the corsage crafts, taping is important. Many flowers have little or no stem, others have very weak stems. Wiring (q.v.) a corsage (q.v.) is rather difficult without first taping the stems. When the stem is weak it should first be wrapped with tape; many types are available. Scotch tape, masking tape and others can be used. The tape should be applied tightly. When the stem has been properly taped, it is ready to be wired (q.v.). Variously colored ribbons can be applied after the corsage has been taped.

tapping: This is the process of cutting a hole in a pipe or surface of a piece of metal; it is then cut in such a way that it will have a threaded hole, which will hold a bolt or screw.

tarlatan: This is a thin material made of cotton, used as a wiping material in etching and printing crafts.

tatami: These are straw mats made three feet by six feet and about three inches thick. Used to make Oriental floor coverings.

tatting: This is a technique of sewing. Threads are pulled through lace with a bobbin or spindle, in such a manner as to form designs on the lace.

tattoo: A process of illustrating on the skin. The purpose is to apply a permanent pigment to the skin. This is done with a needle, the color being introduced under the skin, which of course is a permanent method.

tchama: This is a roll or sheet of papyrus made in ancient Egypt. The summary of the reign of Rameses III was written on a giant roll which measured 135 feet in length and 16½ feet wide. Made completely of papyrus (q.v.).

teakwood: Teakwood from Java is well known. This wood has great strength and has many uses. The wood is well suited for carving; it has a color of a dark gold brown.

technique: The method or mechanical process by which an art or craft is accomplished, usually following a set pattern or rule.

technography: This is a term used to describe the study of the methods of arts and crafts all over the world.

telephoto lens: A type of lens used in photography to bring far distant objects into view and thus record them clearly on film.

temper: A term used in many crafts. To temper clay is to mix and blend in preparation for use. In the metal crafts, to temper is to harden the metal by controlled heating and cooling.

tempera: Tempera painting is a type of painting that has a matte finish (q.v.). This type of paint is mixed with various pigments, glues and gums. Casein (q.v.) may be mixed with the pigments. See egg tempera (q.v.).

template: A pattern or design, cut of leather, metal, cardboard or other material. When doing many copies of the same object in the craft of leather working, a template is a valuable asset. The various patterns are cut out of metal and can be laid right on the leather and a tracing can be made around them. The Northwest Coast Indians used a leather template to carve the figures on their totem poles; this was necessary because some of the figures were done in a set way. Also spelled templet.

templet: A gauge or mold or pattern used to form or create a copy of an object or shape. See template.

tent stitch: A type of stitch used in embroidery (q.v.). Usually done on wool, the resulting design resembles rows of pointed tents.

ternary alloy: A term used in the metal crafts. Ternary alloy is an alloy (q.v.) made from three metals or elements.

terra cotta: A natural color of a clay, rather reddish brown. Terra cotta can be made by mixing burnt umber (q.v.), red oxide and chalk. Zinc oxide and various barytes can be used in place of the chalk.

terra-cotta doll: About the middle of the sixth century B.C., dolls were made of terra-cotta (q.v.). Dolls made at this time had movable legs and arms; their hands often held musical instruments such as cymbals and castanets.

terrace: This is a term used to describe a flaw in marble that is being worked by a sculptor (q.v.), usually cut away and filled in with some other material to match the marble.

tesserae: A term used by craftsmen working in mosaics and in chip carving; these are small odd shaped pieces.

textile: This is a woven material. A textile can be made from any number of fibers or combinations of fibers, such as cotton, wool, silk or synthetic fibers, such as the acetates, glass, nylon, etc.

textile dyes: Textile dyes are made of many kinds of substances, animal, vegetable and mineral. Some textile dyes are very simple and others are involved chemical compounds.

textile size: A solution of a starchy preparation used to impregnate a cloth to stiffen it. Such a cloth could be used in the making of lampshades, etc.

textures: General structure of the surface of a work of art. Fabrics or textiles have a texture when felt or examined; wood and bark have certain recognizable textures, as does leather, stone, etc. Textures of one kind may be duplicated on other objects. An example would be the simulation of tree bark on the surface of a bench that was made of cement or stone.

thallium glass: A type of flint glass, rather dense, made from thallium instead of lead.

thermoplastic: This is a type of plastic which softens when heated, such as plastigraph (q.v.). When cool, thermoplastics become solid or hard, depending on their make up.

thixotropic paint: A term used to describe paint that is very thick, similar to whipped cream. This paint can be stirred, however, and becomes very fluid.

thread marks: Marks that are caused by the ceramist when he uses a thread to separate the clay object from the table or wheel.

thread splicing: Thread or cord splicing in the bookbinding crafts should be done so that the knot will lay flat on the back (q.v.) or the headband (q.v.).

three-quarter binding: A term used by bookbinders. In this type of binding the book has its spine (q.v.) and corners covered with leather.

throw shuttle: A device shaped much like a boat; the throw shuttle contains a bobbin used for holding the thread.

throwing: A term used in ceramics. Throwing is done on a potter's wheel (q.v.). A lump of clay is spun and formed into an object.

thrums: A weaving term used to describe the ends of the warp threads which are waste and are cut from the loom.

thumb-knop: This is a part of a lid on a tankard and also on other containers used to hold liquids. It is pressed with the thumb when pouring liquids; this raises the lid to permit easy pouring. Made of pewter (q.v.) in the early days. Variations of it can be seen today on cream pitchers and syrup containers. First used in the sixteenth century.

tie dyeing: A technique of dyeing cloth. The cloth is tied into knots or sewn together tightly. The cloth is then dipped into a dye and removed. The threads or knots are then removed and the result will be a cloth that has a design partially dyed. This method is also known as batik (q.v.).

timbers: A timber is a sawmill designation and applies to wood that is rough cut (q.v.) and is four to eight inches thick and from six to ten inches wide.

tin white: This opaque white is used in ceramics. Made from stannic oxide.

tint block: A plate or block that is used for the printing of very faint colors on a given area, to tint an area which will later receive printing or other illustrations.

tint tool: The tint tool is a tool made of steel and used in the craft of woodengraving. This tool has four sides, somewhat wedge shaped, one end not quite cut to a point, rather a flat edge.

tintype: An early type of photography. This is a positive picture taken directly on a plate of tin or iron.

tipi: A cone shaped house or tent, made mainly by the Plains Indians of America. The tipi is usually made from the skins of animals, such as the bison, or buffalo as it is commonly known. The tipi is held up by means of long poles which are fastened at the top and are spread wide at the bottom; this is then covered with the animal skin. This type of dwelling is made through necessity because of the lack of other materials. A tipi differs in shape and size from the wigwam (q.v.).

titania: This rather new type of synthetic rutile has a brilliance far better than the diamond. It is, however, a much softer stone.

titanium oxide: A paint pigment of great hiding power. Made from titanium dioxide, this is a very permanent pigment, a pure white pigment made since 1919.

Titanolith: This pigment made from titanium white and

lithopone is a white paint pigment made commercially. The name Titanolith is a trademarked name.

toby jug: Made in the ceramics crafts. This is a ceramic piece made usually in the shape of a squat man. Used as a drinking cup, now mainly a collector's item.

toki: This is a type of Japanese glazed earthenware.

toluidine red: A fire-red aniline color with a yellowish tinge. This pigment is used in commercial paints, not used in permanent painting.

tone: A term used in photography to denote the differences in light and dark in a picture. Also used in the various arts to denote the same general meaning.

tongs: There are many types of tongs in use in the arts and crafts. Tongs used in the jewelry and gem crafts are faced with a slice of clear tourmaline (q.v.).

tooling: A term used in many crafts. The process is the technique of decorating leather, such as on a book cover. The design is pressed into the surface of the leather with variously shaped tools. Sometimes color is added to the design.

toplady ring: A type of ring made in the jewelry and gem crafts. The ring was made of six matched diamonds, arranged in three pairs.

topping: A textile technique. This is a method of dyeing a cloth that has already been dyed. The topping technique is usually done with a lighter dye, thus tinting the fabric another color.

torchon board: A pasteboard (q.v.), made of torchon paper (q.v.), used by water colorists.

torchon paper: This is a type of handmade paper used by artists, especially in the doing of watercolors. The surface is rather coarse.

torse: A term used in heraldry (q.v.). Shown on the helmet, known also as mantling (q.v.); always depicted with six twists of cloth.

tortoise-shell: As used in the ceramic crafts, this applies to the design or finish on the ceramic that resembles the tortoise shell. The slip (q.v.) is made with copper oxide and manganese. This type of ceramic is also known as Whieldon ware (q.v.).

tortoise-shell wood: A type of wood used in carving, also known as snakewood (q.v.).

Toson Koyemsi: The face of this kachina (q.v.) is painted brown, with green lines on its cheeks, round eyes and mouth. The figure has a collar of rags, a black shirt and red shoes. These kachinas accompany the Soyoko (q.v.) after the Bean Dance.

totem pole: A tree carved mainly by the Northwest coast Indians of America. Usually carved from cedar trees, these posts were from three to over ninety feet tall. Carved with grotesque figures of animals and mythical beings. Usually placed in front of a house or tomb. The figures represent legends or special spirits that are identified with a particular family.

tou fang: An art term used in China, to denote a small album of paintings, usually square.

touch: A term used in the metal crafts. A touch is a mark that is placed usually on the underside of a metal object to identify the maker.

tourmaline: This is a gem stone. Only the clear, blue, pink and green varieties are considered useful. The clear mineral is used for the plates in the jaws of a jewelers' tongs (q.v.).

tournasin: A knife used in the ceramics crafts. Used to scrape away the excess slip from a fired (q.v.) piece of pottery.

tracing: A technique of reproducing an illustration on tracing paper (q.v.). Done to copy, reproduce or use for another purpose. Tracing should not damage the original illustration or design.

tracing paper: Paper used by artists and craftsmen. A thin, rather tough paper that has no texture. Pencil or ink can be used on it. A tracing paper can be made by soaking paper in a solution of vegetable oil and balsam turpentine. Hang the paper up to dry before using.

trade binding: A term used in the bookbinding crafts. This is a rather cheap method of binding a book. This trade edition differs from a hand job because all or almost all of the processes are done by machine. This is known as an edition binding (q.v.).

transparency: A term used in heraldry. This is a design on a coat of arms that has been drawn in outline and is not filled in with a solid color. This is done to show that a family is entitled to their bearings but have lost their original land holdings.

trap cut: Used in the gem crafts. This term is used to describe a gem that has a flat table (q.v.) which gradually tapers off to the edge and then comes to a point from the girdle (q.v.) to the bottom.

tray: A tray is usually flat with a hollow depression. Made of metal such as pewter (q.v.), steel, aluminum or wood, fibers or plastic. Trays can be decorated or plain. Used in various parts of the world as receptacles for carrying or holding objects.

treadle: A lever used to raise and lower the threads of the warp on a loom.

triads: A term used to describe any three colors that are arranged in such a way as to form an equilateral triangle, such colors as red, yellow and blue.

trillium: The flower of this plant can be used in the corsage (q.v.) crafts. When picked, use only the bloom, not the leaves. It will last about two days.

trimmed flush: A term used in the printing and bookbinding crafts. A trimmed flush cover is a cover on a book that has been cut or trimmed to the exact size of the pages inside the book. This is the opposite of extended cover (q.v.).

tripod: A three legged device with telescopic legs. Used by photographers to hold a camera in a steady position.

trippant: A term used in heraldry. This is used to describe any animal shown with one foot raised and the other three on the ground.

trolley: This is a variety of lace. The design in this particular lace is outlined with a coarser thread.

tsantsa: The technique of shrinking human heads. This name is applied to heads that are prepared by the Jivaro Indians of the Peruvian rain forests. The skull is removed and the skin is cooked and dried over a hot smoky fire. The result is a rather brittle human head of the size of an orange. The hair remains its original length. The lips are sewn shut, presumably to keep in the spirit of the original owner.

Tsitoto: This kachina (q.v.), also known as the flower kachina, has a body that is painted red and yellow. Has a neck band of Douglas fir. The head is painted with many colored stripes. This kachina appears in the Water Serpent Ceremony of the Hopi Indians of the United States.

tsuikoku: This is a technique used in Japan and is the method used there to carve black lacquered surfaces.

tub size: Used in making paper. This is a size (q.v.) that is applied to the finished paper by passing it through a vat of coating or sizing solution; this differs from the size which is added to the paper pulp during the manufacture.

tulip: A bloom used in the corsage (q.v.) crafts. The flower may be opened wide and used in a bouquet. The bloom may be held in one position by dropping hot wax into the center and then placing scotch tape (q.v.) around in the center so that the bloom will not open. This method will keep the bloom for about a week. Without this method the bloom will last about three days.

tulle: A type of fabric with a mesh weave, used in the making of veils.

tung oil: Also known as China wood oil, this oil comes from the nuts of certain trees found in China, the Aleurites cordata. Trees have been grown in the southeastern United States. Tung oil from China is rather dark and has a noticeable odor. This type of oil is used in commercial paints.

Tungwup Ta-amu: This is the uncle of the Tungwup whipper kachina (q.v.). The Hopi Indians of America use this kachina in bean dance ceremony. The figure is green and the head has a pair of horns like the whipper kachina.

tungwup whipper: This is a type of the American Indian kachina (q.v.). The body figure of this kachina is painted black, covered with white dots. The face is decorated with a mark of a turkey foot. There is also a fox muff on the neck, the feet have red moccasins. There is a whip made of yucca leaves held in one hand and the other hand holds some pieces of the cholla cactus. This figure is used in the Hopi Bean Dance.

tunnel kiln: A type of kiln used in the ceramics crafts (q.q.v.). The pieces move in and out of the kiln on a track or in cars. This type of kiln does not need to be cooled off to remove the fired pieces (q.v.). See periodic kiln.

turkey red: A bright red color used in the painting crafts.

Made from the madder plant. Also known as Adrianople red (q.v.).

turkey red oil. A type of oil made from sulfonated castor oil. Used in coating papers and in the making of textile dye.

turk's head: A type of finishing knot used in leather working.

turmeric: A resin that is prepared from the roots of several kinds of plants found in Asia. This type of resin was used as a yellow dye.

turnbull's blue: A type of Prussian blue (q.v.). Made from potassium ferrous ferricyanide, this type of paint pigment is not generally used.

turner's yellow: This is an obsolete paint pigment, made from lead oxychloride. Turner's yellow is not a permanent pigment and after a time it turns black.

turpentine: Turpentine is distilled from the resins of certain conifers. Distilled turpentine is used to thin oil paints and is also used in many varnishes.

turpeth mineral: This pigment is made of sulphate of mercury. A bright yellow pigment, not permanent and a very poisonous paint pigment. Not generally used today.

turquoise: This is a rather soft stone, used in gem crafts. When cut and polished the shape is cabochon (q.v.). American Indians, especially in the Southwest, use a great deal of turquoise. The very light blue turquoise comes from Persia. There are many types of plastics that look like turquoise and many people buy jewelry that has a synthetic turquoise mounted in it.

turquoise green: A rather expensive green pigment, made from aluminum, cobalt oxides and chromium. A light green with a bluish tinge. Turquoise green is a permanent pigment and is sometimes used in the ceramics crafts.

tuscan red: This pigment is made of an oxide base, also alizarin (q.v.) and Indian red; if these ingredients are included the paint will be permanent. Aniline colors and various earths are sometimes used and these are not as permanent. The pigment is used for industrial purposes mainly.

tweed: A type of soft woolen cloth, a type of twill. The name has been corrupted from the Scottish tweal since 1829. Tweal is the Scotch word for twill (q.v.).

twill: This is a type of weave where two or more of the warp threads (q.v.) pass over and under the weft threads (q.v.). This type of weave is seen on many canvases used by artists and painters (q.q.v.).

twist direction: A term used in the weaving crafts. This term refers to the type of twist given the cords or yarns in a fabric. When held in a verticle position and the twist forms an S, it is said to have an S twist.

type: As used in the crafts of printing, type is a kind of tool having a letter or character on the surface. It comes in various sizes and is cast from lead, antimony (q.v.) and tin. Type is always of a uniform height, .918 of an inch.

type gauge: A type gauge is used to measure type that is used in the printing crafts. This is similar to a regular ruler. Besides measuring inches, it also has a scale of picas (q.v.) and on one side in nonpareils (q.v.).

type metal: Used in the printing crafts. Type metal is composed of lead, tin and antimony and sometimes copper is added to this alloy. Used in the molding of letters because it can be melted rather easily and when cool, it shrinks enough to make a rather smooth hard surface which is needed for type.

typography: This involves the arts and crafts of printing, typesetting and composing; the technique of making up groups of letters into pages to be printed.

Tyrian purple: A purple pigment well known by the ancient Romans. Made from the shells of *Murex trunculis,* many ancient people used these shells to make the well-known color. In 1904 coal tar derivatives were used to duplicate Tyrian purple.

U

uda: A term used in ceramics to describe any glazed pottery that is decorated with a purple brown glaze.

ultramarine: A deep "true blue," originally made by grinding the stone lapis lazuli (q.v.) and then removing the grey rock that was mixed with it. The use of ultramarine was started in the twelfth century in Europe. This pigment is rather costly and the material for its makeup comes from Afghanistan, China, Persia and Chile. Since 1882, ultramarine has been made commercially by mixing clay, sulphur, soda and coal, this is heated and ground. Green ultramarine is produced in the same way and may be called unfinished ultramarine, as this color results before the commercial process is completed.

ultramarine ash: This grey blue pigment is ground lapis lazuli, mixed with the grey rock that it is found in. Ultramarine ash is a permanent pigment.

umber: A brown paint pigment. A dark brown, when burnt it has a reddish hue. This is an earth pigment.

umbrella tools: Old broken umbrellas will provide the craftsman with a fine set of tools that he can use in the block printing (q.v.) and plastigraph (q.v.) crafts. The ribs of old umbrellas are usually made of very fine steel. Their shape varies, but the ribs are usually of two types, and when cut to three or four inch lengths, they will make fine veiners (q.v.) and small gouges (q.v.). They may be sharpened with a file and then honed (q.v.) so that they will be very sharp. These may then be inserted into a wooden handle and used as they are.

umiak: This is a large type of Eskimo canoe. Made large and open and used mainly by women. It carries several people and supplies. This differs in size and shape from a kayak (q.v.). Both, however, are made from the skins of animals, usually seals.

unctuous: A term applied to the greasy or soapy feeling or sensation when certain minerals are touched, such as soapstone, talc, etc. Also applied to certain clays used in ceramics.

uncut: A bookbinding term, used to describe a book that has been rebound but the pages have remained the same and have remained uncut.

undercuts: These are projections in a mold or on an object which prevent an object from being removed from a mold. Care in casting objects which have undercuts must be observed, otherwise the object will be locked into the mold. A ball has undercuts if more than half of it is cast at one time.

underfired: Ceramics that have not been fired properly are underfired or are short-fired (q.v.).

underlay: Used in the printing crafts. This is a thin piece of paper that is placed on the bottom of the form to bring a part of the surface up slightly so that a better impression can be made when printed.

underpainting: A technique of the artist and painter. This is the preparation of a painting or mural (q.v.) prior to the actual painting. Since certain colors will become transparent, it is often necessary to have an undercoating that will blend with the surface in case it should change or flake off.

unopened: A term used in the book arts and crafts. Unopened is a term that refers to the pages that have been folded in a book and have been uncut. They have to be opened (q.v.) in order to see or read the book. These pages are cut by machine or by hand.

unprinted: A term used in the etching (q.v.) crafts. Is used to denote an area that is left white on a plate (q.v.).

upper case: Used in the printing crafts, the upper case letters are located near the top of the job case and are the capital letters.

uranium yellow: This is a rather permanent pigment, made from uranium oxide. The color is a transparent yellow with a greenish tinge, not in great use in paints because of the expense. The pigment is sometimes used in the ceramics crafts.

urinant: A term used in heraldry. This is a fish which is shown on a shield or escutcheon (q.q.v.) with its head down, bent in a half circle with the tail also down.

urn: A term usually used to denote a burial urn. A container used to hold the ashes of the deceased. This is an Oriental art term.

urotropin: This is a material, white and crystalline in structure. Used with resins (q.v.) as a hardening agent.

urushie: A term that defines a picture that is painted completely with lacquers (q.v.).

U. S. Navajo: This stamp was adopted by the Indian Arts and Crafts Board in the United States in 1938, and is placed on all quality silver work done by the Navajo Indians.

U. S. Zuni: This stamp is placed on all quality silver work done by the Zuni Indians of the United States. This stamp was adopted in 1938 by the Indian Arts and Crafts Board.

utakawa yaki: This is a type of ceramic piece made in the Chikuzen province of Japan.

V

Valois doll: A famous sixteenth-century doll. This doll is twenty-two inches tall and is made of wood. The doll is dressed in a typical sixteenth century style, in white silk. The Valois doll was used in 1878 as a crib (q.v.) figure.

value: Value is used to describe the various shades of a color from dark to light or bright to dull.

vambraced: A term used in heraldry. This is a design on a shield or escutcheon (q.q.v.) showing an arm with armour and gauntlet holding a sword.

Van Dyke brown: This pigment is composed of iron oxide and clay with humus and bitumen. Used in pastels and water colors. When used in oil paints, this pigment always turns black, it also cracks the surface and wrinkles. This pigment has the same defects as does asphaltum (q.v.).

Van Dyke red: A paint pigment similar to Prussian blue (q.v.). This pigment made from copper ferrocyanide is a very poisonous color. The color does not fade when exposed to light, but when it is exposed to sulphur fumes, it turns black. The brown shades of this pigment are also known by the name Florentine (q.v.) brown.

varnish: A varnish is usually made from resinous substances (q.v.). Varnish is used to coat the surfaces of wood, metals, sculptured pieces (q.v.) and paintings.

varnish linseed oil: This is a type of refined linseed oil used in varnishes. This oil is refined with alkali instead of acid.

vegetable black: A fine black paint pigment, also known as lamp black (q.v.).

vegetable parchment: This can be made by immersing paper that has no size (q.v.) in a bath of sulfuric acid for a few moments; remove the paper and hang up to dry. The result will be a paper that is tough and resembles real parchment (q.v.).

veiner: A tool of the wood carver and block printer. It has a handle and a curved metal blade that is sharp and is used to cut rounded grooves in wood or linoleum blocks. The grooves cut by a veiner are usually in the form of a V or U as opposed to those made by a gouge or chisel.

vellum: Vellum is a leather of very fine grain. It is made from the hides of lambs, goats and calves. The main use of vellum is in bookbinding; it was also used to write on, then called parchment (q.v.).

Vellum is used in the craft of making gold leaf (q.v.).

velour: A term used in the weaving and sewing crafts. This is any soft material, rather heavy, that has a nap (q.v.). Also used to describe any fabric that has an erect pile (q.v.).

venetian ball: This is a type of glass paper weight that has waste pieces of colored glass imbedded in its base. The paperweight is round on top and flat on the base.

venetian red: An earth that contains up to 40% iron oxide, made commercially by adding calcium sulphate. When mixed as an oil paint, this pigment makes a very hard surface.

verbena: A flower used in the corsage (q.v.) crafts. The blooms are rather red. When used in a corsage they will last about five days.

verdet: A water soluble pigment made from the dark green crystals of copper acetate. Usually made in France, this pigment is poisonous and not very permanent.

verdigris: This is the greenish or bluish color that appears on copper and brass objects that are exposed to the weather. Typical color of copper ore when exposed to the weather. The color of the Statue of Liberty. When used as a paint pigment it is composed of hydrated copper acetate. Used as a paint pigment in early Roman times, not used as commonly today as a paint pigment.

vermilion: A paint pigment made from mercuric sulphide. This bright pure red mixes well in oil paints; it is a very heavy pigment. Some grades are very permanent, others tend to change color and sometimes turn black. The best grades are made in France, England and in China. Cinnabar (q.v.) was used for this color until early in the eighteenth century and was then largely replaced with vermilion.

vernalis: This is a name of a pigment used in ceramics. Vernalis is made by heating viridian (q.v.) and chalk (q.v.); this results in a green pigment, sometimes known as Victoria green (q.v.).

verona brown: This is a type of earth that has been burnt. A permanent type pigment and rather transparent.

veronese green: A pale green pigment nearly like viridian (q.v.). This term also applies to a great many other types of green such as chrome green (q.v.).

verso: This is a term used in the book crafts. The verso is the left hand side of the book, facing the reader. These pages are always even numbered. See recto or odd number.

vert antique: This pale green pigment made from copper carbonate is a permanent type pigment, when used alone. This is used in stippling over brown to imitate copper and bronze finishes.

vetu: A term used in heraldry. This is a design in the shape of a lozenge or diamond with each of its corners touching an edge of the shield or escutcheon (q.q.v.).

victoria green: Made from 40 parts zinc yellow and 80 parts of viridian (q.v.) and 10 parts of gypsum, lithopone or zinc oxides.

vienna white: This is a polishing powder made from chalk. The chalk is produced by air-slaking lime. Vienna white is sometimes used as a paint pigment.

vignette: A small design or illustration, used mainly as a decoration such as would be seen on a page at the end of a book chapter; see tail piece.

vilned: A term used in heraldry. This is a design showing an animal that has been wounded and is bleeding, shown on a shield or escutcheon (q.q.v.).

vine black: This pigment is the result of burning wood and other vegetable matter. All of these pigments have a slight blue tinge. Vine black pigments should not be used in cement or in fresco (q.v.) painting.

violet: This is one of the variations of purple (q.v.).

violet: A flower used in the corsage (q.v.) crafts. A small wild flower, also cultivated. Used in small groups. The blooms will last about two days.

viridian: This paint pigment was first made in France in 1838. Viridian is a bright emerald green, made from hydrated chromium hydroxide. This pigment is a permanent type.

visual arts: Also known as space arts. Visual arts covers the arts and their creators whose works can be seen. This differs from the musical arts which can only be heard.

vitrics: The arts and crafts of the making of glass, history and design.

vitrified: A term used in the ceramics crafts (q.v.). Meant to be any ceramic piece that has a glaze (q.v.). Also applied to tiles.

vitro-di-Trina: In the craft of glass blowing, this is a technique of making diamond or lozenge-shaped pieces which are lacelike in texture.

volant: A term used in heraldry. This is a design on a shield or escutcheon (q.q.v.) showing a bird in flight.

vorant: A term used in heraldry. This is a design showing an animal eating another animal. The design is placed on a shield or escutcheon (q.q.v.).

vulcanizing: This is a method of curing and preparing rubber for molds and other uses. Vulcanization temperature is 300° F. The time for the vulcanization to take place is about a half an hour, depending on the size to be vulcanized. Vulcanizing may be done at home in the kitchen oven.

W

walling wax: Used in the etching crafts. A type of wax which is built up around a plate (q.v.), used to keep the etching acid on the surface of the plate.

walnut oil: The mature and stale kernels of the English walnut are crushed and pressed and the result is an oil used in paints. Walnut oil is used as a dryer in paint.

wampum: The making of wampum is rather difficult. The beads were made from the shells of clams, the white part made the white beads and the purple beads were made from the purple part of the shell. The beads were small and polished and strung on belts. Used as a medium of exchange by American Indians and the early settlers.

warm colors: A term used in the painting crafts. The colors of red, orange and yellow are considered to be warm colors. These colors are associated in the mind with the heat of the sun and fire.

warp: A term used in the textile crafts. The warp is the yarn or thread that runs the length of the fabric. The warp interlocks with the woof (q.v.).

warped record dish: A novel dish can be made from a melted phonograph record. Place the record in a flat pan and fill with very hot water. When the record becomes soft and pliable, remove the water and shape the record as you wish, form it over a block of wood or bowl. When cool, paint a design on it.

water color paint: These paints are composed of transparent pigments. Water color paints come dry, in cakes and in tubes; the form that they come in is optional to the artist, some prefer one to the other. To make your own water colors the following method may be used: Powdered gum Senegal about 1 oz., ⅓ oz. pure glycerin, and about 2 oz. of distilled water. Other materials in about the same amounts are gum arabic, glycerin and honey or other sugar and oxgall, oxgall helps to break the surface tension of the water. Homemade water colors are not as good as manufactured types because they are rather coarse.

water gilding: A technique of applying thin layers of gold on an object. The gold is prepared sufficiently thin to be applied by brush.

watermarks: These are marks that can be seen through paper when it is held in front of a light. A watermark is a design, usually of the maker of the paper; designs or names are shown. The design is formed because of the construction of the paper. The design has fewer fibers and thus shows up more clearly.

water lily: A bloom used in the corsage (q.v.) crafts. This flower will last about three days. When freshly picked, they may be made to last longer by dropping a bit of warm wax into the centers.

wawarus: This is a name given to several Hopi Indian kachinas of the United States. These kachinas run races. If they win, they will insult whomever they win against; if they lose, then they will give the winner a present. They sometimes carry yucca whips, shears, mud balls, or rabbit sticks which they will use on the loser of the foot race. See kachina.

wax casting: In the jewelry crafts, wax casting is a method used to duplicate metal parts of pins, figures, etc. Simply, the method is this: If a rubber mold is used, first powder the mold lightly with any type of talc or use some type of oil or green soap. The wax is poured or forced into the mold, depending on the type of object. When the wax has become hard, remove the mold. You now have a wax duplicate of the object you will cast in metal. Next, coat the wax with a mixture of plaster of paris and quartz, this is called investing. You now have the figure completely covered; cut a small hole and heat the mold until the wax has all run out. The mold is now ready to receive the metal which is poured into the small hole; the mold is then broken away, leaving a perfect duplicate of the original, now in metal.

waxed leaves: Leaves of the fall months can be preserved by dipping them in hot wax or paraffin (q.v.). Hold the leaf by its stem when it is dipped in the hot wax; next, as you remove the leaf, twist or twirl it between the fingers so that the excess wax will be thrown off. The leaves can be pressed in a notebook.

waxing: In the craft of making stained glass windows, waxing up is a process of placing stained glass in various designs on a flat piece of glass and holding it in place with wax. It is at this time that the desired shading and changes are made before the windows are actually placed in their lead frames.

weaving: This is a textile craft. It is the process of interlacing threads, yarns or cords in such a way as to form a fabric such as a rug, blanket, etc. Weaving is done on a loom (q.v.).

wedged: This term is used in the ceramics crafts. Wedged clay is clay that has been pounded and cut until all air bubbles are removed from the clay. If bubbles are present in the clay when it is fired (q.v.) it will crack and may even explode.

weft: A term used in weaving. This is the thread that is carried by the shuttle (q.v.) through the warp (q.v.). This ties in the surface of the cloth or rug that is being woven.

weld: This method is used in metal working. Two parts are fastened together by welding, which is done with heat; the two parts are melted together, the resulting part that is welded is usually much stronger than the rest.

In the painting crafts, this is a yellow color, made from a plant known as Reseda luteola. Not in great use at the present time for paints. Also called yellow weed (q.v.).

we-u-u: The head of this kachina (q.v.) is painted purple; the face has a white line across it bounded by red. Wears a blanket and red shoes. The body of this kachina is painted white. This strange kachina follows Soyoko on its visits but says nothing, a rather lazy kachina, it often falls asleep.

whatman paper: This is a type of drawing paper, used for the special printing of special editions of books.

Whieldon ware: A type of earthenware (q.v.). This type of ceramic was made in England in the 18th century. The surface of this ware is mottled and resembles tortoise shell (q.v.).

whirling table: Used in the ceramics crafts and by sculptors. This is a table with a turning top; see gentleman (q.v.).

white: A term used in ceramics. This describes a piece or biscuit (q.v.) that is ready to be fired (q.v.). The name is derived from the fact that the piece has become lighter in color, due to drying, etc.

white birch: The inner bark of this tree was used by the Ojibwa Indians of the Great Lakes region of Canada and the United States. Dogwood (q.v.), oak bur and cedar bark ashes (q.q.v.) were used to make a red dye. Used mainly on porcupine quills.

white earth: This is a type of white clay that is used in certain types of paints as a pigment.

white lead: This paint pigment is made from lead carbonate; it is poisonous and mixes well with oils. This pigment turns brown when exposed to the fumes of sulphur. White lead has been in use since the days of ancient Greece.

white space: A term used in the printing crafts. This is the area on a printed page that does not carry any printed matter. This is filled out with blocks which do not register, known as furniture (q.v.).

whiting: This is a white amorphous (q.v.) powder, a form of calcium carbonate (q.v.). Whiting is used as a filler or as an adulterant in many crafts. Used with a mixture for the gilding of picture frames, used with glue as a paint ground. Used with plaster, dextrin (q.v.) and asbestos shreds, this is mixed with water and used to make small figures and the bases for dioramas (q.v.). There are three grades of whiting in use: (1) the best grade, known as "Paris White," used in museums to make models with mâché (q.v.); (2) the second grade, known as "Extra Gilder's," is the type in most common use; (3) "Commercial" grade, which when mixed with oil forms putty (q.v.).

whittling: A term used when referring to carving (q.v.) when it is done on a small scale, with only a sharp knife, as opposed to large scale carving done by a sculptor (q.v.) or by the Indians of the Northwest who carve totem poles (q.v.).

wickiup: The wickiup is a type of hut or shelter that was constructed of brushwood by the Indians of the Plains in the United States. These houses differ from the wigwam (q.v.) and the tipi (q.v.).

wigwam: A type of dwelling or house made by the American Indian. Usually made of bark, round or arched in shape, a wigwam differs in shape and material from a tipi (q.v.).

Wiharu: A type of kachina that is all white, has a beak and horns. The figure carries a bow and arrows and a saw. The Wiharu helps the Soyoko Kachina (q.v.). Wiharu is a Kachina (q.v.) of the Hopi Indians of America.

Wikchina: This kachina (q.v.), also known as the greasy kachina, is seen in the spring cleaning ceremony. He has a head painted black, his body is also painted black. He wears a fox skin around his neck. His eyes and mouth have white circles around them and he has red hair. This is a wawarus kachina (q.v.) and when he catches someone in a race, he smears him with black paint. This is a kachina of the Hopi Indians of the United States.

wild plum (Prunus americana): This plant when used with bloodroot (q.v.) produced a dark red dye. When used with dogwood red-osier (q.v.) and alder (q.v.) a bright red dye was produced. This dye was made by the Ojibwa Indians of the Great Lakes region of the United States and Canada.

wilkinite: This mineral is used in the ceramic crafts (q.v.). Wilkinite swells greatly when mixed in water; this clay comes in various colors.

wimple: The wimple was a type of head covering for dolls made in Nuremberg, Germany, in the thirteenth century. Dolls at this time were made of terra-cotta (q.v.).

wiping: A term used in the etching crafts. The plate that has the etching on it and is ready to be inked, must be clean and on a flat surface. The ink is applied on the entire surface and then scraped off. The remaining ink is then wiped away; this is done with a tarlatan (q.v.) cloth. After the plate has been wiped on its surface it is now ready to print; the ink that will do the printing has remained in the grooves or etched surface.

wire drawing: In the jewelry crafts, it is necessary to thin wire at times for making chains, etc. The wire is drawn through a gauge which is numbered for certain sizes; bees wax (q.v.) is used to lubricate the wire as it is pulled through the draw plate.

wire sewing: A term used in the bookbinding crafts. Wire sewing is the method or technique that is used to fasten the sections of a book together.

wire-stitcher: A machine used in the bookbinding crafts. The wire-stitcher has a roll of wire which feeds into a machine which in turn cuts it into staples. The staples are pushed through the back of a folder and hold several sheets in place to form a booklet or pamphlet.

wired glass: This is glass that has wire mesh imbedded in it at the time of its manufacture.

wiring: In the crafts of corsage making, wiring is important. Various types of wire are used. Wire replaces the stems of the flowers in many cases; others re-enforce the stem. Wiring of the corsage should be done so that the wires will not show. The use of green covered wire will help to conceal its use. The covered wire will be less likely to rust. If the stem is weak, it may be taped (q.v.) and then wired; if no tape is available, wrap a small piece of wet cotton around the stem first and then wrap the wire around this. Sometimes it is necessary to push the wire through the flower to make a stem when none is available; to make this wire hold, bend it to form a hook.

wisteria: This plant grows on trunks of trees, sometimes as a bush. The blooms of this plant are purple and have a very sweet scent. When used in a corsage (q.v.) they hang and give a drooping effect. The blooms last about two days.

wivern: A term in heraldry, an animal with the forepart the shape of a dragon with legs and wings and the hind part of a serpent with a barbed tail.

woad: A rich blue dye made from the plant Isatis tinctoria, a European plant. The blue dye is extracted from the leaves of the plant. Woad is used with the dye known as indigo, and also used as a substitute for indigo.

wood tanning: Chestnut wood, as well as hemlock and oak bark, are used in the process of tanning of leathers.

woodcut: This is a type of carving on wood which results in a surface on the wood that forms a design or picture. The raised surface that is left on the block may be rolled with ink and then placed on a surface and with pressure exerted, a print may be made, known as a wood-block print (q.v.). Woodcuts are usually made on hard wood. Woodcuts are many in size and shape; some woodcuts may be used along with regular type in a printing press. Designs, letters, etc., can be cut on wood and then printed on paper, cloth and many other surfaces. See wood engraving.

woodcarving: A craft done with a sharp knife or small mechanical tools. Usually done with hard woods, depicting small figures of animals, and men.

woodcraft: Generally, this term is used to describe crafts (q.v.) that are done in the woods, such as building a shelter, starting fires by the use of two sticks, making one's own fish traps, etc. Woodcrafts are usually done with simple tools, such as an ax or camp knife. With these simple tools, many useful objects are made from material found in nature.

wood-engraving: This craft is similar to block print cutting (q.v.). It is a more difficult craft to do. Tools used in wood engraving are called gravers (q.v.). Wood engraving is done on hardwood. The end wood or end grain is used only. The process of wood engraving is similar to etching, at least as far as the design goes, as quite fine work can be done on a hard block. The wood used is usually boxwood; this fine-grained wood comes from Russia and Turkey. Maple, pear and cherry wood can also be used. Because boxwood takes so long to grow, it is necessary to glue several ends together to form a block of the size needed. The wood block is printed and inked in much the same manner as a block print or Plasti-Print (q.v.).

wooden tablet: An ancient Egyptian craft used from 1000 to 200 B.C. This wooden tablet was used as a writing tablet, also known as ostraka (q.v.). A wooden panel was covered on one side with a thin layer of plaster or white lime.

woof: A term in the textile crafts, this applies to the yarn that runs across the fabric from selvage to selvage (q.v.). The woof interlaces with the warp (q.v.).

wool: Used in the weaving crafts, this soft textured, curled hair, is the coat of a sheep. The wool is sheared from the sheep and is cleaned and then spun into long firm threads. The use of wool by weavers goes back to at least 2200 B.C. in Ur. Sheep were first brought to America in 1609. The merino sheep are the parent stock of American, European and Australian sheep used for wool.

woold: A type of dye, also known as weld (q.v.).

woolder: A device of the rope maker. This is a wooden shape made in such a way that it can be turned and thus twist the fibers into a rope.

Worcester: In the ceramic crafts, this is a well known porcelain (q.v.). Made in England from 1751, were decorated with oriental figures and the colors were many, on a creamy-white background. Worcester pieces have a registration number and a script letter W. Also known as Royal Worcester.

worming pot: A term used in the ceramic crafts. A worming pot contains slip (q.v.) which is forced out of small holes or tubes to apply a worm-like pattern on a ceramic as it is rotated on a potter's wheel (q.v.).

wove paper: A type of paper made in a mold; the wire marks which are seen on most papers do not show on wove paper.

wrapping paper: A tough brown paper used for many crafts; used for covering craft tables, making kites, lampshades, etc.

wreath: A term in the making of a roll or chaplet (q.v.) in heraldry.

wreath glass: This is a defect in the making of glass. The wreath is the wave-like appearance in the finished glass, especially in flint glass.

wriggled: As used in the metal crafts, this term is applied to a method of decoration that is done on pewter (q.v.). The design is made by rolling or rocking an incising tool (q.v.) to give an ornamentation to an object. This is known as "wriggled work."

writhen knop: A term used in the metal crafts. Writhen knop is applied mainly to pewter made in 16th century England. See knop.

writing reed: This was a reed pen made by the ancient Egyptians, also known as a gash (q.v.).

wrong draw: A term used in textiles. This is a defect in the weaving where the warp (q.v.) and the filling (q.v.) did not combine correctly to complete the design.

Wrotham ware: A type of slip-decorated ceramic, made in England in the early 17th century. The finest pieces were made from 1627 to 1717 and were red with a white slip, sometimes decorated with ornaments and incised. There are some that were decorated with a lead glaze of yellow.

wupomo: The body of this kachina (q.v.) is painted red, with one green shoulder and the other shoulder yellow. The top half of the head is painted yellow and the bottom half is painted black. This kachina has a long beak with a tongue that hangs out. Around his neck he wears a fur piece, in his hand he carries a bow and arrows. This kachina stands guard at the kiva during very special ceremonies.

wuyak-ku-ita: This is a type of kachina (q.v.). Used in the Hopi Indian Bean Dance. The face is black, sprinkled with fragments of gypsum (q.v.). The teeth of this kachina are made from the twisted husks of corn.

X

xanthic: This is a general term that is applied to any material, vegetable or mineral, that is used to make a substance that is yellow and used as a color with dyes or other pigments. The color itself is derived mainly from the madder plant and is known as madder lake (q.v.).

xanthometer: This is a scaled instrument used to measure the precise color hues of liquids.

xanthorhamnine: A yellow dye made in Turkey and Persia from berries and from a grain known as Avignon.

xanthorrhea: A resin from Australia. This resin comes in two colors, a yellow gold and a ruby red. It forms a film somewhat like shellac. Xanthorrhea is used in industry to color varnishes. Other names for this resin are, Botany Bay gum, blackboy gum and gum Accroides. It is used as a size for many types of paper and also in the manufacture of certain waxes.

xanthosiderite: This is a type of ocher (q.v.), the color is a yellow to a golden brown.

xerography: This is a recent process of printing. A method of reproducing many types of printed matter with the use of dry powders and static electricity. This is also sometimes known as dry writing (q.v.).

xihuitl: This type of turquoise (q.v.) was used by the ancient Aztecs of Mexico. Xihuitl is used in the lapidary crafts.

xylenes: These are a large group of coal tar products from which many paint pigments and various dyes are made. Xylenes are also used as thinners in many lacquers. Also known as xylol.

xylography: The process of making a type of wood cut that was developed in the early 15th century. The surface of the wood block is incised (q.v.) and the smooth surface is then coated with special pigments that soak into the wood. The surface is then polished or covered with an enamel. This is now known as a xylograph.

xylol: A coal tar derivative. Belongs to a large group known as xylenes (q.v.).

xylolin: This is a type of fabric made from wood pulp. Xylolin is woven into drapes, rugs and upholstery. The yarn is made after the pulping process in paper making, it is then twisted into thin strips.

Y

yellow lake: This transparent yellow pigment, made from aniline dyes, is used mainly in printing inks.

yellow ultramarine: This is a term that was used for barium yellow, now an obsolete term for this pigment.

yellow ware: A type of earthenware (q.v.) with a yellow color. Yellow ware is usually covered with a lead glaze.

yellow weed: A type of dye made from the plant known as Reseda lutetola. This plant is grown in Europe and now in the Eastern United States. Yellow weed is also known as weld (q.v.).

yew: A type of wood used in carving. The wood is soft and has a straight grain. The tree belongs to the family Taxus.

yoko: This is a type of Japanese wood block print. It is made on a block of about ten inches thick and about fifteen inches wide.

yoro yaki: This is a type of oriental ceramic made in the Mino province, Japan.

Z

z twist: A term used in weaving; the cord is woven in such a way that the fibers slant in the direction of a Z.

zaccab: This is used in Yucatan and is a mixture of a white earth and lime. The natives of Central America use it as a plaster for their walls.

zaffer: This is a term used in the making of smalt (q.v.), it is the next to the last stage in making smalt.

zaffre: This is an ingredient used in the making of stained glass (q.v.). Zaffre gives the glass a deep blue. It is made from an oxide of cobalt.

zarf: A type of receptacle used in the metal crafts, used to hold a cup without handles. Used mainly in the Orient.

zaroche: Used in the metal crafts, this is a type of impure gold. Zaroche usually contains silver.

zebrawood: This type of wood is used in fine woodworking and cabinet working. Zebrawood can be given a high polish; also known as snakewood (q.v.).

zein: This is a protein substance made from corn, which can be dyed in any color. Zein is used to make the plastic covers on booklets and other materials that have a thin cover or finish on them.

zeze yaki: This is a type of ceramic made in the Omi province of Japan. It is a type of earthenware (q.v.) with a practical use.

zimba: This is a type of game that is made by various Indian and Eskimo tribes of the world. There are many variations. Simply, the game consists of a cord of string or rawhide (q.v.), a sharp pointed stick, a triangular piece of leather and some large hollow bones. The game is made as follows: Tie the sharp stick on one end of the string, next, string about ten slices of bone along the cord and at the end, tie the triangular piece of leather. Cut several small holes of various sizes in the leather. The object of this game is to swing the cord and catch the bone rings on the pointed stick or catch the leather on the stick. Score should be kept, so much for each ring or bone that is caught.

zinc: Used in many crafts. A metallic element, used in alloys (q.v.), printing, etc.

zinc etching solution: About four ounces of pure gum solution, two drops of nitric acid and about a half an ounce of tannic acid. Mix well. This solution will etch an average size zinc plate (q.v.).

zinc green: This is a paint pigment known as cobalt green and made from zinc yellow (q.v.), Prussian blue (q.v.) and various barytes.

zinc half-tone: This is a cheap method of making printing plates instead of using copper. The zinc half-tone is used to make plates for use in newspapers.

zinc oleate: This greasy white powder is used in paints as a dryer.

zinc white: This is a paint pigment made from pure zinc oxide. It is nonpoisonous and does not change color when exposed to sulphur fumes. Zinc white was first made in France near the end of the eighteenth century. This was not a popular pigment until it was sold under the name of Chinese white in the early twentieth century.

zinc yellow: Made from zinc chromate, this is a pale yellow paint pigment. This pigment is poisonous and not a permanent color.

zincography: This is a printing craft. Zincography is similar to lithography (q.v.). The zinc plate is etched (q.v.). This type of printing is also known as anatastic printing (q.v.).

zinnia: A type of flower used in the corsage crafts. The blooms come in many colors. The stems should be scalded and then the flower placed in cool water. The blooms last about four days.

zinnober: This is a vermilion (q.v.) color, a pigment.

zinnober green: An olive drab or brownish green shade of green, made by mixing Prussian blue and any of the chrome yellows (q.q.v.).

zinn-stahl: This is a type of pewter (q.v.). Zinn-stahl, used in the metal crafts, is a pewter that has been reinforced with steel to give it strength, used mainly in eating utensils—knives, forks, spoons and ladles.

zircon: This is a gem stone used to imitate diamonds. A zircon is the heaviest transparent stone known. Zircons are white and blue; this color is man made by heating the stone, which changes the color of brown and yellow that is found in the stone. Zircons are cut and polished by the jewelry craftsman.

zircon white: Used in the ceramic crafts. This material, zirconium oxide, is used in ceramic glazes; it is white in color.

zirconium: This is usually a heavy powder, used in the making of glass and several kinds of enamels.

zo: This is a term applied to the image of a deity. Zo applies to Japanese sculptures of any deity.

zogan: This is a type of inlay work, done mainly in Japan. Zogan uses gold or silver applied to wood, metal and on many other materials.

zoisite: This is a kind of mineral that is used in gem crafts. This mineral comes in several colors—grey, brown and some of the crystals are green and red. The red or rose-colored type is used in costume jewelry.

zola: This substance is a natural borax or sodium borate. Zola is used in many crafts. Used in casting to harden plaster of Paris (q.v.). This substance is also used in the leather crafts as a preservative, to fireproof textiles, used in the making of glass and is also used in the making of glue and printing inks.

COLLEGE OF THE SEQUOIAS

REFERENCE

LIBRARY